Joy to the World

Joy to the World

INSPIRATIONAL
CHRISTMAS MESSAGES
FROM AMERICA'S
PREACHERS

Edited by

Olivia M. Cloud

ATRIA BOOKS

NEW YORK LONDON TORONTO SYDNEY

ATRIA BOOKS

1230 Avenue of the Americas
New York, NY 10020

ISBN-13: 978-1-4165-4000-7
ISBN-10:   1-4165-4000-8

First Atria Books hardcover edition November 2006

Copyright permission information appears on pages 397–401.

10   9   8   7   6   5   4   3   2   1

ATRIA BOOKS is a trademark of Simon & Schuster, Inc.

Manufactured in the United States of America

For information regarding special discounts for bulk purchases,
please contact Simon & Schuster Special Sales at 1-800-456-6798
or business@simonandschuster.com.

Preface

"Joy to the World, the Lord is come!" That's good news to us today, just as it was good two thousand years ago. But Isaac Watts had not yet been born to write those words, when Mary got the news of the coming Messiah, so Mary expressed her joy at the Savior's coming through a personal song of praise, known in Christendom as the Magnificat (Luke 1:46–56).

Mary broke into a spontaneous song of praise after the angel Gabriel revealed to her that the Lord would use her as a vessel for His miracle. Mary begins "My soul doth magnify the Lord" (Luke 1:46, KJV).

In her "freestyle" song she extols the virtues of her God. But even in offering this most magnificent song of praise, could Mary have known the magnitude of the gift that had been given to her?

"Mary, Did You Know" is a beautifully moving song written by Mark Lowry and Buddy Greene. The song poses a series of reflective questions to the Mother of our Lord regarding the miracle baby she birthed.

Today we can only wonder, "Did Mary recognize the breadth and depth of the gift that had been bestowed upon her?"

When God places gifts or blessings in our lives, often it is through a process that we discover their true magnificence. Do any of us fully recognize the magnitude of the gift that God has given us in Christ?

Clearly, at the time of Gabriel's revelation to her, Mary knew that God was doing something miraculous and wonderful in her life, but in her humanness she couldn't have comprehended how it would impact the lives of all humanity.

The miracle of Christmas would continue to unfold for Mary long after Gabriel's appearance to her and long after her son was born.

Mysteries in the Christmas story continue to unfold, and the meditations offered by the preachers in this book give evidence to that fact. There is only one true and authentic Christmas story, and it takes up very little space in the Bible. Still, no two messages in *Joy to the World* are exactly alike.

Each piece adds new insights into the miracle of Christmas. Each preacher gives a fresh and original perspective. The story never changes, but it never gets old. Reading these meditations will increase your joy during the Christmas season, and throughout the year.

—Olivia M. Cloud, editor

Contents

CONTENTS

CONTENTS

Joy to the World

The King with Four Names

Daniel Akin

BASED ON ISAIAH 9:1–7

Suppose that an alien from another planet, or even another galaxy, were to come and visit our earth during the holiday season. What do you think that alien would discover and conclude about Christmas? Would he conclude that it is more about Santa, or Savior? Rudolph and reindeers, or a Redeemer? Jingle bells, or Jesus? Happy Holidays, or Merry Christmas?

During the 2005 Christmas season in Denver, a Christian group was denied permission to participate in the city's annual Parade of Lights because they planned to sing hymns and say "Merry Christmas" on their float. A part of Denver's holiday celebration for over thirty years, the parade was open to the vast majority of the community, including homosexual American Indians, belly dancers, and, of course, Santa Claus among its participants.

In McHenry County, Illinois, children, parents, and teachers gathered for a time of holiday celebration at school concerts. They sang of Hanukkah, gave a rendition of a Jamaican folk song, and made their list for Santa. In the "spirit of inclusiveness," however, there was no mention of Christ and no word about the Christmas story. Later it was reported that the slight of our Savior was "inadvertent."

Even *Time* and *Newsweek* magazines entered the debate with cover stories about Christmas, though the observations from *Times*'s "Secrets of the Nativity" and *Newsweek*'s "The Birth of Jesus" probably would not impress those of us who take the Bible seriously. For they question the reality of the Virgin Birth. They question whether or not the shepherds ever came or the Wise Men ever showed up, and they questioned, "Did it ever really happen?"

Well, from Genesis through Malachi, the Word of God paints for us a beautiful portrait of the Savior who is to come, the Christ of Christmas. The Old Testament unfolds the drama of redemption and the true essence of what Christmas really is all about. There, painted for us in magnificent detail, is a king with four names.[1]

The year is approximately 725 B.C. Israel, the Northern Kingdom, faced an ominous and perilous situation from the north, as an evil and aggressive Assyrian empire was growing and expanding. Tiglath-pileser III had built Assyria to its zenith in power, and now Shalmaneser V was poised and ready to attack and to morally bankrupt a militarily weakened Israel.

It's important to note here that just three years later, in 722 B.C., Israel would be sacked, overrun, and crushed in humiliating defeat by the Assyrian empire. Loved ones would be brutally killed, families would be broken up and destroyed; the land would be devastated, and economic havoc would be rampant. The once-proud nation of Israel would be brought to its knees in shame, humiliation, and judgment. And yet, in the midst of their despair and hopelessness, they received a Word from God.

In Isaiah 9 we are told that sorrow would turn to rejoicing. The distress of verse 1 would turn into the joy of verse 3.

The oppression of verse 1 would turn into a broken yoke in verse 3.

The darkness of verse 2 would turn to the light of verse 2.

The shadow of death of verse 2 would be overcome in verse 6.

In these verses, all of the verb tenses are in the perfect tense. In Isaiah's mind, these things had already happened; they were a settled reality. Why? Because there was to come, in a wonderful new day, a king with four names.

E. J. Young, a wonderful Old Testament scholar, notes that these verses find initial fulfillment in Matthew 4:14–16. There is going to be great rejoicing among God's people because God has broken the yoke of burden and oppression! The burden and the oppression are removed because the weapons and garments of the warrior are destroyed. The basic reason for these blessings is that a child has been born.

And so, seven hundred years before the Wise Men gave, before the angels sang, and before the shepherds arrived, Isaiah explains for us in wonderful detail what Christmas is all about. He tells us about a king with four names.

What would Isaiah have us understand from this wonderful text? There are three truths that I want to put before you as we walk through these verses.

HE IS MARVELOUS IN HOW HE CAME

Verse 6 reads, "For unto us a child is born. Unto us a son is given." Now, it is imperative that you see the flow of Isaiah's argument in this section of his book. Here Isaiah intimately connects to the virgin-born Immanuel of Isaiah 7:14—this Wonderful Counselor and Mighty God, Everlasting Father and Prince of Peace of Isaiah 9:6, who we learn later is the bloodline or the stem of Jesse (Isaiah 11:1), and ultimately is the Suffering Servant of the Lord in Isaiah 53.

There is something particularly marvelous and majestic about His coming, something that is indeed mysterious as we try to unfold the truth of what we have before us. He is marvelous in how

He came for two reasons. First, He came in the form of earthly humanity. "For unto us a child is born . . ." And literally, in the Hebrew language, the phrase "a child" is fronted for emphasis: "A child is born unto us."

Isaiah is not looking at his day but to a new day—a wonderful day, a day out there in the future of unparalleled joy and blessing for a one-of-a-kind child, when a king with four names is born for us. A child is born. "A child is born" draws us to the baby in Bethlehem. It was unto us, for us, and for our good that this child was born.

Hebrew 2:14 (KJV) helps us understand why it was necessary that this One be born as a human baby. There the Bible says, "Inasmuch as the children have partaken of flesh and blood, he himself, likewise, shared in the same."

Paul adds his commentary in Galatians 4:4, where he says that when the fullness of time had come, God sent forth His Son, born of a woman, born under the Law.

Isaiah, under the inspiration of the Holy Spirit, is quite clear and quite precise in his prophecy. He did not say, "A child is born," but rather, "A son is born." [2] No. Isaiah, the inspired seer of messianic prophecy, wrote words that he may not have fully understood, but words that were clearly, specifically, and precisely true. Indeed, it's been well that God's Christmas gift came in the person of deity, wrapped in the package of humanity.

Now, please understand that Jesus' birth in Bethlehem was not the beginning of the *Son*. There was a time when Jesus was not; His beginning was Bethlehem. But there was never a time when the *Son* was not. Indeed, John 1:1 reminds us in the beginning was the Word, and the Word was with God, and the Word was God.

Hebrews 1:1–2 says that God—who in the past spoke many times and in many ways through the prophets of old—has in this last day spoken to us by His Son.

John Phillips, that wonderful expositor, explains it beautifully: "The great mystery of the manger is that God should be able to translate deity into humanity without discarding the deity or distorting the humanity." Yes, indeed, the incarnation was a true and genuine wedding of perfect deity and sinless humanity.

I love the way R. G. Lee, that wonderful pastor for many years at Bellevue Baptist Church in Memphis, Tennessee, explained it: "Jesus is the only one born with no earthly father, but an earthly mother. He had no heavenly mother, but a heavenly father. He was older than his mother, and as old as his father."

John would add in his gospel, "For God so loved the world that he gave his only begotten Son" (3:16). Yes, He is marvelous in how He came. He came in earthly humanity; He came in heavenly deity.

HE IS MAJESTIC IN WHO HE IS

And now see with me that He is also majestic in who He is. From Genesis to Revelation there are more than 250 names and titles given to our Lord; but here, Isaiah does something utterly unique. Here, Isaiah brings together four names in a concise package—names that appear nowhere else in the Bible.

Indeed, more names are crowded together in Isaiah 9 than anywhere else in all of Holy Scripture. Taken together, they encapsulate in a beautiful way the totality of both the person and the work of Jesus—who He is and what He does. And when these four titles are coupled with the fact that He is the child who is born, He is the Son who is given, the result is nothing less than the God-man Immanuel, "God with us."

In the ancient Semitic mind, names, titles, often constituted the character of the person and the activity of the person—who they are and what they do. Jesus Christ will show Himself to be absolute perfection in terms of these four names that describe Him.

What can we say about these four names?

Wonderful Counselor

This name tells us He is a wise counselor who solves my confusion. "Wonderful counselor" could perhaps be translated as a "wonder of a counselor." In other words, He is glorious and He is wondrous as a counselor, unfailing in His wisdom. It's interesting to note that the word translated "wonderful" there is never used in the Bible to describe humankind, but always as an attribute of God.

Of course, we live today in the day and the age of the counselor, of the psychiatrist, the psychoanalyst, and the therapist. It has been said that a counselor is someone who will help you organize your hang-ups so you can be unhappy more effectively.

It was by a counselor that the world fell into sin. Satan got Eve involved in psychoanalysis. She got Adam involved in group therapy; together, they plunged the whole world into insanity. Yes, the world was ruined by a counselor, but the world is also redeemed by a counselor.

In 1 Corinthians 1:24, we are told that Jesus Christ is the wisdom of God. This phrase tells us He is our adviser and He is our teacher. He is our friend and He is our confidant. And Jesus Himself said in Matthew 11:28 (KJV), "Come unto me all ye who labor and I will give you rest." Jesus gives rest for your body, rest of your mind, and rest for your soul. He is a wise counselor who solves my confusion.

Mighty God

Jesus is a worthy defender who shelters us from conflict. He not only is a wonderful counselor, He is a mighty God. It is the Hebrew phrase *El Gabbor.* Some translate this the "hero God," or the "warrior God."

Here you have a title that causes severe discomfort and agitation among liberal and Jewish scholars. He is the mighty God, and so they try to tell us this is nothing more than popular exaggeration, royal hyperbole or court flattery. However, when taken in its context, and in the greater context of Isaiah's book, we are inescapably driven to the conclusion that here is an affirmation of a Child and a Son who is nothing less than deity.

The argument is indeed settled quite clearly, I believe, in Isaiah 10:21; for there the Bible says of the remnant of Israel, "the remnant will return to *El Gabbor,* the mighty God."

It's been well noted that the term "mighty God" conjures up images of warfare and the battleground; indeed, the king with four names is a warrior God. He is a hero-God who would fight a battle far greater than Waterloo or Valley Forge and more decisive than Gettysburg or D-Day. This warrior-God, whom Hebrews 2:10 calls the "captain of our salvation," will take the field of battle at a place called Calvary.

There he would engage the titan forces of sin and Satan, death, hell, and the grave. And when the dust had settled, an empty tomb stands as a monument to the victory of *El Gabbor,* the mighty God. He is a worthy defender who shelters me from conflict.

Everlasting Father

He is a watchful father who showers me with compassion. He is father of eternity; He is eternally a father. Of course, the idea of eternity speaks of the fact that He is the source and the origin of eternity. In John 1, we have had that affirmed. And then, in Revelation 1:8, we are told of this one who is the Alpha and the Omega. And amazingly, in Hebrews 1:8, God Himself declares, "but to the Son he says, your throne, O God, is forever and ever."

And so here is a child who is also a father—fatherly in His love, fatherly in His care, fatherly in His goodness, fatherly in His compassion. He acts toward us like a father, a good father, a perfect father, a provider and a protector. And as the eternal Father, the everlasting Father, His provision and His protection are forever. He is a watchful father who showers me with compassion.

Prince of Peace

Jesus is a wonderful comforter who soothes my conscience, for he is the Prince of Peace. In Luke 2:14, the angels sing to the shepherds of One who will bring peace on earth. And as the Prince of Peace, or *Saar Shalom* in Hebrew, He is the supreme giver of peace. He is the one who is going to see that the warrior's boot and the garments rolled up in blood are nothing less than fuel for the fire (verse 5).

He is, indeed, the greater Gideon of Judges 7, where in the day of Midian He put an end to the forces of evil who stand against and oppose the people of God.

When *Saar Shalom* shows up, darkness, despair, and death will come to an end and the boots and the blood of battle will cease to be, never ever again to appear.

Of course, we are informed in the New Testament that He is the one who gives us peace with God (Romans 5:1).

In Philippians 4:7, He is the one who gives us the peace of God. He is the one who brings about universal peace—peace between God and humanity, peace among humanity, and peace even within humanity. He gives us peace in the present, and He will give us peace in the future.

In verse 7 Isaiah tells us, "Of his peace there will be no end." And so He is marvelous in how He came; He is majestic in who He is; but there is one final thing.

HE IS MIGHTY IN WHAT HE WILL DO

Our God is a promise-keeping God. He will fulfill what he says He will do. And in 2 Samuel 7:12–13 (NKJV) is found one of the key covenant texts in the Bible. There, God said to David, "I will set up your seed after you who will come from your body . . . and I will establish his kingdom. I will establish the throne of his kingdom forever."

Building up on the inside of those two texts, Isaiah tells us that He is mighty in what He will do; for he will rule completely (verse 6). It says there, "And the government will be upon his shoulder."

His unending reign is reaffirmed in the New Testament in Luke 1:32–33 (NKJV), where the angel Gabriel appears to Mary and says, "Behold, you will conceive in your womb and bring forth a son and shall call his name JESUS. He will be great, and he will be called the son of the highest and the Lord God will give him the throne of his father David. And he will reign over the house of Jacob forever and of his kingdom, there will be no end."

His rule will be universal. His rule will be unending. His rule will be unparalleled. The government will rest upon His shoulder.

Respected theologian Herbert C. Leupold said "the government . . . upon His shoulder" speaks of the golden chain that hangs around the neck of and lies upon the shoulder of the great ruler as a symbol of his authority.

And my good friend James Merritt says this text "makes one thing clear, no one will vote Him into office, and no one will vote Him out of office. When He comes, He comes to take over. He comes to rule completely. He will rule completely. This child is a king; this son is a sovereign lord. He will rule completely."

Verse 7 (NKJV) tells that He will rule eternally: "Of the increase of his government and peace there will be no end." No end in time; no end in space. His government will increase and grow and flourish, never, ever to be brought to an end.

Hope is going to burst forth out of hopelessness, and it will just keep on growing. Peace will come forth out of "peacelessness," and it will keep on growing. Justice will burst forth out of injustice, and it will keep on growing—and the character of His kingdom, judgment and justice, now and forever. "Of the increase of his government and peace there will be no end."

He also will rule powerfully, according to verse 7: "From that time forward, even forever. The zeal of the Lord of Hosts will perform it" (NKJV).

Bring about the kingdom of this child, the kingdom of this Son—this king with four names is not left to the devices of humanity. God Himself, Jehovah, will see that His Son is rightly enthroned and rightly honored.

It has been well said, "The Father is jealous and has a passion to establish the rule and reign of His Son. And He is certain to see that it will come to pass."

In heaven, there is no confusion about Christmas. In heaven, there is no confusion about who belongs on the throne forever. And, indeed, God is burning. He has always burned with a passion, a zeal, for one thing and one thing only—the glory of His beloved Son in whom He takes great delight.

Martin Lloyd Jones says, "Ultimately, nothing matters but what we think of Jesus." Isaiah says that we should think He is marvelous in how He came; He is majestic in who He is; and He is mighty in what He will do.

A gift tells us much about the giver. In this passage in Isaiah, which almost has a magical quality about it, we discover and we try to remember at this time of the year that we are the recipients of a surprising Gift, and a supreme Gift; a humble Gift and the highest Gift. Indeed, we learn that God will never, ever be able to outdo Himself in the gift that He gave at Christmas.

Dr. W. A. Criswell has said well, "The shoulders that bear the government of the universe are the shoulders that bore the cross to Calvary."

What, then, should be our response? We can join with Paul in 2 Corinthians 9:15 and say, "Thanks be unto God for his unspeakable gift." We can join with Isaiah and say, "Thank You, Lord, for the king with four names."

🌿 PRAYER 🌿

Heavenly Father, we have stepped into and upon holy ground in a text that I recognize that no human lips are adequate to fully and completely describe all the truth, all the glory, and all the majesty and awesomeness that we find there.

And yet, Lord, even though we may be infants in our understanding, and though we may not be able to know you exhaustively, we can know you truly.

I am so grateful for that Child who was born and that Son who was given. And I thank you so much for the Wonderful Counselor, the Mighty God, the Everlasting Father, and the Prince of Peace, who is the Lord Jesus.

May we, if no one else does this time of the year, remember the truth and the essence about Christmas. May we be courageous and faithful, not to be intimidated by a secular culture, not to be cowed by skeptical writers and theologians who scoff at the reality of the Incarnation.

But may we, out of our own experience of having met you personally, share with them about the Child who was born and the Son who was given, not only for us, but also that others might come to know Him as their Wonderful Counselor, their Mighty God, their Everlasting Father, and their Prince of Peace. This we ask and pray in His name. Amen.

NOTES

1. We are told in Genesis 3:15 that He would be the seed of a woman. We are told in Genesis 12:1–3 that He would come from the seed of Abraham. We are told in Genesis 49:9–10 that He would come from the tribe of Judah.

We are taught in Deuteronomy 18:15 that He would be a prophet greater than Moses. In 2 Samuel 7:12, we are told that He will be a son of David who will reign forever.

In Psalm 2, He is called "God's anointed"; in Psalm 22, "the righteous sufferer." In Psalm 110, he is a king-priest after the order of Melchizedek.

In Isaiah 7:14 He is the virgin-born Immanuel. In Isaiah 53, He is the "suffering servant of the Lord."

In Daniel 7:13–14, He is the coming Son of Man.

In Micah 5:2, He is the babe who will be born in Bethlehem.

But adding to that glorious portrait we find Isaiah 9:1–7—an additional picture, a greater Gideon who is to come—a king with four names.

In the ninth chapter, the prophet Isaiah wrote:

> Nevertheless, the gloom will not be upon her who is distressed, As when at first He lightly esteemed the land of Zebulun and the land of Naphtali, and afterward more heavily oppressed her, by the way of the sea, beyond the Jordan, in Galilee of the Gentiles. The people who walked in darkness have seen a great light; those who dwelt [dwell] in the land of the shadow of death, upon them a light has shined. You have multiplied the nation and increased its joy; they rejoice before You according to the joy of harvest, as men rejoice when they divide the spoil. For You have broken the yoke of his burden and the staff of his shoulder, the rod of his oppressor, as in the day of Midian. For every warrior's sandal [boot] from the noisy battle, and garments rolled in blood, will be used for burning and fuel of fire. For unto us a Child is born, unto us a Son is given; and the government will be upon his shoulder. And His name will be called Wonderful, Counselor, Mighty God, Everlasting Father, Prince of Peace. Of the in-

crease of His government and peace there will be no end. Upon the throne of David and over His kingdom, to order it and establish it with judgment and justice from that time forward, even forever. The zeal of the Lord of hosts will perform this. (NKJV)

2. E. Y. Mullins, president of the Southern Seminary, said of this text: "Christ's spotless humanity, as a finite drop of dew reflects the glory of sovereign holiness and love taking the initiative in saving man. 'For unto us a child is born.' He came in earthly humanity. But we should also see in this text that he came in heavenly deity. 'For unto us a child is born. Unto us a son is given.' Again, the phrase 'a son' is fronted for emphasis. Literally, the text 'a son is given' to us. A son is given now addresses his eternal being. It speaks of the God of glory. It tells us of God's greatest gift. And do not run past the text too quickly."

Keeping Christ Central to Christmas

MELVIN BANKS SR.

BASED ON COLOSSIANS 1:15–19; 2:9–10

Without Christ there would be no Christmas, so one would think that stressing the centrality of Christ to Christmas would be a non-issue. Yet due to the subtle ways that Christ in our day is frequently marginalized and reduced to being just another good teacher, it is appropriate to address the issue of who Christ really is. An example of this reductionism of Christ can be found in the recent hype surrounding *The Da Vinci Code,* book and movie.

The Da Vinci Code is the story of a curator at the Louvre Museum, located in Paris, France. The curator is mysteriously murdered, and his granddaughter discovers that he left a secret, which she and a friend are determined to uncover. She follows one clue after another, in a kind of scavenger hunt, until she finally discovers the secret—Mary Magdalene and Jesus were married and had a family whose bloodline continues to the present day, living in France!

Both the book and the movie are, in reality, just another

not-so-subtle effort to resurrect and popularize the old Gnostic teaching.

Gnosticism holds that we become Godlike without being accountable to God. It is the same proposition Satan offered Adam and Eve in the garden of Eden (Genesis 3:4–5): "If you eat this fruit you will become like God, knowing good from evil." People attempting to live independent from God is echoed by the psalmist: "Let's get rid of this bondage to God" (Psalm 2:1–3).

Today, many believe we are living in a postmodern age, that the conventional method of distinguishing right from wrong must give way to the new thought that nobody really knows what is right and what is wrong, that we are free to do whatever seems right.

People—not God—become the measure of what is right and wrong. They say, "If it feels right, do it." God is viewed as a "genie" to give us what we want when we want it, without our submitting to Him.

Without necessarily knowing how aligned they are with Gnostic thinking, bumper stickers that insist health and wealth are birthrights abound on cars across America. Such thinking discounts God's sovereign right to arrange our circumstances as He sees fit. We sometimes even hear it said that we can command God to give us what we want. People and their selfish needs take center stage, not God and His purposes and plans.

We need a biblical perspective to inform this way of thinking. Bible scholars are agreed that the early stages of Gnosticism manifested during the first century. God's spokesperson, the apostle Paul, became furious when he discovered that the person of Christ was being distorted by certain Christians of his day. In letters to the Christians in Galatia and Colossae, he declared emphatically the centrality and superior place Christ should have in the thinking of God's people (Colossians 1:15–20).

And at this Christmas season, when we pause to reflect on the Incarnation of Christ—that is, of God becoming human in Jesus—

we reemphasize that Jesus Christ should remain central to the celebration.

In Colossae, Christians were falling victim to certain teachings similar to Gnosticism, or what is currently called New Age thinking. This teaching denied the deity of Christ, teaching that Jesus "the man" was human only, but not the Christ. They believed that God came upon Jesus at His baptism and left before He was crucified, so He ministered as "the Christ" but died as a man, not as the God-man.

Second, they denied the existence of sin. And because there is no sin, they espoused that people don't need salvation in the way the Christian community understands it. To their way of thinking, people are not sinners in need of an atoning sacrifice for their sin.

They didn't believe that everyone can know God based on the truths set forth by God's revelation in the written Word. Instead, they asserted that God can be known through having a series of experiences in which one moves from one degree of inferior knowledge to a higher degree of knowledge, which was available only to a select few.

Gnostics taught that the body was unimportant. Some even taught that in order to know God, one had to punish the body through asceticism: "Don't touch that," or, "Don't eat this," and, "For God's sake don't touch that!" (Colossians 2:16). Others taught that since Christ has set us free, we're at liberty to do anything our hearts desire. We can indulge ourselves through gluttony or immorality—eat all you want, have all the sex you want with whomever. You're free to do whatever you please.

In response to such distorted thinking, Paul said, "Wait a minute! Let me tell you who Christ really is and what He has done to provide a salvation that is neither a license to sin nor one in which you need any addendums or add-ons."

In order for believers to respond to today's removal of Christ from Christmas and to the Gnostic philosophy sweeping our world, we need to remind ourselves of who Christ is, His person and His work. We need to examine our relationship with Him, lest we find ourselves adding unnecessary burdens to our lives, or lest we allow ourselves to become victims of the philosophy that says we are free to do what we please as long as it doesn't harm anybody else.

Paul addresses this issue in Colossians 1:15–19 by reminding Christians of who Christ is.

Paul teaches that Christ is the visible image of the invisible God—the exact representation of God's likeness (verse 15). For example, when you use a cookie cutter to make cookies, you cut the dough with the cutter and the shape of the cookie is the exact shape of the cutter.

Paul says Jesus is the exact representation of God. That's why Jesus could tell Philip (when Philip asked Jesus to show them the Father), "The person who has seen me has seen the Father" (John 14:9). Paul was saying the same thing.

Second, Jesus is in the position of Firstborn (verses 15–17), a position of authority over all creation—a position of priority, preeminence, and sovereignty. What does that mean? It means that Jesus preceded everything. He is above everything. He controls everything. He created everything that exists, and keeps everything together today.

When you reflect on the magnitude of our universe, the extent of Christ's power to keep the world together becomes mind-boggling. Scientists tell us that our universe contains some 1 billion galaxies, and that even to travel at the speed of light (186,000 miles per *second*!) to the outer limits of what we now know as the universe would take some 20 million years. Christ keeps all that together, just by His Word! That's what Paul means in saying that Christ is the Firstborn over God's creation. He is in charge.

Third, Jesus is the Head over the church, which is His body (verse 18). This means that just as the body is the vehicle through which the human personality performs and expresses itself, as directed by the brain, so the church is Christ's instrument—His body—to perform His work here on earth and also into eternity!

Finally, Jesus possesses the fullness of the Godhead—nothing is left out (verse 19). What a strong statement for Paul to make regarding the divinity of Christ! All of God is present within the person of Christ. Jesus is God with human flesh wrapped around Him.

This is all the more reason we must give our undivided loyalty and worship to Jesus the Christ.

The significance of the Christ of Christmas is that through Christ's becoming human, and through His death and resurrection, we have been given the matchless gift of becoming reconnected with God!

Honoring Gifts fr…

Nathan D. Baxter

Based on Matthew 2:1–12

After Jesus was born in Bethlehem of Judea, wise men from the East came to Jerusalem, asking "Where is the child who has been born king of the Jews? For we observed his star . . . and have come to pay him homage." [King Herod had them brought to him and asked that they find the child on his behalf so he too could pay respect.] . . . *When they saw the star had stopped they were overwhelmed with joy. . . . When they saw the child they knelt down and paid him homage. Then, opening their treasure chests, they offered him gifts of gold, frankincense, and myrrh. (NB)*

A friend of mine who likes putting a feminist spin on things says: "If there had been three wise women instead of Wise Men, they would have asked for directions earlier, gotten there on time, helped deliver the baby, and brought useful gifts!" Useful gifts? The wise men offered the Christ Child gold. Whether the gold was in the form of coins or jewelry or little household idols called teraphim,

know. But what we do know, as did they, is that gold is a
symbol of wealth.

They also offered frankincense, a perfumed incense used in religious rituals; and myrrh, a precious spice used in embalming the
dead. Now I hasten to note these are not normal baby shower gifts.
However, I see in the act of offering these gifts a compassionate
prayer for this little Prince of Peace, a prayer we must offer for every child if this world is ever to know peace and goodwill.

And what is the unspoken prayer in the Wise Men's offerings?

Gold: a prayer that this child might have sufficient material
resources for living.

Incense: a prayer that He might have spiritual strength for fulfilling God's purpose in His life.

And finally, a precious burial spice: a prayer that the hour of
His dying might be experienced and remembered with dignity.

Is not the Magi's prayer a universal petition offered on the
world's behalf by people of peace and goodwill for children and
their families no matter what their religion? Although most scholars believe that the Wise Men came from Arabia or Iran, we cannot
know with certainty their nationalities or language. We do not
know their religion. Were they Zoroastrian priests or indigenous
shamans?

It is also important to remember there is no evidence that as a
result of their visit these Wise Men converted to Judaism or embraced a faith in Jesus as their own Messiah. Remember, these were
learned stargazers and mythologists from the East. They were looking for the prophesied Jewish king, the royal heir, whose star they
came upon in the course of their normal research of the heavens
and related cultural myths.

In fact, in his gospel, Matthew uses the Greek word for "paying
homage to a ruler" rather than a term for divinity.

And what had the Wise Men expected to find at the end of

their long transcontinental expedition: a child in a palace attended by courtly servants or a member of a priestly caste surrounded by temple eunuchs?

Whatever the Magi may have expected, what they found was a vulnerable peasant family with a tender child—a child who was an object of political intrigue, an enemy of the state even before He was born; a child soon to be a political refugee in a foreign country, Egypt.

But the Magi clearly dismissed any disappointments they may have had and acted with adoration and compassion through their gifts of gold, frankincense, and myrrh. But perhaps their greatest gift was their fourth offering—the gift of justice, by refusal to return to King Herod and collaborate in his diabolical scheme to find and kill the child whom he believed to be his rival.

Whatever their religious convictions, they refused to be accomplices to evil and oppression by choosing, at great risk, not to report the child to Herod as he had commanded them. This reminds me of what Saint James wrote in his epistle: "Religion that is pure and undefiled before God, the Father, is this: to care for orphans and widows [those most in need] in their distress, and to keep oneself unstained by the [evil and political intrigue of the] world" (James 1:27, NAB).

I believe that the integrity of religion in the new millennium (Christian or otherwise) will not be measured by doctrinal orthodoxy, but rather by compassion and the spiritual courage not to be complicit with injustice, bigotry, or oppression, but to stand firmly and clearly for human dignity.

Therefore, in this Christmas season, I deeply believe that the story of the Wise Men must mean more to us than the submission of other religions to ours. Rather, it is also a call to remember that there must be peace and mutual respect among the great religions. For if there is anything we have learned in the years since the birth of Christ, it is that there is no world peace without peace among the religions. Should we not as Christians lead the way—nationally and in our own communities?

THE INTEGRITY OF RELIGION in the new millenium will be measured by compassion and the spiritual courage to stand firmly and clearly for human dignity.

In light of September 11, I think many of us now recognize that there are times in the human experience when the universal does—yes, even must—transcend the particular of religious and cultural boundaries. I believe there are circumstances—great moments in our collective and personal lives—when the transcendence of God (the God who "so loves the world") shines so brightly in the interest of peace and goodwill that the moral and spiritual integrity of men and women of peace and goodwill are drawn together beyond their own cultural traditions and religious orthodoxy. In such moments, it should never be a question where Christians stand.

Shortly after the World Trade Towers attack, a major Christian denomination sought to expel some of its clergy for participating in an interfaith service held on September 23 in Yankee Stadium in New York City. In a ten-page petition, church leaders accused the participants of idolatry by "participating with non-Christians." The document went on to call their participation "an egregious offence against the love of Christ" that diminished the priority of the Christian faith by giving the impression that it was one among many by which people can pray to God. The pastors under criticism said they saw the event as a "blessing; an opportunity to join other religious and civic leaders in offering comfort to a nation raw from the recent terrorist attacks" (*Washington Post*, December 2, 2001).

Well, I will let you decide which behavior most truly represents the love of Christ. But personally, I believe that as never before we are mindful that we live in a global village. Therefore, we must find ways to witness to the integrity of our Christian faith, accepting that, until Christ Jesus returns, there will not be agreement on religious revelations, doctrines, or practices.

Christian integrity also means we must grow to recognize and respect that the divine light of peace and goodwill—which we know as the light of Christ—can be found in people of other faiths as well. My brothers and sisters, we must do this! For as Martin Luther King Jr. said, "Either we will learn to live together as brothers and sisters, or perish together as fools."

CHRISTIAN INTEGRITY MEANS we must grow to recognize and respect that the divine light of peace and goodwill can be found in people of other faiths as well.

To know this truth, we need only look at the effect of religious intolerance in this past century. When religions do not work together out of the truest courage and compassion of their spiritualities, we get Nazism, Fascism, anti-Semitism, Communism, apartheid, slavery, Jim Crowism, and the tragedies of September 11. But when Christian people risk working with other people of peace and goodwill—religious and secular—systems of oppression fall, freedom and human dignity find new expression, and the joyous hope for peace and goodwill is again alive in the world. Just think of Poland, East Germany, and South Africa as examples.

I am Christian. I believe Jesus is the Son of God, the only begotten of God. Jesus is my Lord! I live to invite others to see the beauty of God through my faith. Through His death and resurrection, I have found salvation and hope for life everlasting. Intellectually, in Jesus I see and hear most clearly God's universal call to justice and human liberation; and through Jesus, we have come to know God as intimate and personal—as Abba, "Our Father, who art in heaven." I also believe in the Great Commission found in Matthew's gospel (28:19, NAB): "Go into all the world and proclaim the gospel of Jesus Christ, baptizing in the name of the Father, Son, and Holy Spirit."

But if there is compelling power in the gospel of Jesus Christ, it is the message of my life: my life revealing the spirit of Christ's love and compassion, His respect for the human dignity of others, and His courage to stand for justice and truth. These are the witnesses that will inspire the world. These are the compelling aspects of Jesus' earthly life that made disciples; and these must be the compelling aspects of my own life and message. The same spirit of God that was in Christ Jesus must be seen in you and me. It is not our dogma or doctrine that will change others or contribute to peace in the world. It is the Spirit of Christ in all we do.

And remember, it is God's Spirit to which Jesus came to testify; therefore only God determines where, how, and through whom glimmers of that divine Spirit of hope and peace will be revealed.

As Jesus said to Nicodemus, "The Spirit of God, like the wind, blows where it chooses" (John 3:8). The light of Christ shines where God wishes it to shine, bringing hope and truth. The light of God's love and justice is most pure and radiant in Christ, but it is also present wherever we see efforts for peace and goodwill among people.

A few years ago I had an opportunity to visit Saint Paul's Cathedral in London, one of the greatest monuments to Christianity in the world. The north transept of that enormous cathedral is dominated by an early-twentieth-century painting called *The Light of the World*, by William Holman Hunt. It is the familiar depiction you have seen many times on church bulletins and other Christian literature of Christ knocking at a darkened door holding a lantern of light: "Behold, I stand at the door and knock" (Revelation 3:20, NAB).

As depicted by Hunt's famous painting, the light from the lantern shines through the shapes in the lantern's design, shapes that are not only Christian crosses but Muslim crescents as well. Historian Ann Saunders interprets this peculiarity as meaning that the message of God is "for all the world, not only for those already nominally Christian."

Think for a moment of those who have so powerfully shown us the way to God's vision of shalom. Think of those whose lives have spoken and continue to speak so powerfully to the spirit of humanity across generations—across lines of culture, language, politics, race, and religion. Think of those who make us all see so vividly what the kingdom of God's love and justice and God's peace is really about. Can we honestly distinguish between the Christian Desmond Tutu, the Buddhist Dalai Lama; the Christian Mother Teresa and the Hindu Sister Dodi; the religiously eclectic Nelson Mandela or the Salvadoran martyr Catholic Archbishop Oscar Romero; the Hindu Mahatma Gandhi or the Baptist Martin Luther King Jr.?

Who, I ask you, among these people, was a greater living portrayal of the light of peace, the dream of God for human dignity?

In this regard I am always moved by those poignant questions in the Baptismal Covenant on page 305 of the Book of Common Prayer. The church asks: "Will you seek and serve Christ in all persons, loving your neighbor as yourself? Will you strive for Justice and peace among all people, and respect the dignity of every human being?"

We must say "yes" more boldly and more effectively in this new millennium. Yes, dear Christians, we must expand the sense of who is in God's family beyond our own religious identities. And we must remember that those "from the East"—Hindus, Sikhs, Buddhists, Muslims, and other peoples of faith, non-Christians—also can bear gifts that glorify God. We must grow beyond any bigotry or arrogance that keeps us from loving and respecting others as God would have us do.

Now I am sure there are some who say, "This Wise Man thing is all nice, but where does one find the spirit of Christ in Muslims who preach jihads and terrorism around the world, or Hindus in India who kill priests and missionaries and rape nuns?" But if these are the measure of other faiths, then we must apply the same standard to Christian radicals who bomb abortion clinics, Christians who preach that homosexuals should be put to death, or America's white supremacist Christian movements.

In recent years some prominent Christian leaders have spoken publicly of other religions as "evil." None of these is the true measure of Christianity any more than the evil of hateful radicals are the measure of other great faiths.

So, only together can we stand against the evil uses of religion. Only together can we find a global ethic against poverty, illiteracy, and disease. Only together will we find a spiritual and moral basis for the ever so crucial tasks of caring for this fragile earth, our island home. Only together can we address poverty, the sickness of children, and create a world where they can grow in safety and "study war no more." Only together can we learn and share what is uniquely the gift that God has given each community of faith for the glory of God. Yes, we must honor our religious distinctions, but we must never allow them to obstruct God's dream for the world.

ONLY TOGETHER CAN WE *learn and share what is uniquely the gift God has given each community of faith for the glory of God.*

I know this is hard work, but I believe it is the most essential work that we must do in these times. For, whatever the writer of the gospel of Matthew might have intended by preserving this scene of the Magi, with two devoutly Jewish parents (Mary and Joseph), and the infant Lord of Christendom, and these strangers "from the East," what I see is a powerful moment of peace and mutual respect between religions. Yes, the story of the Magi reminds us that in this new millennium we must all bring our gifts to the fragile infant of peace and goodwill. Jesus said, "Blessed are the peacemakers, for they will be called children of God" (Matthew 5:9, NAB).

And indeed, those who work for the vision of peace—for understanding, for reconciliation, human dignity, and justice—the peacemakes, they shall be called "children of God" whether their name for God is Adonai, Atman, Allah, Great Spirit, Jehovah, or "Our Father, who art in heaven."

Over twenty years ago, John T. Walker, episcopal bishop of Washington and dean of this National House of Prayer for All People, founded the Interfaith Conference of Greater Washington. It is an organization of many leaders of the great faiths around the metropolitan D.C. area. They continue in their twenty-first year to gather monthly in task forces, lobby groups, and discussion groups to address problems of our communities; to understand, share their faith experiences and beliefs; and (where possible) learn to respect religious differences. Every year this interfaith organization hosts a great concert offering performing religious arts from each tradition.

I shall never forget that in my first year as dean, the concert was held in the Washington National Cathedral, with almost three thousand people in attendance. In this great Christian cathedral I heard a Muslim imam chant the call to worship, I watched painted Hindu dancers, and listened to Jewish cantors. Then there was a Sikh instrumentalist accompanied by sacred singers. As the concert continued, a Vietnamese Roman Catholic youth choir danced and sang music from their culture. A black Baptist choir with drums and bass guitar rocked the pillars of the nave with the sounds of gospel music. Buddhist chanters rang little prayer bells, and barefooted Krishnas danced down the aisle.

I must admit that the experience was all too much for my traditional Anglican sensibilities. How could I, as a Christian, accept this?

At the end of the concert they all came together as one choir—more than two hundred voices: turbans of many colors, saffron robes, African kente cloth robes, and beards and painted faces. And in a great harmonious chorus they sang:

Joyful, joyful, we adore thee,
God of glory, Lord of love;
Hearts unfold like flowers before thee,
Praising thee their sun above.

As I beheld this strange crèchelike scene, my eyes began to fill with tears. I was overwhelmed with a strange and beautiful peace. Like the Magi, these strangers from afar were all offering their gift to the vision of divine peace on earth, goodwill to humankind. And like a great heavenly host of angels, they continued singing:

Thou art giving and forgiving,
ever blessing ever blest.
Wellspring of the joy of living,
ocean depth of happy rest.

Thou our Father, Christ our Brother,
All who live in love are Thine:
Teach us how to love each other,
lift us to the joy divine.

It was then I heard the voice of God saying deep within me, "Nathan, whatever your view of heaven may be, this is my dream for the world."

My brothers and sisters, as we contemplate our crèche scenes this Christmas season—the Child of Peace surrounded by Mary,

Joseph, shepherds, and angels—may we be inspired to bring our gifts of faith to the dream of God for peace and goodwill in the world. And may we also be inspired to honor the gifts of peace and goodwill offered by wise men and wise women from the East. Amen.

Vision Is a Process

A. R. BERNARD

BASED ON ISAIAH 53

The question posed by the prophet Isaiah in chapter 53 is reiterated in a conversation between Philip the evangelist and an Ethiopian eunuch who was part of a caravan under Candace, queen of Ethiopia.

The Holy Spirit instructed Philip to attach himself to that caravan, and when he got there, he found an Ethiopian official reading from the prophet Isaiah.

After reading Isaiah 53, the official wanted to know: "Is the prophet talking about himself, or is he talking about some other man?"

In response, Philip asked the man, "Do you know what you are reading?"

The Ethiopian replied, "How can I know unless someone teaches me?"

At that, Philip continued to expound on Isaiah 53.

But the question "Who has believed our report?" is an interesting query coming from the Almighty. Why would God even make a statement like that? Who would have trouble believing God's report with regard to redemption? Well, the reality is that there are still folks today who don't believe the Lord's report.

Then Isaiah poses another question in verse 1 (KJV): "To whom is the arm of the Lord revealed?" That's a powerful statement, to call Jesus "the arm of the Lord."

What does the arm do? The arm resides between the hand and the body. When you extend the arm, the hand is able to go far from the body because of the arm; yet it is attached.

So the whole imagery in Isaiah 53:1 is God extending Himself to the earth to reach humanity. So, to whom is God's arm revealed? Who understands what God is doing, reaching out to humankind? The birth of Jesus Christ was God reaching out to humanity.

So Isaiah asks two questions: "Who believes the report?" and, "To whom is what God is doing revealed?" Then he begins to explain the very questions he has asked.

The arm of the Lord, which is Jesus Christ, grew up before the Lord like a tender shoot, or plant, a root out of dry ground. He had no beauty or majesty to attract us to Him, nothing in His appearance that we should desire Him.

He was despised and rejected, a man of sorrows and familiar with suffering. Like one from whom men hide their faces, He was despised, and we esteemed Him not.

But then Isaiah says of this One whom we despised, "Surely he took up our infirmities and carried our sorrows." In the *King James Version,* verse five reads: "But he was wounded for our transgressions, he was bruised for our iniquities: the chastisement of our peace was upon him; and with his stripes we are healed."

Notice the words: "our . . . our . . . our . . . we." Everything Christ was engaged in while extending Himself had nothing to do with Him. It was not for His own benefit; rather, it was for the benefit of those to whom He was extending Himself.

In Genesis 1:26 (NIV), God said, "Let us make man in our image, in our likeness, and let them rule over the fish of the sea and the birds of the air, over the livestock, over all the earth, and over all the creatures that move along the ground."

God created humankind in His own image; male and female He created them. God blessed Adam and Eve, who represented all of humankind, and said to them, "Be fruitful and increase in number; fill the earth and subdue it. Rule over the fish of the sea and the birds of the air and over every living creature that moves on the ground."

Then God said to them, "I give you every seed-bearing plant on the face of the earth and every tree that has fruit with seed in it. They will be yours for food. And to all the beasts of the earth and the birds of the air and all the creatures that move on the ground—everything that has the breath of life in it—I give every green plant for good." And it was so.

Humanity is the focus of God's attention. God did all of this for humankind. In Genesis 14:1, God said, "let there be lights in the expanse of the sky to separate the day from the night, and let them serve as signs to mark seasons and days and years, and let them be lights in the expanse of the sky to give light on the earth."

Who would need to know about the passage of time? Humankind. Who would need signs and markings for seasons, day and night? Humankind.

Without human beings, the earth has no reason for existing. God did not create the earth for Himself, as though it was the only spot in the universe available for Him to reside.

God owns everything, but it doesn't mean that He created it for Himself. To understand that humanity is the central reason for the creation of the earth, you have to go beyond the earth and take a good look at the entire universe. The universe is much, much bigger than this speck called planet earth. We've just been so caught up in our environment that we think we are it.

There is a vast universe. Our solar system is but a speck in a galaxy of billions of stars in a stellar space of millions of galaxies. When we consider this, our mind goes "Whoa!" So we've got some nerve!

But we have to put it in perspective. Everything God did—everything He arranged on this planet—was not for Himself, though He gets glory out of everything He does. The reason for the formation of the earth is humankind.

Isaiah says that God did not create the world in a topsy-turvy fashion. Genesis 1 explains it in the same way: God created the world, and it was chaotic. Darkness was on the face of the earth. The term there was chaotic, as though some cataclysmic event took place that disrupted everything. The prophet Isaiah said that God did not create the world to be chaotic; He created it to be inhabited. And the inhabitant that He wanted on the earth was a creature that would reflect His image.

The truth can scare you sometimes! Take the truth about your potential—that will scare you! Right now, some folks are so afraid of their true potential that they're paralyzed and not getting a thing done.

You must always respect and reverence your own power. If you don't, you'll abuse it. But the other side of that is you can be negatively fearful to the point of paralysis. You have two extremes: Either you abuse it or you don't use it. Balance being the key to life, you want to realize it, recognize it, use it and be very reverential with it.

You must count the cost, but don't count too long. And the reason why we don't count too long is because if you're waiting for perfection conditions, you'll never get anything done. So if it says count the cost on one hand, and if you wait for perfect conditions on the other hand, you'll never get anything done there must be a balance.

THE BALANCE IS THIS: after you've counted the cost, you still must come to a point where you make a decision based on faith as to whether you go forward or not. Anything you do with God requires faith, because if you don't need faith, you don't need God.

It is God who puts vision and desire in the human being who has surrendered to Him. That's why God can give them the desires of their heart—because when that heart is surrendered to Him, that heart is open to the infusion of His own desires. So that person ends up desiring what God already has desired.

Jesus is the reason for the season, but we are the reason for the creation. Without humanity, the earth has no reason for existence. Jesus confirmed it when He said, "fear not, little flock, it is your heavenly Father's good pleasure to give you His kingdom."

Some religious-thinking folks have a problem with that because when they hear "to give you His kingdom," they think Jesus was talking about the great by-and-by, when we get to heaven.

To believe that you can only enter the kingdom of God when you die is to believe that Jesus' death was not enough to get you in; that it also requires your own death. It is best you never put yourself on that level. You went to the kingdom of God the moment you were born again.

JESUS SAID, "Except a man be born again,"—not "except a man die"—he cannot enter the kingdom of God and he cannot see the kingdom. So the new birth takes you into the kingdom and the kingdom begins in you, and will ultimately manifest itself to the rest of the world. But it begins inside the believers.

So you don't die so that you can get into the great by-and-by over there, the great kingdom of God. No, the moment you were born again you entered the kingdom. And the kingdom to you is presently a system of thought and conduct, which makes you a channel to bring a revelation of God into the earth's realm.

It took Jesus' death to get you into the kingdom, not yours. For too long, too many Christians have never had any kingdom expectations while they were here on earth. All of their kingdom expectations were in heaven. Don't become so heaven bound that you're no earthly good.

Because we have been so religious in our thinking, we take Scripture and conform it to what we think it should say, instead of realizing what it does say. Psalm 8:1–2 (NIV) reads:

"O LORD, our Lord,
how majestic is your name in all the earth!
You have set your glory
above the heavens.
From the lips of children and infants
you have ordained praise
because of your enemies,
to silence the foe and the avenger.

Then David writes in verses 3–5:

When I consider your heavens,
the work of your fingers,
the moon and the stars,
which you have set in place,
what is man that you are mindful of him,
the son of man that you care for him?
You made him a little lower than the heavenly beings
and crowned him with glory and honor.

David relates everything God has done to humanity. When God created all of what David describes in this psalm, He had humankind in mind. In verse 4, the term "son of man" is a double reference, because it also refers to the Incarnation of God in human form in Jesus Christ.

You made him ruler over the works of your hands;
you put everything under his feet:
all flocks and herds,
and the beasts of the field,
the birds of the air,
and the fish of the sea,
all that swim the paths of the seas.
O Lord, our Lord,
how majestic is your name in all the earth!

This is consistent with what He said in Genesis: He did it for you and me. And the worst thing that could happen is for you to have all of this accessible to you and do nothing with it but complain. To prove my point, let's look at the Prodigal Son's experience.

The Prodigal son took off from home, depleted his fortune, found himself in a pigpen, and then decided to go back home. The father was so happy at his son's return that he said, "My son was dead. He's alive from the dead! Kill the fatted calf. Let's have a feast! Let's party! Take out my best robe and put a ring on his finger to show his identification with me. Bring him in!"

Meanwhile, what did the other son do? Instead of rejoicing at his brother's return, he got an attitude. He was angry and jealous. The father tells him, "Hey man, while you were here, it was yours all the time. How could you get mad with your brother? You failed to enjoy what was yours."

We have to accept that humankind is the reason for the earth. God did all of this for us. We are the reason for redemption.

Why did God come in human form—to redeem the animals? No. He specifically took on the form that He wanted to redeem. The Incarnation of God in Christ immediately testifies to the importance of human life.

Now, the fact that God Himself would come into His own creation to identify with it—its pain and its suffering, for the purpose of delivering it from that pain and suffering—tells me that we are mighty important to God.

I'm with David: "What is man that You are so mindful of him, God?" What puts me on Your mind, God? Why am I on God's mind? Everything that God did, from Genesis to Revelation, was for me.

It's easy to sit back and be religious: "Praise the Lord! He did it for Himself!" No! He did it for you and me. And if I put it off on somebody else, I cannot fully appreciate what He did for me.

God does not go around to Christians and say, "Hey, you! Praise Me! You over there, praise Me!" God doesn't operate like that. When He does something in your life—opens a door for you, gives you favor here, creates a miracle over there—He doesn't have to say a word.

God does His work in your life and then makes you aware of who did it. Suddenly, from deep down inside, something rises up and you begin to say, "My God!" And then you go run and tell somebody, which further testifies to His power and greatness.

But you have to understand how it works, otherwise you'll be looking for God to work in a way that He doesn't work, and He won't be there. Without humanity, the earth and everything in it and about it has no reason for existence.

I appreciate people who are concerned about the abuse of animals. They're spending billions of dollars to save these animals, but sometimes, not far from their headquarters, are homeless people, people lying in the street, and people who don't have anything to eat.

If you save humanity, you save the animals, because the redemption of all of creation rests upon the redemption of humankind. All of creation grows and is in travail for the redemption of humanity. Because even creation knows that if humankind is redeemed, they will be redeemed and set free.

Hebrews 2:5–7 (NIV) tells us: "It is not to angels that he has subjected the world to come, about which we are speaking. But there is a place where someone has testified: 'What is man that you are mindful of him, the son of man that you care for him? You made him a little lower than the angels; you crowned him with glory and honor.'"

Does that sound familiar? Absolutely! Right out of Psalm 8. Paul the apostle, writing under the inspiration of the Holy Spirit, referred back to this Scripture passage on the importance that God places on humanity.

God put everything under the authority of humankind. God has not left anything that is not subject to humanity.

You have to take some time to absorb that, because there's a whole lot of stuff in this world that doesn't appear to be subject to humankind. It gets a little confusing sometimes. You know, you're supposed to be in control when stuff and circumstances just rise up and say, "No!"

God has not left anything that is not subject to humanity. Yet, at present, we do not see everything as subject to us. But we do see Jesus, who was made a little lower than the angels and crowned with glory and honor because He suffered death.

So what does this mean? What we see in Jesus Christ was the original intent for humanity. And though we cannot see the subjugation of creation to humankind, we can see it in Jesus Christ, who is a symbol of what God intended in Adam.

So if you want to know the kind of dominion that God wanted you to have, look at Jesus. For what you fail to see in other people, you will find in Christ. What you fail to see about God in other people, you will find in Jesus Christ.

In verses 14–16 (NIV), Paul continues, "Since the children have flesh and blood, he too shared in their humanity so that by his death he might destroy him who holds the power of death—that is, the devil—and free those who all their lives were held in slavery by their fear of death. For surely it is not angels he helps, but Abraham's descendants."

The King James Version reads, "He took on him the seed of Abraham," which is simply human nature. Why did he take on human nature? Why did He incarnate in that little manger scene that we call Christmas? To identify with humanity for the purpose of redeeming us, bringing us back to the original intention of God.

God was simply saying that God created it all—He made it beautiful—because it is a reflection of His own tastes. I believe that our environment is a reflection of our self-image, so when God created the garden for Adam, it had to look good. Because if God made us in His image, He knew what human beings would like, because it would be simply what He would like. And what God would like for Himself, He knew humankind would like for themselves.

The Bible says that in the fullness of time, God sent His Son, born from a woman. What was the fullness of time? Well, in Genesis 3:15, God makes a promise that a seed would come from the woman who will actually bruise the serpent's head. Got it? And the serpent would bruise the heel. And that seed, we now know, is Jesus Christ.

God would have to bring that seed through forty-two generations, a period of over four thousand years, before he would reveal in Christ the plan that he spoke of in Genesis. That's why every nation that oppressed Israel tried to commit genocide against them—

because of the seed. If you wipe out the nation that's carrying the seed, you wipe out the seed. So even when Israel rebelled against God, which caused them to come under oppression, He always made sure there was a remnant. There had to be somebody left of that nation to carry the seed into the next generation.

So there was a process—God engaged in over four thousand years of human history to bring about the Incarnation of Himself in Jesus Christ. In Matthew 23:34, Jesus said, "Behold I sent to you prophets; you killed them; you killed the priests; one you slew right at the altar." He said, "And then, He sent His own son, and you killed him, figuring that if you kill the son, you'll take it all."

Human redemption is a process that God went through. That's important in terms of vision because God sets the pattern. Israel was in bondage to Egypt for 430 years before the Lord showed up and said, "I heard your cry."

You heard us crying for 430 years? Couldn't you have made it a little sooner? But there was a process. He had to bring a family together—a man and woman who would give birth to a boy named Moses.

He would have to create a situation where there was pressure on the male children. That seems to be God's style, because when he brought forth Jesus, He did the same thing. So the pressure came on that family to save their baby. They put him in a little basketlike raft, and sent him out to safety.

Why is it that Pharaoh's daughter just happened to be out on the river that day and just happened to see that baby floating down? And she just happened to take the baby in, raise him, and give Him an education and upbringing that his parents were too poor to give, an education that he would need in order to lead several thousand people? It was a process.

Here's the principle: change is not an event; it's a process. And if you don't realize that, you will think that all you need is a major event to change your life. The event simply puts you in a place to make a decision and then commit to that decision—but the event does not create the change.

And yet there are people who think like that. Vision is the end result, but process takes you to the end result. What is process? It is a systematic series of actions that direct you to an end. Whatever that end result is, whatever that vision is, it's systematic, which means it's organized activity. They go in a certain order, a systematic series of actions that directs you to the vision, the end result.

The majority of people are committed to the end result, but they're not committed to the process. So they talk about losing weight, and have a picture of what they want to be like, but they're not committed to the process—the systematic series of actions that will take them to that end result, like a change in diet and exercising.

And we're good for talking about the end result, especially at Christmas. But if you are committed to the vision, the end result, but not committed to the process, then forget about it—because it is the process that takes you there.

If you want to be wealthy, you see yourself financially well off, but there is a process that takes you there. You cannot skip the process and jump to the vision. It won't work.

Process is a requirement in order to get you where you want to go. Change is a process, not an event. A process takes you to the end result. You must be as committed to the process as you are to the end result.

You want a better marriage? There's a process that will take you there. Be committed to the process.

God is a God of order and process. This Christmas season, think about the process God used to bring His Son into the world to save humanity. It took God four thousand years, but He was committed to the process.

You are made in His image. Whatever it is you want to accomplish, or achieve, there is a vision, an end result, and the process. You must be just as committed to the process as you are to the end result.

All the Christmases to Come

GEORGE G. BLOOMER

BASED ON MATTHEW 1:18–25

Joseph had a divine encounter that came from God Almighty, a visitation from the Lord. There are no long stories about Joseph; he could not handle all of the negative talk before the birth of his fiancée's child. When you're birthing something, there are going to be contractions.

When you're birthing something, there is going to be pain.

When you're birthing something, there are going to be climate changes, but you have to stay true to what's in your womb.

It's December 24, the day before Christmas, the day that every child waits for, dreams for. It's the big payoff. The year was 1970. Mattel had released a new toy called the Generator, a flashlight that generated its own electricity when you turned the handle. No need for batteries. There was also a chemistry set out that came with test tubes, a microscope, a dead frog, a turtle, and a bird—all perfectly preserved specimens to be dissected by "Dr." George Bloomer, the nine-year-old with a great imagination.

My father had promised that he would get these things for me. He'd told one of my friends, named Jon-Jon, who lived on the second floor of our building, in apartment 2-D. This little boy was the envy of every child in the projects because his mom and her live-in boyfriend lavished him with gifts that we could only dream about—a big wheel, a ten-speed bike, a Duncan yo-yo, a G.I. Joe doll, a train set, tons of play army soldiers, a badge, and a Lone Ranger gun with silver bullets. Jon-Jon had all the things that I could only wish to have one day.

But things changed when, around December 20, my dad promised me that on Christmas Eve he would come and take me shopping and buy me anything that I wanted—which for me was the Generator and the chemistry set. Finally, I would be able to compete with Jon-Jon—the crown prince of presents, the guru of gifts.

So early on Christmas Eve, about 7:00 A.M., I woke up to the smell of fresh bacon, scrambled eggs with cheese, grits, smoked sausage, and pancakes—the traditional Christmas Eve breakfast. It was the start of the Christmas festivities, with the big breakfasts, a little shopping, final gift wrapping, huge Christmas Eve dinner, and finally, waking up with excitement on Christmas morning, seeing that Santa had arrived.

About 9:00 A.M. on Christmas Eve, however, I became concerned. By 11:00 A.M., my sisters started laughing at me because I had been sitting by the door for the past three hours with mittens, a coat, and a hat on, awaiting the arrival of my dad, my Christmas genie who would grant me one wish.

By 3:00 P.M., I was waking from the nap that I'd taken while sitting at the door, sweat pouring down my brow. My mother urged me to take off my coat and mittens, encouraging me that my father would come. This was the same man who had abandoned her and never did what he'd promised her; yet she was able to hide her hurt and to hope silently that the rejection inflicted on her would not be transferred to her son.

"It takes a long time to get from Hempstead to Brooklyn, George," my mother told me.

"Do you think he's coming?"

"Sure. Did he say he was coming?"

"Yes."

"Then give your father a chance."

The word "chance" was a two-edged sword. If he didn't come, I would be devastated, but at the same time, this devastation could scar me for years to come. It's now 12:01 Christmas Day. He never showed up. I would not realize the extent of this devastation until years later, when I began to experience the residual effects of my father's rejection—having problems with trust, anger, and rejection. My past almost caused me to destroy my future.

Nevertheless, what the devil meant for evil, God would later allow me to use for good. There was great destiny being birthed in my womb, which I did not realize at the time. But today, it is what gives me the ability to minister more effectively to others who are going through the same thing.

Getting gifts and sharing in celebration at Christmas are wonderful for young and old alike. But we should never lose sight of the true meaning of Christmas. While I was seeking acceptance from someone who was rejecting me, I was unable to see the One who was covering me—Jesus Christ. While I was waiting for the chemistry set and the Generator, my mother was forced to conjure up words of comfort to protect my destiny. It was at this door of rejection that my mother preserved all the sermons that were yet to come from inside of me.

Can you imagine the decisions that Mary had to make to protect Jesus, hearing the decree that all the firstborn would be put to death? Knowing what was in her son? In Him were all the Christmases, the "Christ-mases" to come.

Herod's decree had no power over the life of Jesus. Likewise, the devil's decree that my destiny be destroyed that Christmas Eve, while I was sitting at the door waiting on my father, had no power.

While the devil sought to cripple my mind with the rejection that I endured, by the power of Christ I am able to preach the glad tidings of the kingdom of God.

My success today is directly attributed to the blessings and miracles of God. No longer do I allow one day to define who I am in comparison to others. I am now able to celebrate God's goodness throughout the year.

As parents we should instill within our children the true meaning of Christmas. While gifts are always fun to receive, we also should teach them the blessing of giving to others. One of the greatest blessings that I've had the privilege of experiencing is giving gifts to kids in the community—not just during Christmas, but also throughout the year. It's a story of success that I'm not only able to articulate by mouth, but also able to demonstrate by action.

The Forgotten Man at Christmas

CHARLES E. BOOTH

BASED ON MATTHEW 1:18–22; 2:13–15

Nobody likes to be forgotten. This is particularly true at this time of the year when the idea of remembrance is so prevalent with the giving of gifts. Regardless of how strong we say we are, everyone wants to be remembered at Christmas.

Brown v. The Board of Education of Topeka (1954) eradicated the "separate but equal" doctrine of *Plessy v. Ferguson* (1896) for education. The dominant name associated with this historic decision is Thurgood Marshall, and rightly so because his was the lead voice that argued this landmark case before the Supreme Court. However, Marshall was not the only force and dynamic behind this historic drama. By his side was an attorney who would later become president of Howard University—James Madison Nabrit Jr. In my opinion, Nabrit is a forgotten person in the *Brown v. Board* drama. The most forgotten man in this historic saga, however, was Charles Hamilton Houston, former dean of the Howard University Law School, who taught Thurgood Marshall.

It was Charles Hamilton Houston who inspired Marshall and

all of his law school students to be more than attorneys. He drilled in them the notion that they must become social engineers whose sole goal was to overturn *Plessy v. Ferguson.*

We talk about Thurgood Marshall, and rightly so, but the forgotten men in *Brown v. The Board of Education* are James Madison Nabrit Jr. and Charles Hamilton Houston.

I BELIEVE THAT Joseph is the forgotten man of Christmas. Joseph is mentioned in the Nativity narratives of Matthew and Luke, but material about him is scant. He is never quoted directly. He disappears from the gospel story following the holy family's return from Egypt. Even though we know precious little about Joseph, still there is sufficient information to make the claim that he must be remembered as well as emulated. Why should Joseph be remembered?

JOSEPH WAS NOT IMPULSIVE

Joseph was not a man to act on impulse. When Joseph is informed of Mary's pregnancy, knowing the child is not his, he is understandably disturbed and upset. The text says Joseph did not want to expose Mary to public disgrace, and he considered a quiet divorce. Notice the language of the text: "But after he had considered this . . ." (Matthew 1:20, NIV).

Joseph was not the kind of person to make snap decisions or hasty judgments. He considered his options but did not act on his initial impulse to divorce her. To have acted on impulse would have been to go against the grain of holy destiny. He was not, as we can sometimes be, a person who acted before thinking or speaking.

Not thinking before acting can be dangerous. Take a quick glance at your life! Have you ever acted in haste? Have you ever said or done something in haste, thus causing irreparable damage? Do you wish you could go back and reclaim a word or deed, knowing that with such reclamation life might be different today?

Nobody was more impulsive than Peter—always putting his mouth in motion before putting his mind in gear. When Jesus was arrested in the garden of Gethsemane, it was Peter who acted impulsively and dismembered a Roman centurion's ear. Peter was a man of impulse, not one who gave thought and consideration to his deeds.

I cannot help but raise the question: How much thought actually went into the decision to go to war against Iraq? The cold hard facts are that we had faulty intelligence, and weapons of mass destruction have never been found. The evidence causes one to question: Was the impulse to go after Saddam Hussein on the part of our president more personal than prayerful and thoughtful? Is it possible that all of the death and destruction we currently are witnessing in Iraq is the result of an impulsive act and not a well-thought-out and calculated strategy? Joseph thought before he acted.

JOSEPH WAS OBEDIENT TO THE ANGELIC COMMAND

Notice that when Joseph did not succumb to his emotions the text says, "Behold, the Angel of The Lord appeared to him in a dream . . ." (Matthew 1:20, NIV). God shows up with direction, if one will stop, think, and consider before acting impulsively. It is rather difficult for God to intervene and assist us if we are caught up in the emotion of impulse.

The Angel of the Lord explained to Joseph that Mary's pregnant condition is of the Lord and not human activity. Joseph understood that even though the Holy Spirit was responsible for Mary's impregnated condition, this did not erase the reality of public embarrassment and humiliation. Joseph still would live with the reality that people would talk and point the finger of blame at him for Mary's premarital pregnancy! Despite angelic explanation, Joseph would live with the stares, gossip, finger-pointing, and what would become a marred reputation. His character remained in check even though his reputation was now suspect. Whether we like it or not, what people say sometimes hurts and sticks, even if what is said is not true. Dr. Robert Franklin of Emory University pointed out in a *Time* magazine article (December 2005) that there is a similarity between Joseph and many of the African American men of slavery. Joseph had to raise a child whose paternity he could not claim. How many African American men during slavery thought their impregnated wives were giving birth to their son or daughter, only to discover at birth it was the master's child! The black man could do little or nothing because both he and his wife were chattel—property. This was more than embarrassment and humiliation.

This was for the African American man emasculation! At least Joseph was informed of his wife's pregnancy by the Holy Spirit. Black husbands in slavery were, in most instances, not. It is not always the easiest of tasks to raise another man's child. Many blended families can attest to this. Joseph deserves immense credit for not getting mad with God for putting him in such a precarious position. Joseph loves Jesus as his own, and never is there inferred or pronounced animosity or antagonism toward mother or child.

JOSEPH WAS A PROTECTOR

Joseph is to be remembered because he was a protector. Once again he was obedient to the angelic command and took Mary and Jesus into Egypt, where they as a family were told to remain until the death of Herod the Great. Joseph did not leave his family or vacate his responsibility as husband and father. He understood his role as the family protector.

50

Our women and children are to be protected by our men. From a biblical perspective, the man is to be both priest and protector in the home. How sad and tragic that we have come to a day and time when our communities, schools, and homes are no longer safe. In the African American community, our women are not safe. There was a time when black women feared sexual, emotional, and psychological abuse from racist men. Today, in unprecedented numbers, many of these abuses come from black men who may well be husbands, sons, and grandsons. Our sons and daughters tell horror stories of fathers, stepfathers, uncles, priests, and preachers who abuse and do so under the guise of kin, office, and title.

I believe Joseph is the original "Promise Keeper"! The Promise Keeper philosophy has to do with strong masculine role models in the biblical tradition. Such men bond together for the purpose of guiding and mentoring younger men in their quest for responsible manhood. Joseph bonded well with Jesus. Joseph protected Jesus as an infant, guided him as a child, taught him as a youth, and helped him develop his skills as a carpenter.

One need not think that Jesus' dazzling performance before the elders in the Temple at age twelve was the sole result of budding omniscience. He had been well taught by Joseph—father and priest of the home. Joseph not only taught his son the sacred truths of Hebrew Scripture but impacted Jesus in such a profound way that Jesus plied Joseph's trade and became a carpenter. Long before people called Jesus the Christ, Messiah, Redeemer, or Son of the Most High God, they called him "The Carpenter's Son"!

Thank God for Joseph, the humble carpenter from Nazareth— The Forgotten Man at Christmas!

Christmas Past, Present, and Future

Mark G. Boyer

Every Sunday and holy day at Saint Francis of Assisi, after the homily, we stand and recite the Profession of Faith. After declaring that we believe in one God, we begin a series of statements regarding what we believe about Jesus Christ, "the only Son of God, eternally begotten of the Father."

There was never a time when the Son of God did not exist. He has always been begotten by the Father.

We continue the Profession of Faith, saying: "For us men and for our salvation he came down from heaven: by the power of the Holy Spirit he was born of the Virgin Mary, and became man."

We believe that God, in the human person of Jesus of Nazareth, descended from heaven and was born on this earth. Through the intervention of the Holy Spirit, He was conceived in the womb of the Virgin Mary, and after nine months He was born. God became man; God entered into His creation a creature. Thus, every time we make our Profession of Faith we say that we believe in Christmas.

The Roman Catholic Church instructs us to make a profound

bow at the words professing the Incarnation on every Sunday and solemnity: "He was born of the Virgin Mary, and became man." However, on Christmas we genuflect, because Christmas celebrates the birth of God among us.

And who can't bow his or her head? Who can't genuflect when mentioning such a stupendous divine act? The Creator has become one of His own creatures.

CHRISTMAS PAST

It is easy to get stuck in Christmas past. Christmas past is depicted as Baby Jesus in a manger. Mary and Joseph stand guard while shepherds approach, sheep slumber, and Magi from the East make their way. That's Christmas past. It presumes that Christ's birth two thousand years ago was a once-in-a-lifetime-of-the-world event.

After he was born, he grew up. Then, after preaching about God's kingdom for a few years, He died on the cross and was raised from the dead. He ascended into heaven; He returned to God. And the purpose of the Incarnation was finished. But Christmas past is not all there is to Christmas. There is also Christmas present.

CHRISTMAS PRESENT

See, while Christmas remembers the birth of Jesus, the emptying of the Son of God into human form, the descent of God to the earth, that's not all there is to Christmas. Christ's resurrection and ascension do not mean that the Incarnation was finished. There is no such thing as a "dis-incarnation." Once the Incarnation was begun, it could not be stopped. That means that Christmas continues. Christmas is present.

Christmas is present in that Christmas continues in every mass. That's the meaning of the very word "Christmas"—Christ's mass. Christ's real, incarnate presence continues in the breaking of the bread and the sharing from the cup. During mass, recalling the words of the Last Supper, the priest says, "This is my body. This is my blood." That means that the bread is the body of Christ; the wine is the blood of Christ. In that sacrament, our God is upon our altar, emptying Himself for us over and over again. Here is the Incarnation taking place sacramentally. Here is Christmas present.

Then we come forward to eat the body of Christ and to drink the blood of Christ. We become what we eat and drink.

We become the body of Christ. The Eucharistic minister says: "The body of Christ." We answer: "Amen."

We say, "Yes, this bread is the body of Christ." Each of us says, "Yes, I am a member of the body of the Christ. And together all of us are the body of Christ. Amen."

We become the blood of Christ. The Eucharistic minister says: "The blood of Christ." We answer: "Amen."

We say, "Yes, this wine is the blood of Christ." Each of us says, "Yes, I am a member of the blood of the Christ. And together all of us are the blood of Christ. Amen."

Here, in eating the body of Christ and drinking his blood, we make the Incarnation present in our own flesh. Here is Christmas present.

And there is still more of Christmas present. Wherever we go, whatever we do, whomever we meet, we bring the Incarnation to others. In other words, we bring Christ to other people; we are the walking Christ to others.

Others should see Christmas in us. Others should see the Incarnation in our lives. It's who we have become.

Through the gifts we give, through the cards we send—through us the Incarnation continues. We recognize and honor the fact that the Incarnation begun two thousand years ago is now taking place here in one another. Here is Christmas present.

CHRISTMAS FUTURE

And what about Christmas future? Christmas future is not yet revealed. Through God's self-emptying in the person of Jesus Christ, everything—everything and every person—has been transfigured. The Incarnation changed everything.

We do not know what we will become. We believe that Christ will come again and that His kingdom will have no end. We believe that the Incarnation, once it was begun, will never end. One day God will be all in all. And that will be Christmas future.

"By the power of the Holy Spirit He was born of the Virgin Mary, and became man." At those words we genuflect at Christmas. Who wouldn't, or who couldn't, genuflect or bow at those important words? How awesome the mystery of Christmas past!

In the Catholic tradition, we believe that we all can be the incarnate Christ over and over again. And we believe that we can participate again in the Incarnation when we come forward to eat the body and drink the blood of Christ and make Christmas present here in this place. How awesome the mystery of Christmas present!

And as we wait in joyful hope for the coming of our Savior, Jesus Christ, we trust that Christmas future will one day be ours—when God will be all in all and complete what he started two thousand years ago. How awesome the mystery of Christmas future!

See, we are surrounded forever in Christmas. It is past, it is present, and it is future. We remember the past, we celebrate the present, and we await the future.

That's what we say every time we in the Catholic tradition make our Profession of Faith: "By the power of the Holy Spirit He was born of the Virgin Mary, and became man."

We Have Something to Give

CECELIA WILLIAMS BRYANT

BASED ON 2 CORINTHIANS 4:5

The season of Advent brings with it a wonderful word of encouragement and hope for these times of terror. In the midst of our holiday maneuverings, we interrupt our shopping mania and ceremonies of indulgence to reclaim the mystery and the wonder of God's redeeming love.

As United Methodist bishop Reuben Job explains, "We are the window through which the world sees God." Therefore, the Christian community must endeavor to let the world see through us that a beloved community is possible—a place where forgiveness dismantles revenge; where compassion eliminates poverty; where love is greater than class, nationalism, or gender; and where prevailing prayer heals our hurts, awakens us to prophetic purpose, and keeps us together.

Advent is not for cowards. The "Coming One" while camouflaged as an infant, the Messiah is actually the Warrior Prince of Peace whose only assignment is the healing of the nations. And so it is that the redeemed can never be as others are. We have been waiting for Advent—waiting to remember again the light that shines from a broken lamp. Indeed, something good *has* come out of Nazareth! Now we are waiting to see again the star that shines in the East so that we might remember again that the Advent journey leads home. The One who was born has been born again in us and we "fear no evil."

As the "Coming One" is gifted to us by the Almighty God of the universe, we who are redeemed become the gifting in every generation. Let's get it right this time! The whole world is watching. The whole world is waiting. We are well able to make sure that, according the prophecy of Isaiah 11:9, the earth is "filled with the knowledge of God, as the waters cover the sea."

Our gifting is not for our personal use or glorification. As the apostle Paul explained it, "We don't go around preaching about ourselves; we preach Christ Jesus, the Lord. All we say about ourselves is that we are your servants because of what Jesus has done for us" (2 Corinthians 4:5, NLT).

In order to affirm that we have something to give, we must recognize that faith is the power that unleashes the gift of God. What we have to give does not involve shopping malls, credit card debt, catalogs, or eBay. Contrary to the picture-perfect expectations the media feeds us regarding the Christmas gift-giving season, what we have to give is not stress inducing or anxiety provoking, nor does it drive one to suicide. The gospel is first of all a spiritual thing, accomplished by the Spirit—communicated in the power of the Holy Spirit—and visits spiritual manifestations in the congregation of faith. The intent of the gospel is the inner life of the disciple.

There is an incomplete theology in our time that parades itself as the gospel. You can recognize it because it promotes wealth without compassion, success without justice, grace without sacrifice, or praise with no prophetic burden.

This is not the gospel of Jesus Christ. The gospel teaches, "No cross, no crown."

The gospel teaches, "You will have power when the Holy Ghost is come" (Acts 1:8, KJV), but it also teaches that "men shall revile you, and say all manner of evil against you falsely" (Matthew 5:1, KJV).

According to Old Testament scholar Walter Brueggemann, "The people of God are marked by visionary concerns," and this must be the driving force in our lives. In other words, when my inspiration comes from the Holy Spirit, my aspirations become supernatural. What wakes me up in the morning is the knowledge that I have something to give. I no longer see things as they are; I see things as they can be!

Only when the Source of my inspiration became spiritual could I grasp what Dr. Martin Luther King Jr. got out of this song:

If I can help somebody as I pass along,
If I can cheer somebody with a word or song,
If I could show somebody he's traveling wrong,
Then my living shall not be in vain.[1]

We have something to give! It is the spiritual product of our inner life! It is because of what Jesus has done for us. It's time we understood exactly what Jesus has done for us; then we will know why we are so gifted.

To discover what Jesus has done for us, we cannot look solely to the Incarnation—Christmas, the Virgin Birth, the Word becoming flesh—because the Incarnation is nothing more than a promise, a sign pointing beyond itself to something greater!

To learn what Jesus has done for us we must look past the angels, the shepherds, the Wise Men, and the manger.

To learn what Jesus has done for us, we must follow the sign that leads to Calvary.

Why do we have something to give? To answer this question further, let us deconstruct the crucifixion of Jesus of Nazareth. For the sake of historical justification you can leave the crown of thorns, but take away His sonship, His divinity. You can leave the flogging, but take away His covenant sacrifice. In fact, you can leave the nails; just remove His redeeming love. Since we have gone this far, go ahead and pierce Him in the side, but extract His ministry of atonement. What do we have left? A first-century Rodney King episode!

But if we allow the will of God to remain uncontested, and thereby the gospel to be unmarred (John 3:16), we discover what it is that Jesus has done for us. We need only consult the prophet Isaiah 53:5: "He was wounded and crushed for our sins; He was beaten so that we might have peace. He was whipped, and we were healed" (NLT). All of us have gone astray; yet the Lord laid upon Him our guilt and sin.

This is why we preach Jesus and not ourselves. Popular religion would have us embrace a theology that has been emptied of suffering and rejection. But it is not so if we embrace the whole gospel, which means, "Although I have something to give, I cannot escape the midnight of the Lord."

There are times when I find myself in the wilderness. When I am least able to endure it, I will face the silence of God. Because of what Jesus has done for me, disappointment does not make me bitter; it makes me better.

Paul says to the Corinthians, "We are pressed on every side by troubles, but we are not crushed and broken. We are perplexed, but we don't give up and quit. We are hunted down, but God never abandons us. We get knocked down, but we get up again and keep going" (2 Corinthians 4:8–9, NLT).

Why? Because we have something to give.

The way we give is sometimes called special abilities or spiritual gifts, or even grace gifts.

Former missionary and scholar Peter Wagner once said, "No local congregation will be what it should be, or what Jesus prayed that it would be, or what the Holy Spirit has gifted and empowered us to be until it understands spiritual gifts."

First Corinthians 12:4–7 explains that there are different kinds of spiritual gifts. But all the gifts have the same source—the Holy Spirit—and the same purpose: to bless the church.

Not only do you have something to give, but Proverbs 18:16 declares that your gift will make room for you.

Your gift will open doors you thought were shut and raise up friends for you in high places!

If anyone had asked him, Ray Charles would have said blindness cannot handicap your gift.

Nelson Mandela will tell you that being a convicted felon does not put your gift on lockdown.

Oprah will tell you that not even incest can pervert your gift.

Venus and Serena are proof that growing up in the 'hood does not mean you have to impoverish your gift.

But greatest of all, Jesus has conquered all things (Romans 8:37); and just as Paul taught, we have this gift "in earthen vessels that the excellence of the Power would be of God and not of us" (2 Corinthians 4:7, NKJV).

The gift of God is spiritual power. Because of what Jesus has done for us, we can say with Paul, "Thanks be to God for His unspeakable gift" (2 Corinthians 9:15, KJV).

We have something to give! Give it now; give unconditionally. Give with your whole heart.

Don't allow your past or your circumstances to intimidate you. Don't be discouraged because you didn't get it right the first time or even the second time.

Paul wrote Timothy, "Stir up the gift" (2 Timothy 1:6). You've still got it! Time cannot erase it. Failure does not cancel it. You've still got it!

You have something to give! Give it now, unconditionally, with your whole heart.

Give until weapons of mass destruction are extinct.

Give until toxic wastes no longer threaten humanity.

Give until deforestation and global warming are reversed.

You have something to give! Give it now! Give unconditionally, with your whole heart.

Give until a new day dawns.

Give until HIV/AIDS is eradicated.

Give until justice rolls down like water, and righteousness like a mighty stream (Amos 5:24).

You have something to give. Give it now. Give unconditionally. Give with your whole heart.

Give until Ethiopia shall stretch forth her arms (Psalm 68:31).

Give until men beat their swords into plowshares and their spears into pruning hooks (Isaiah 2:4).

Give until nation shall not rise up against nation (Matthew 24:7).

Give until we study war no more.[2]

Like the Corinthians, the only reason we come together is because of what Christ has done for us.

Advent is a season of joy! Don't let Advent find you mourning, despondent over memories of the dead, obsessively engaged in acquiring debt, and thereby sustaining humiliation. In this season, don't be seduced by self-pity into isolation or wandering in a stupor of indulgence. Allow the spirit of Advent to place you at a new center of awe and amazement as you give yourself anew to the One who comes. You have something to give!

During Advent, let each heart pray to the Lord to bring joy to the world as together we allow the Word of God to awaken, transform, and disciple us, in the wonderful name of Jesus.

NOTES

1. A. Bazel Androzzo, copyright © 1945.

2. Negro spiritual.

Have You Seen Jesus?

JOHN R. BRYANT

BASED ON LUKE 2:25–30

I remember watching the six o'clock news during one Advent season while visiting in Saint Louis, Missouri. A lead-in to the news announced, in a very serious voice, that Baby Jesus was missing; he had been stolen. After the commercial, the lead story of the evening news reported that in a nearby community some unidentified person or persons had stolen the Baby Jesus figure from the community's Nativity display.

The television reporter interviewed a couple of people who were in the vicinity. Both expressed how awful it was that someone would do such a thing. The reporter went on to say that the police could not determine the exact time that the theft took place, but it was noticed about midday that the Baby Jesus was missing. Everything else was left intact. The Nativity scene included Mary, Joseph, shepherds, animals, manger, but there was no Jesus.

They ended the report by asking the viewing audience for their help with leads on the theft. The news team asked that everyone be on the lookout for the missing Jesus; anyone having information on the whereabouts of Jesus should contact the television station. The lead reporter looked right into the camera and asked whoever took Jesus to return him, and also announced that the person would not be prosecuted.

Aligning myself with those appalled by the theft, I decided then and there to become involved in the search. I, too, am outraged that Jesus has been stolen from the Christmas scene. And because I have joined the search-and-rescue team, I am compelled to ask you, "Have you seen Jesus?"

Have you even noticed that Jesus is missing from Christmas?

Jesus has been stolen—snatched right out of the miraculous imagery of Christmas. He has been stolen by commercialism. During the Sundays of the Christmas season, there are more cars at the shopping malls than there are in church parking lots. In the name of spreading the Christmas spirit, more money is collected at the malls than in the churches of the Lord Jesus Christ.

Yes, Jesus has been stolen. He has been stolen by a secular culture that doesn't even believe in Him. They have gone so far as to remove His name, and replaced it with an *X*. Have a merry "Xmas."

Jesus has been stolen right before the eyes of apathetic believers. Wake up! Jesus has been stolen! Can't you see that?

It was reported that a Wal-Mart store near Grand Rapids, Michigan, opened its doors for a Christmas sale, and when a crowd of people rushed in, some of them fell down. Those who were still standing simply stepped over them in their rush to buy "Christmas" presents. Jesus is missing from Christmas.

Once they were inside, customers broke out into fistfights trying to buy the latest popular video games and the units used to play them. Jesus is missing from Christmas.

It was also reported that at another Wal-Mart, a high school choir was singing Christmas carols in front of the store. The store's management called the police to come and remove the young people because they were blocking the entrance, making it difficult for paying customers to come in and shop. Jesus is missing from Christmas.

I know some of us have not noticed that He has been stolen because, as the Saint Louis news telecast reported, everything else is in place. Santa Claus is in place, along with his reindeer. The sleds, Christmas trees, lights, mistletoe, eggnog, parties, and big dinners are all in place. The presents have all been bought. Are they presents for Jesus? Oh no, presents for us, not for Jesus, because Jesus is missing.

Personally, I do not want to spend another Christmas without Jesus. I want Jesus back, so I need to know: have you seen Jesus? He gives better gifts than Santa Claus. His gifts do not break or go out of style. His gifts are of the highest quality.

The Bible tells us that every good and perfect gift comes from our God (James 1:17). I need more than what is sold at department stores. I want the gifts that Jesus has to give. Jesus gives abundant life, eternal salvation, peace, joy, and much more. But since these things are missing from so many people's lives, it is important that we find Jesus.

The Christmas story, as told in the gospel of Luke, introduces us to a believer named Simeon. This man is described as righteous, devout, and one upon whom the Holy Spirit rested (Luke 2:25).

Simeon actually saw Jesus (Luke 2:28–30). The Bible teaches us that if we too are to find Him, we must be like Simeon. If we are to see Jesus, we too must be righteous. To be righteous is to be in right relationship with God. To believe in God and to be determined to obey God makes one righteous.

Simeon was also devout. This man filled his life with spiritual disciplines. To find Jesus today you need to develop a prayer life, study God's Word, and be a worshiper. Luke tells us that Simeon had the Holy Spirit upon him. We too must have this relationship with God. The Holy Spirit makes us determined to be in the presence of Jesus (Luke 2:26).

We, like Simeon, must live our lives on tiptoe. We must believe we will find the Word, and live daily expecting to see Him, hear Him, and feel Him.

The Holy Spirit revealed to Simeon that he would find Jesus in the Temple (Luke 2:27). Our search for Jesus ought to also be centered in the house of the Lord. Every time we come to church we ought to expect to see Jesus. Do not be satisfied with anything less.

This Christmas I want to see more than family members. I want to see more than trees and lights. I want to see more than brightly wrapped presents. I want to see more than mistletoe and holly. I want to see Jesus! I want to experience His Spirit—in my church, in my home, on my job, and in my community.

If Jesus is in your heart He cannot be stolen. If He is in your heart, not even a secular age can remove Him. Jesus is the light of the world, and the darkness of this world cannot dominate Him or understand Him (John 1:5).

This Christmas I challenge you to follow the light. Let us consciously seek Jesus daily. Let us make Jesus the focus of our prayers.

The Bible promises that those who diligently seek Jesus will find Him. Simeon teaches us through the text that the Lord responds to human devotion. If you praise Him, He will come.

This hymn encourages each one of us to look for Jesus:

Look and live, my brother, live!
Look to Jesus now, and live;
'Tis recorded in His word, hallelujah,
It is only that you "look and live."[1]

Have you seen Jesus? If you search for Jesus you will find Him. Those who find Him will experience the same joy that Simeon did.

This joy that comes from finding Jesus is a gift that comes from above.

It is a gift that Madison Avenue can't create, that no business can manufacture, that a credit card can't acquire, and most important, that an unbelieving world cannot steal.

> *This joy that I have,*
> *The world didn't give it to me . . .*
> *The world didn't give it;*
> *The world can't take it away.*[2]

NOTES

1. "Look and Live," by William A. Ogden, Ph.D.

2. Negro spiritual.

Giving Is the Mark of Greatness

KEITH A. BUTLER

BASED ON ISAIAH 9:6

Our heavenly Father sent us that baby in the Bethlehem manger for one specific purpose, which can be rendered in one verse. First John 3:8 reminds us of why we celebrate Christmas. It's about God's love for you, delivering you, and setting you free. It's about you being able to have eternal life: "For this purpose the Son of God was manifested, that he might destroy the works of the devil." Sin, sickness, poverty, fear, depression, lack, want—all of those things Jesus came to rid us of.

Now, because God loved us, He showed us the mark of greatness, which is giving. Thank God that we are able to receive, but giving is the mark of greatness. God gave His only begotten Son, that whosoever shall believe in Him should not perish, but have everlasting life.

Now in Acts 20:35 (KJV), Paul tells us, "I have shewed you all things, how that so labouring ye ought to support the weak, and to remember the words of the Lord Jesus, how he said, 'It is more blessed to give than to receive.'"

Our tradition of giving gifts to one another at Christmas comes from us replicating God in giving gifts to others—gifts not just to loved ones, but to those we may not want to give to. Show love to them anyway.

In Luke 12:32, Jesus said, "Fear not, little flock, for it is your father's good pleasure to give you the kingdom." God takes pleasure in giving you joy, great pleasure in prospering you financially, great pleasure in providing healing for your body, and great pleasure in giving you eternal life.

Don't ever think that God doesn't want you to have anything. The Bible tells us that all good things come from God. He gives us good things because God wants to have pleasure. He takes great pleasure in blessing you, so why deny God His pleasure? Receive His blessings for you.

Giving is the mark of greatness when the gift is given properly, from a right heart. In Luke 6:38, Jesus says, "Give and it shall be given unto you." But what giving is He talking about?

Beginning at verse 33, Jesus said:

> "And if ye do good to them which do good to you, what thank have ye? for sinners also do even the same. And if ye lend to them of whom ye hope to receive, what thank have ye? for sinners also lend to sinners, to receive as much again. But love ye your enemies, and do good, and lend, hoping for nothing again; and your reward shall be great, and ye shall be the children of the Highest: for he is kind unto the unthankful and to the evil. Be ye therefore merciful, as your Father also is merciful. Judge not, and ye shall not be judged: condemn not, and ye shall not be condemned: forgive, and ye shall be forgiven: Give, and it shall be given unto you; good measure, pressed down, and shaken together, and running over, shall men give into your bosom. For with the same measure that ye mete withal it shall be measured to you again." (Luke 6:33–38, KJV)

So if you give big forgiveness, it's coming back to you in a big way if you ever need it. If you ever need to be blessed financially, and you've helped other people when they needed it, it'll come back to you in a big way. If you aren't judgmental and quick to kill people with your judgment, if you ever need mercy, then mercy will be extended to you in a big way.

Jesus said, "Give and it shall be given unto you." Giving is the mark of greatness. When you give with the right heart, it will come back to you in good measure, pressed down, shaken together, and running over. Then people will give to others.

What I like about God is that He treats us all equally. God doesn't have any big favorites. He gives people different jobs to do and different anointings. Sometimes people think He has favorites because He calls certain people to do certain things. God holds people accountable for whatever He calls them to do. Unto whom much is given, much is required (Luke 12:48).

Matthew 20 begins a parable about the kingdom of heaven. Jesus compares the kingdom of heaven to a landowner who went out early in the morning to hire laborers to work in his vineyard. He agreed to pay the laborers a penny a day. He went back out about at around 9:00 A.M. and saw others standing idle in the marketplace. He said to them, "Go into my vineyard. Whatever is right I will pay you," so they went to work for him.

He went back out at noon and again at around 3:00 P.M., and got more workers. With all of them he did the same thing; he found idle laborers and gave them an assignment. To all of them he said, "I am going to give you what is right." Then about the eleventh hour, or about five o'clock in the evening, he went out one last time and found others at the marketplace standing idle. He asked them, "Why are you standing idle around here all day?" They responded, "Because no man hired us." So the man made the same promise to the men he met at the eleventh hour—that he would pay them what was right.

At the end of the day, the man instructed his stewards to call in all of the laborers who had worked for him that day. He paid all the workers, beginning with those who were hired last. When it came time to pay the workers hired first, seeing how much the other workers had been paid, they thought that they should receive more because they had worked longer.

But when they had received their pay, the workers who had been there all day were disgruntled and began to speak against their employer. But the landowner told one of them, "My friend, I haven't been unfair to you! Didn't you agree to work all day for the usual wage? Take it and go. Is it against the law for me to do what I want with my money and pay the last workers as much as I did the first? Am I wrong for being kind?"

Jesus concludes His parable with, "So the last shall be first, and the first last: for many be called, but few chosen" (Luke 20:17, KJV). God is saying that even though some have come into the fold just this year, and others have been laboring for almost thirty years, God will bless everyone the same, because He is good.

There are people who have gone on into glory after having given themselves to Jesus on their deathbed. Heaven is going to be their home just as it will for those who have lived for Him all their lives, because God is good. Not only is He good, He is good all the time.

Giving is the mark of greatness, and that child in the manger was a display of God's greatness and goodness, regardless of who you are or where you come from.

The kingdom of God is equal, for God has made us all equal. Race, creed, color, gender, nationality, and economic status do not matter. With God there are no big I's and little you's, because God loves us all.

Psalm 29 begins: "Give unto the Lord, O ye mighty, give unto the Lord glory and strength. Give unto the Lord the glory due unto his name; worship the Lord in the beauty of holiness" (Psalm 29:1–2, KJV). What happens when you do that? Psalm 29:11 tells us: "The Lord will give strength unto his people; the Lord will bless his people with peace." Nothing missing, nothing broken; that's what peace means.

Psalm 85 also affirms that giving, the mark of the greatness, is modeled for us by the Father Himself, and He expects us to imitate Him in giving—giving in love, giving of joy, giving when people don't deserve, but doing it anyway.

Psalm 85:12 reads: "Yea, the Lord shall give that which is good; and our land shall yield her increase." Our Lord is good, and so for us, our land is going to yield increase. Then, verse 13 tells us that righteousness shall go before Him and shall set us in the way of His steps.

God is good, giving, and generous in His blessings. That is why Psalm 92 tells us to praise God:

> *It is a good thing to give thanks unto the Lord, and to sing praises unto thy name, O most High. . . .*
> *But my horn shalt thou exalt like the horn of a unicorn, I shall be anointed with fresh oil.*
> *My eye also shall see my desire on my enemies, and my ears shall hear my desire on the wicked that rise up against me.*
> *The righteous shall flourish like the palm tree, he shall grow like a cedar in Lebanon.*
> *Those that be planted in the house of the Lord shall flourish in the courts of our God.*
> *They shall still bring forth fruit in old age. They shall be fat and flourishing*
> *To show that the Lord is upright. He is my rock and there is no unrighteousness in him.*
>
> (Psalm 92:1, 10–15, KJV)

He is our rock; He is upright. He's so good to us. We can trust Him.

That baby in the manger signifies God's undying love for humanity. He signifies God's undying commitment to you and me. So lift your hands before the heavenly Father and praise Him for the Gift He has given.

Open your mouth and give Him praise, glory, and honor; for He is good, and His mercy endures forever.

Giving is the mark of greatness. The Gift that God has given us is the mark of His greatness. He has given us Himself.

PRAYER

Thank You, Father, for sending your Son, Jesus. Thank you, Jesus, for loving us enough to come down to us.

The Fullness of Christ Revealed

Anthony Campolo

BASED ON EPHESIANS 4:13

Although it's not a traditional Christmas story text, Ephesians 4:13 really captures what Christmas is all about. In Jesus, the fullness of Christ was revealed; the fullness of God was made known to us. If you want to know what God is all about, if you want to talk about the nature or the essence of God, it's not some philosophical statement; it's not some theology. Christmas is God incarnated in a human being. All that God is, is revealed in Jesus. But that's just part of the verse.

Not only is He the revelation of the fullness of God; the rest of the verse goes on to say that in Him is the revelation of the fullness of our humanity. That means we're supposed to be like Jesus. Not that we've already attained this. We haven't yet reached that goal.

Every once in a while somebody comes to me and says, "The church is full of hypocrites." And I always tell them, "You're going to feel right at home there."

The truth is we are hypocrites who are trying to overcome our hypocrisy through the grace of God and the power of the Holy Spirit.

Paul writes in Philippians 3:12 that it's not as though we've already attained this; we're still pressing toward that goal, the high calling of God in Christ Jesus our Lord.

The Bethlehem Jesus is not only the full expression of God, He is the manifestation of what each of us is supposed to become. That's the goal. And, it has not yet appeared what we shall be, says 1 John, but one day, when we meet Him face-to-face, we shall be like Him. Between now and then, however, we're pressing on the upward way.

As we press on, we look to Jesus and see what we're supposed to become. In Him, we see several things.

LOVE TRUMPS LAW

That love is more important than the Law was Jesus' great conflict with the Pharisees. These legalists were into a religiosity that was rules and regulations, do's and don'ts. Nevertheless, Jesus does not minimize the importance of keeping rules, or the significance of keeping the law. He simply says, you can do all of these things, but if you don't have love, it doesn't amount to anything.

Charles Spurgeon, the great Baptist preacher, once went to Oxford to visit a wealthy Turkish gentleman who wanted to make a contribution to a missions project. Spurgeon went to Oxford with two of his deacons. When they entered their host's living room, the man, who was not a Christian, opened a box of cigars and offered a cigar to each of these Baptists. Now, for those of you who don't know, you have to understand that Baptists are "types." We don't dance, we don't smoke, we don't chew, we don't even go to Disneyland; we are very straight people. You can imagine the deacons' great indignation at being offered cigars. However, Spurgeon, this great evangelical preacher, reached out, took a cigar, lit it, sat down, and they had a pleasant conversation.

On the way back to London on the train, the deacons really reeled out Spurgeon and said, "How could you compromise the testimony of our church by smoking a cigar in front of that Turkish man who isn't even a Christian?"

And Spurgeon answered, "Well, one of the three of us had to act like a Christian." Certainly, Spurgeon was not advocating smoking. The issue was not whether smoking cigars is a good thing or a bad thing. The fact is there's something more important—being kind and gracious to people, reaching out to them with thoughtfulness, and respecting them and their dignity.

We are called to live love in action, and we all have our place to fulfill this calling. You don't have to go off to the mission field to do it; you can do it right where you live.

A woman who had been deserted by her husband visited a pastor friend of mine one day. Her husband had run off with a younger woman, leaving her bereft, troubled, and broken. My friend suggested that she put some time into missionary work, thinking that doing something for others might help her forget herself for a little while and alleviate her pain. Taking his advice, the dejected wife wrote to Mother Teresa in Calcutta, India. (It was very easy to write to Mother Teresa. All you had to do was write, "Mother Teresa, Calcutta, India," and it would get to her.)

The woman waited and waited for a reply, but nothing came to her, not for a week, not for a month, not for two months. Then, one day, a brown envelope arrived. She opened it and the note contained inside simply read:

> Dear Joanna,
>
> Find your own Calcutta.
>
> Love,
> Mother Teresa

In a sense, that's what we all have to do—each person has to find his or her own Calcutta. There is a place where you can express love. It may be in the office or in the neighborhood, but that's your Calcutta. That's the place where you're supposed to live out the love of Jesus Christ. That's where you're supposed to do service for the kingdom, through putting love in action and doing justice. Justice is love simply expressed in social policy.

Perhaps you've had an opportunity to see the movie *To Kill a Mockingbird*. Gregory Peck portrays Atticus Finch, a lawyer who defends an African American man who's unjustly accused of rape. Clearly, the man is innocent, but the prejudicial jury votes for conviction. Following the verdict, the people exit the courtroom, except for the African Americans sitting in the balcony. With them is Finch's son and daughter. As Finch packs up his belongings and picks up his briefcase, obviously feeling dejected, beaten down, he walks the aisle to exit the courtroom of injustice. As he passes under the balcony, all of the African Americans rise to their feet in solemn respect. The pastor of the church nudges Finch's daughter, Scout, who does not realize the totality of what has transpired. "Stand up, girl. Your father is passing."

What a statement! Indeed, to live out love, to live out justice—this is more important than keeping religious rules and regulations. That's what Jesus was about. The legalists' religiosity had all the forms, but didn't have the love or the compassion. The laws had been established by people whose hearts had not been broken by the things that break the heart of Jesus.

PEACE OVER ACTIVISM

Not only do we find in Christ love taking precedence over law, we also find peace taking precedence over activism. I'm an activist—"Go! Go! Go! Go! Run! Run! Run! Run!"

It's hard to live in peace; certainly around Christmas it's hard to have peace. Go to the shopping centers and see the people running to and fro, hustling, bustling. Just stand in line at the checkout counter, and everybody, especially the women, are saying things like, "I hate Christmas. I just can't keep up. It's driving me crazy. I can't wait till this is over! The meals, the decorations, the visits, the wrapping, the presents; it's more than one can handle."

And in the midst of it all, Jesus comes and says, "Come unto me, all ye that labour and are heavy laden, and I will give you rest" (Matthew 11:28, KJV). Jesus was very busy, but he was never so busy that He couldn't find time for rest. One time, He was surrounded by people demanding to be healed; He had been working all day long, ministering to people, healing people, and it was time for rest. His disciples said, "You can't rest. Look, there are people who are sick, there are people who need your help." He said, "Get me on a boat and get me to the other side of the lake" (Luke 8).

There is a time to stop. There is a time to rest. And I have to tell you that during the busy season, if you do nothing else, a godly responsibility, a spiritual necessity, is to stop what you're doing and go out for a walk, find a quiet place. Sit down and just be still.

A Chinese philosopher said, "You cannot make a muddy pond clear. But if you'll just let the water remain still for a while, it will become clear." With our minds rushing, and with the tensions, and with the 101 things to be done, and travel arrangements to be made, the Voice comes and says, "Peace. Be still. Be still."

Corrie Ten Boom said once, "If God cannot make us bad, he will make us busy." What a good statement. God is incapable of causing us to do bad things, but doing the things of God can keep us so busy that we can have no time for God Himself. God's business can take us away from God just as much as sin can take us away from God.

Are you so busy that there is no time for God? No time to be still? I have to carve out time each day to get up before I have to and be still in the morning. I carve out time in the morning for stillness. There's an old gospel song, "Turn your eyes upon Jesus, look full in

His wonderful face, the things of earth will grow strangely dim." And I do that; I say the name Jesus over and over and over again.

You may wonder, "Why do you keep saying that name?" Because there's something about that name that drives back all the extraneous thoughts and all the things that are waiting to be done. I have to drive back all the pressures that are coming in to sweep me away, and create the still quiet place where I need to rest. I need to be still and know that He is God.

We don't have enough stillness. We don't have enough quietude and surrender. It's not just a psychological thing; it's not just a Buddhist thing. It's surrendering. It's saying, "Here I am, Lord. I'm letting go of my ambitions. I'm letting go of all the things I have to do. I'm going to let go and let God; I'm going to let you come into my life."

When was the last time you invited Jesus to invade you, to possess you? You say, "Well, I'm theologically sound." We may be theologically sound and have committed our creeds to memory. But on Judgment Day—when He says, "I was hungry. Did you feed me? I was naked. Did you clothe me? I was sick. Did you care for me?"—will you say, "I believe in God, the Father Almighty, maker of heaven and earth, and in Jesus Christ . . . ," and so on and so forth?

He's going to say, "Come on, did you know how to be still and quiet and surrender to Me and allow My Spirit to invade you?"

Some Christians talk a lot about receiving Jesus. Not just believing in Jesus, but receiving Jesus. Have you come to that point where you've received Jesus? That's what Billy Graham tries to do at his revival meetings: he draws people, most of whom already believe in Jesus.

Most people who believe in Jesus have never received Jesus. They have never, in quietude, surrendered. Jesus said, "If you want to pray, go into the closet and shut the door. Let the world go away" (see Matthew 6:6).

· · ·

AMID THE FRENETIC ACTIVITY associated with the Christmas season, there's so much to do. There's no time for peace; but with Jesus, peace takes precedence over activism. One of the great missionaries of our time was heard to have said, "I have so much to do today. Instead of a half hour, I'm going to have to spend a whole hour in stillness and prayer." The quietude and the invasion of the Spirit, as much time as it takes, enables you to do the rest of the day with a level of efficiency that would not otherwise be possible. Jesus says, "My peace I give unto you. My peace I leave with you" (John 14:27, KJV).

Activism, activism, activism. There is a story Fred Craddock tells of a man who used to rescue greyhound dogs from the race-track. When Fred went to visit this man, there was a greyhound dog lying on the floor playing with the man's children, rolling and laughing. They were hugging the dog and having a great time with this retired greyhound. Fred said, "I spoke to the dog and said, 'Dog, why aren't you racing anymore? Is it because you stopped winning?'

"And the dog said to me, 'Oh no, I was winning, I was winning every race.'

"So then I asked, 'Well, weren't you earning enough money for your master?'

" 'Oh, no, I was making a lot of money.'

" 'You weren't getting recognition?'

" 'Oh, no, they were writing me up in the racing journals. I had it all.'

" 'Well, why did you stop racing?'

"And the greyhound said, 'Because one day I realized that rabbit I was chasing wasn't real.' "

In all of the activism, and all the chasing, and all the endeavors to go after what we think is important, there is a voice that echoes down the corridors of time and says, "That rabbit isn't real."

All the while Jesus is asking us, "Why do you spend your money for that which satisfieth not? Come unto me. Let me give you some rest, let me invade you, let me possess you, let me make you fully alive" (see Isaiah 55:2 and Matthew 11:28).

Nineteenth-century philosopher and theologian Søren Kierkegaard well said in a personal illustration: "When I was a little boy, I was learning how to swim. I was splashing in the swimming pool with both arms and one leg, yelling at my father, who was at the edge of the pool, yelling, 'Daddy, look at me! Look at me! I'm swimming! I'm swimming!' And all the time I was holding on to the bottom of the pool with my big toe."

Isn't that the way we all are? We all do the motions, but we won't totally surrender to a God who in Christ wants to flow into our lives.

The same Jesus who was born in Bethlehem and lay in a manger has ascended into heaven and has come back to be among us. The Holy Spirit is with us. And if you will allow Him, "Behold," He says, "I stand at the door and knock. If you open up, I will come in" (see Revelation 3:20).

I invite you not only to believe in Jesus, not only to be an activist, but in stillness and quietude, to surrender to an invasion of His Spirit. When was the last time you felt God invade you—felt the spirit of God radiate within every nerve and sinew of your being? When was the last time you experienced God?

The Christ who lived and died and is among us now in Spirit, waiting to invade our lives—this same Christ portrayed for us the model of hope. No matter what the circumstances, He said, it's not what it seems. There is hope. When there was a situation where death became evident, His point was very clear: "This isn't the end. I am the resurrection and the life." In the face of death, there's hope.

There is hope beyond this life. Paul writes that if we have hope in this world only, we are a people most miserable.

I was in England, and a man there told me this story. When he was a boy he lived in a small town, and they had a telephone operator who put the plugs into the switchboard. He said his telephone number was six. He said, "One day my mother explained to me how the telephone worked. She said, 'You see this zero here? If you dial that, that's the operator. You dial that if you want information.'"

One day, the boy's canary got very sick; his mother wasn't home. He dialed zero and told the operator what his problem was. "My mother said if I had any questions I should call you because you have information. What should I do about my sick bird?" The operator told him what to do.

After that, every time he had a problem and nobody was around, he would dial zero and the same woman would answer. When his bird died, he called the operator and said, "What do I do now? My bird is dead. What do I do now?"

And the operator said to him, "Son, there are other worlds in which to sing. There are other worlds in which to sing."

My friend told me he went off to the university several years later. When he returned home, just out of curiosity he went to the phone and dialed zero again. He told the operator who he was. He asked, "Are you Mrs. Creighton?"

She said, "No, I'm not. But I know who you are because I was there at her deathbed when she passed away and she told me that one day you might call. And that, if you did, I should tell you this: 'There are other worlds in which to sing. There are other worlds in which to sing.'"

Death hath no sting. The grave has no victory, even in the face of death, and Christmas is particularly hard when there's death. So many people seem to die around Christmas that I have to tell you there are other worlds in which to sing. There are other worlds in which to sing. There's hope out there, not only in the next world, but also for this world.

People have troubles. Sometimes the troubles can be so overpowering that they despair, believing that there is no hope. A married couple says, "There's no hope for our marriage. It's a disaster; it's a loss."

Parents say, "There's no hope for my child. I don't think there's anything that can turn my child around from what she's doing—what he's doing. Life is too messed up. Things have gotten so bad that there's no turning back. There is no hope."

During the 1950s there was a movie called *The Seventh Seal,* a very artsy movie with great symbolism. It was built around a medieval knight who plays chess with Death. The movie ends with Death making a move and saying to the medieval knight, "Checkmate," and the curtain comes down. A friend of Bobby Fischer, the world champion chess player, said that Bobby turned to him and said, "Why is he giving up? Why is that knight giving up? The king has one more move."

Is your kid messed up and you think it's hopeless? I've got good news: the King has one more move.

If your marriage is in trouble and you're saying, "I think this thing is doomed to destruction," I've got good news: the King has one more move.

If you're saying, "I'm sick. I'm not sure there's any hope for me. I don't think there's a future for me. I'm so troubled. I'm so messed up." I've got good news: the King has one more move.

We are people of hope, not only in our everyday lives, not only when this life comes to an end, but even for our world. You may say, "Not this world. I'm giving up! This world is in a mess. That Iraq mess will never get straightened out." But the promise of Romans 8:28 is that even when we mess up, if we call upon God, if we surrender our lives to Christ and say, "We've messed up. Now, God, show us what You can do in the midst of this," then He will.

Are you old enough to remember Jose Melis, bandleader on the old Jack Paar show? Paar would go over to the piano and just smash down on the keyboard. And with that terrible discord, he would say, "Okay, Jose. Let me see what you can do with that." Jose would put his finger on that discord and blend it into a beautiful piece of music. It was a trick they would do about once a month. It was a beautiful thing.

No matter what discords you may strike in life, you can say, "Okay, God. Come in. Take my discords. Let's see what You can do." But it all begins by admitting that we've messed up.

We can, at any time, admit that we've messed up and ask God to show us what we can do to make the situation right. When we don't know the steps we should take, God does. God calls upon us to surrender and to look to Him for wisdom, guidance, and direction.

I believe in tomorrow. When we look at the perilous international conditions, it's challenging to have faith and to believe in a better tomorrow.

I heard the bells on Christmas day
Their old familiar carols play,
And wild and sweet the words repeat
Of peace on earth, good will to men.

And in despair I bowed my head.
"There is no peace on earth," I said,
"For hate is strong and mocks the song
Of peace on earth, good will to men."

Then pealed the bells more loud and deep:
"God is not dead, nor doth He sleep;
The wrong shall fail, the right prevail
With peace on earth, good will to men."

Christmas is about a God who not only reveals Himself to us but also reveals what we should become—people of love, people of peace, people of hope, people who at this time in history need to shout loud and clear.

You say it's time to give up? One time, Winston Churchill, after the battle of the Bulge, was told by his advisers, "The battle of the Bulge proves one thing. That British soldiers are braver than the German soldiers." To which Churchill responded, "Oh, no, they're not. The German soldiers are just as brave as the British soldiers, but the British soldiers were brave five minutes longer."

Hang in there. Hang in there, for there is a God, says Romans 8:28, who worketh in the midst of everything that's happened to bring about His good. Be people of hope. Be people of peace. Be people of love.

May the love of God, the peace of God, and the hope of God revealed in Jesus abide in you and with you forever. Amen.

Christ's Concern for Current Concerns

Joseph Champlin

During the month before Christmas, I customarily visit with several young people, seeking their input for my Christmas sermon. I always ask them the question "What are people's concerns or issues today?"

One year, I got a rather candid response from a young husband and father who owned his own business and who worked part-time as a bartender. His survey of his customers revealed their concerns as the local economy, global conflicts, and family life. This is a trying time for us globally, as fears of terrorism abound. But matters of funds and family are always a concern during the Christmas season.

CHRIST'S CONCERN FOR ECONOMIC CONCERNS

Skyrocketing gasoline prices, job insecurities, and sharply rising utility costs cause worry, especially at Christmas, when people are trying to find money to buy toys and gifts. Families on limited budgets try to fulfill their children's expectations for Christmas as they strive to continue meeting everyday expenses. Trying to do both can cause a great deal of stress and worry.

The Christ Child, who is Emmanuel, or "God with us," by His example and teaching offers reassurance to those who are worrying.

The story of Jesus' birth reminds us that there was no room at the inn when it was time for His mother to give birth. But Mary and Joseph had no reason to worry because their heavenly Father took care of them.

Later, during His adult preaching days, Jesus cautioned about fretting over food and clothing (Matthew 5). "Look at the birds in the sky and the way wild flowers grow. God cares for them. Are you not more important than they?"

Just as God provided that first Christmas, Matthew 6:25–34 reminds us to seek God first and know that the Creator will provide for all our needs and for many of our wants as well.

But as He is calling us out of worry, Emmanuel would also tell us to work hard, check our spending habits, and distinguish between our needs and our wants.

CHRIST'S CONCERN FOR GLOBAL CONCERNS

Global conflicts, especially in the Middle East, deeply trouble people. They find it hard to be hopeful, even during this season of hope.

Some visionary leaders maintain that the hunger for freedom among people in our contemporary society conquers their fear of terrorism. And two experiences confirm that view.

First, a *Time* magazine survey revealed that two-thirds of Iraqi voters preferred a democratic government to a dictatorship or an Islamic state.

Second, elections in Afghanistan likewise prove the point. Despite transportation difficulties and death threats, over 70 percent of those eligible voted, a remarkable response, particularly compared to our usual 50 percent voter turnout during a presidential election year.

But the price of freedom is high. Mel Gibson's movie *The Patriot* dramatized the painful sacrifices required during the American Revolution.

George Washington had a hard struggle bringing the many colonies together to form one nation.

Abraham Lincoln gave all his energies, and even his life, to keeping the nation united and ending slavery.

Toward the end of World War II, during the battle of the Bulge, at Christmastime, eighteen thousand American soldiers were killed or froze to death and twenty-five thousand were captured.

Pope Paul VI said to the United Nations, "War no more, war never again."

In our search for peace, we must offer ourselves to the Christ Child, who is the Prince of Peace. His mission is echoed in the words of Pope John XXIII, who said, "In peace, nothing perishes; in war, all is lost."

Amid threats of terrorism and war, the Prince of Peace still reigns supreme, giving us hope for the future.

CHRIST'S CONCERN FOR FAMILY CONCERNS

The busyness of modern life infects families, sometimes weakening or even severing relationships between its members. At Christmastime, the Holy Family teaches us that only by making relationships a priority can we solve the problems that would otherwise tear us apart.

An incident from James Patterson's novel *Suzanne's Diary for Nicholas* dramatizes that need for priorities in relationships.

Suzanne, a thirty-five-year-old physician, had worked for eight years at Massachusetts General Hospital in Boston when she suffered a heart attack and, the next day, underwent a coronary bypass.

While she was recuperating, a doctor friend told her this story of five balls: Imagine life is a game in which you are juggling five balls. The balls are called work, family, health, friends, and integrity, and you're keeping all of them in the air. But one day you finally come to understand that work is a rubber ball. If you drop it, it will bounce back. The other four balls—family, health, friends, and integrity—are made of glass. If you drop one of these, it will be irrevocably scuffed, nicked, and perhaps even shattered.

Once you truly understand the lessons of the five balls, you will have the beginnings of balance in your life. Even Jesus needed balance in His life. He rested, ate, prayed, and spent time with friends and family.

Bud, a retired police officer, worries somewhat about economic concerns, global concerns, and family concerns. But grief over the death of his wife—he cared for her at home for a long period until she succumbed to cancer just prior to their fortieth wedding anniversary—dominates his thoughts and feelings.

The Christmas immediately following her passing, he sent a poem as part of his Christmas letter to relatives and friends, verses that mean a great deal to him.

If I knew it would be the last time that I see you fall asleep,
I would tuck you in more tightly and pray the Lord, your soul
*   to keep.*
If I knew it would be the last time that I see you walk out the door,
I would give you a hug and a kiss and call you back for one more.
Tomorrow is not promised to anyone, young or old alike,
And today may be the last chance you get to hold your loved one
*   tight.*

Christmas is a time to remember our blessings—spending time with family, sharing gifts and times of fellowship—even amid our day-to-day concerns. It is not God's desire that we be consumed by these matters, serious though they may be. The Bible tells us to cast our cares upon Emmanuel, "God with us," because He cares for us (1 Peter 5:7).

Christ is concerned for our concerns. He has felt our concerns, as He became one of us. Christ came to the world and lived on earth during a time when people were concerned about the economy. The Roman government exacted a heavy toll and taxes were high. During Jesus' earthly ministry there was global conflict in the world as they knew it. There was political tension and talk of insurrection. During His earthly ministry, families were threatened by the ravages that could tear them apart.

Emmanuel, God with us, knows all about these concerns because He came to us. Christmas is a time of remembering and celebrating that we do not serve a distant God who watches us in our concern from far away.

At Christmas, we can celebrate the fact that He came to us because He loves us. And He is concerned for our concerns.

The King Has One More Move

DAN CHUN

In nearly every story, in both film and literature, we can discover a hidden message from God. One of the best can be found in a 1957 black-and-white movie called *The Seventh Seal*, directed by Ingmar Bergman.

It's a story about a medieval knight who, against the backdrop of villagers battling the black plague, plays a metaphorical game of chess against the Grim Reaper, with high stakes—his own life. If Death checkmates him, the knight dies.

In the last scene, Death indeed checkmates the knight's king, and the knight dies.

However, my friend Tony Campolo told me that after the movie was released, a Russian chess master studying the final move discovered a mistake. He said, "If you look closely at the pieces on the chessboard, you'll see that the knight wasn't really checkmated. The knight's king had one more move!"

So I rented the DVD, and when I came to that closing scene in which Death apparently traps the knight's king and says, "Checkmate," I freeze-framed it. Being a chess aficionado, I looked, and lo and behold, it was true! The king had one more move!

This old black-and-white movie holds an important truth for all of us.

No matter how bleak the situation looks, no matter how trapped and hopeless we feel, the King, our Lord, always has one more move.

In essence, this is what Christmas is all about. God in His love and grace came down to earth in the form of Jesus to say to us that there is a better way to live life, both here and for eternity. No one needs to feel trapped or checkmated.

If you follow the way mapped out by God's Son, if you travel in the footsteps of Jesus, King of Kings, then you will always have hope. Why? Because no matter how deep our despair, King Jesus has one more move! God can make good out of bad and bring hope in the face of despair.

When there appear to be irreconcilable differences, financial hardship, or heartache and pain over the loss of a loved one, have faith in what we cannot see. Don't give up! For as long as there is life, the King has one more move.

In my church, I often share airport stories. Airports can give you a lot of stress—delayed flights, missed connections, lost luggage, big crowds, a fear of flying. As George Carlin says, "It is hard to feel optimistic when just before landing the pilot announces, 'We are making our final approach.' And that when you walk into the airport, it is called a terminal."

At the height of 9/11, security was so tight you couldn't take anything pointed on board—knitting needles, scissors, or pocket Swiss army knives. I once got my nail clipper taken away! "You want my what? Gee, how dangerous can that be? Look out! That pastor has a nail clipper. Get away, get back! My gosh, he has a nail clipper!"

But when we follow Christ we can always be optimistic, even

amid illogical irrational circumstances, for the King has one more move.

When I was making a trip from Honolulu to California, my mom gave me a lamp at the last minute to take to my brother who lives in California. It was a huge lamp, three feet high and fragile. It needed to be taken as hand luggage because I couldn't fit it into my carry-on. Plus I already had two carry-ons. I was doomed.

When I got to the gate, I was number seventy-two in line. (I know because I counted.) My luggage was cumbersome and heavy. I was transporting a lamp and I had too many bags! What was I going to do? And with all these people in front of me, I knew there would be no room for my stuff on the plane. There would be no empty overhead bins near me.

But then, out of nowhere, this short, thin Filipino man appeared wearing what looked like an airport employee uniform. I reveal the fact that he was Filipino to give you a visual for the story and to illustrate how God shows up in all colors and forms.

He walked up to me and asked if I needed help. I said yes, and with that he swooped up my lamp and said, "Follow me."

He led me through the crowd, and we cut in line in front of everyone (a terrible sin, but I had to follow him—plus, he had my lamp!). We walked onto the plane. He put the lamp in the overhead, and when I turned to thank him, he was gone. He disappeared! An angel! The King has one more move!

When my wife, Pam, and the kids and I moved back to Hawaii from California a few years ago, I showed up at the airport with eighteen boxes. I had decided I would pay for them to get on the plane. I knew I was doomed because of the cost, but for reasons too hard to explain, I just wanted them to come on board with me with the rest of the luggage.

An African American skycap came up and asked if I needed help. Boy, did I! He took all of my boxes, big and small, to the counter and checked them in. I needed to tip him so I figured that would be about $3 a box. That meant tipping him big bucks, so I pulled out some cash. He looked at me and said, "No, that's okay. You don't need to tip me." And then he walked away. Amazing! No one turns down a tip! The King has one more move.

Three months ago, my flight from Orange County airport arrived late at the Los Angeles airport. I needed to get to my gate in another terminal, a fifteen-minute walk away, to make a flight that was already boarding.

I ran as fast and as hard as I could in my suit and dress shoes and I realized I wouldn't make it. Suddenly, out of nowhere, I saw an airport employee driving in a cart and she pulled up about fifteen feet from me.

I gambled and went for possibility thinking and said to her, "Gee, I don't know if this is allowable: you look kind of busy, but, you see, my flight is leaving and I am late, so I was wondering if you could give me a ride to the other terminal. But if it is not okay, then . . . ," and before I could finish my pitch, this wonderful African American woman, who looked like Queen Latifah, said, "Get in!"

She hit a switch that turned on a flashing yellow light (and I thought, "That's embarrassing!"), and out came a blaring, loud *beep-beep-beep* sound. She hit the pedal to the metal and off we zoomed at high speed.

We wailed down the corridor of the Los Angeles airport, twisting and turning and dodging passengers. We were hauling so fast that my hair was blowing in the wind. People were staring at me, wondering, "Who is this VIP? Who gets this kind of treatment?"

I felt tempted to wave at them as a king would to his people. "Take care. Have a nice trip. Bless you. *Vaya con Dios.*"

I made it just before the doors closed. God saved me! I wanted to tip the cart lady, but off she went. The King had one more move!

Then there was the time the school needed my daughter, who

was around eleven at the time, to bring in an anole lizard, a five-to-eight-inch chameleonlike lizard that is all over the island.

I don't like holding lizards. I hate catching live creatures. It doesn't seem Christian, but I figured I would do it this once to help my daughter and then release the lizard the next day after class.

Do you realize how hard it is to find an anole lizard in Honolulu when you need one within twenty-four hours? Why do schools do this to parents? And to lizards?

So I thought maybe I could find one in the schoolyard near my house. I looked and found nothing. But then, by a miracle of miracles, I saw one on the back wall of my house. What were the chances?! So I picked up my little fishing net and with lighting speed went for the chameleon—but I missed.

But by God's grace, I saw another one. Again, I tried to get it with my lightning gung fu speed, but my lightning gung fu speed was more like turtle speed, and so I missed again. I couldn't believe it! It was right there and I missed it! Such rare chances and I blew it. Jackie Chan I am not.

An hour later, still no luck. I was truly bummed and frustrated. What a horrible school assignment, the kind where dads try to help their daughters and come up empty. But here is how the story ends, and this is no fooling.

I walk into my house to put away the net and then I walk outside through the front door, totally frustrated, when something falls off of the ceiling and onto my head, and I go, "Aaugh!" I grab for it because it's in my hair. I knock it and it falls to my shoulder and onto the floor, stunned. It is an anole lizard! I catch it and throw it in a cage, which happens to be on my front porch. The King has one more move!

Because Christ exists, I figure I can always be optimistic. I always drive into parking lots even when it says, "Lot is full," figuring there has got to be one space. Nine times out of ten I find one!

Once I was at a store and I asked for a product from a salesperson, who went back in to the storeroom to look for it, came out, and said they didn't have it.

I figured the King has one more move, so I asked another employee and she went to a shelf and said, "Sorry, we don't have it."

So I went to a third employee and asked the same question. Lo and behold, he went to a third shelf and found it! The King has one more move!

With Jesus we can always live with optimism, a never-give-up attitude.

You may think, "Oh, easy for you to say that, Dan. You don't know the disappointment that I have faced. Maybe you just lead a charmed life, a Pollyanna life. Besides, that stuff you're talking about is minor, unimportant. You don't know real hardship."

That's a fair response. However, never say to a pastor that he or she doesn't see hardship, whether personally or professionally. We see more every week than most people.

Personally, I know disappointment like any one else. I remember, thirty years ago, living with little money in a different city and wondering if I would have to rely on food stamps to get by.

I have gone through some difficult medical operations that have not all worked and actually made my life harder.

Before I became a pastor I went through a gut-wrenching divorce. My ex-wife married someone thirty days after our divorce, someone who I didn't even know existed. Talk about the King has one more move! God then sent me my wonderful wife, Pam, and we have three great kids. But through that divorce, I have known betrayal, heartache, loneliness, and depression.

During Thanksgiving dinner one year, at the exact moment when I put the turkey down on the table, my mother, who lived with us, had a seizure and went into a coma. She died three days later.

She had endured a four-and-a-half-year battle with lung cancer. Much of her last year involved me taking care of her, driving her to the hospital for treatment, tests, doctor's appointments, and at her lowest point, cleaning and feeding her.

As a pastor I say good-bye every year to about ten to twelve people who pass away, and often I am with them in their last days or hours after struggling with disease or injury. Then I have to bury them—they who were my friends.

I tell my church that sometimes I feel I have a low-grade depression all the time because while not all the members know every deceased or sick member, I know them all, and I grieve with their families and miss them when they're gone.

In addition to the deceased and the ill, there are all the others that the church is trying to help in their marriage, parenting, finances, addictions, grief, or depression.

But because of Jesus Christ, I have hope. We all can have hope because the King always has one more move.

Because of Christmas, because of God coming to earth in the form of a man—fully human and yet fully divine, Jesus Christ—we all can have hope. We all can be optimistic.

When we believe in the One who is greater, the One who knows all the moves and then some, when we have even the smallest amount of faith, we can look for the possibilities.

So, people going through financial hardship must still believe that the King has one more move.

People facing a life-threatening disease must affirm and believe that the King has one more move.

People going through disappointment should not give up but, rather, believe that the King has one more move.

When Christians lose loved ones, we know that heaven waits for them. The King has one more move.

Those who live with grief and pain must believe and the King has one more move.

Because I believe that God always has one more move, I can pray in faith. In the last few years I have prayed in faith and have seen two people come out of comas, one of whom did not have brain waves.

I have prayed and seen people freed from arthritis and deafness. I have heard from our members who prayed for people who were then healed of blindness, fibromyalgia, and other diseases, sore necks, injured knees, and painful hips.

In the case of a longtime friend of mine who suffered fifty-two years from polio and a nerve atrophy disease, God healed him of it instantly during a prayer session. He thought he would live all his life in leg braces and with crutches, but the King had one more move. Today my friend walks without any walking aids.

Do you have faith at Christmas that God has one more move, one for each of us?

Might He perform a miracle in your life? This is the Christmas season, when the Holy Spirit is here in power, helping us to remember this because we are celebrating Jesus' birthday. When the Holy Spirit falls upon us and fills us, miracles happen.

Do you believe that God might perform a miracle in your life or on your loved ones? That God does have one more move?

No, God doesn't heal everyone all the time in the way that we would want. If he did, no one would die and none of us could experience all that heaven holds for us. But God does heal. I believe He chooses to do so, not because we deserve it but because of grace.

Believing that the King has one more move, I have offered many prayers of healing. I have seen God perform many miracles. I like to know when God miraculously answers prayer, so I invite people to write me and let me know. I ask them to make it a part of their thanksgiving and gratitude to God to let me know how the Lord has healed them. Jesus often told people in the Bible who were healed to immediately go and tell the pastor.

In our Christmas Eve services we pray for miracles. I like for each person in the congregation to have a symbolic reminder of the prayer that was prayed for them. Each person in attendance is given a rose to take with them. When that prayer is answered I ask that they send their rose back to me with a letter explaining what happened. All the returned roses are added to our wreath of hope, a wreath full of roses, each one representing a miraculous answer to a prayer said during a previous Christmas Eve service. Each of the roses represents an answered prayer—healing, reconciliation, adoption, release from addiction or depression.

Every answered prayer is a reminder that the King has one more move! And because we know that He always has another move, we can always say in our hearts, "Joy to the world, the Lord is come. Let earth receive her King!"

PRAYER

Lord, our prayer is that we seek Your will. And as we pray for the miraculous, we pray that You will answer in a way that is best for us. Your answer might surprise us, but we believe You will somehow answer it. We pray against all odds. And we pray that a year from now, every person who has prayed for You to offer one more move will have a rose to add to our wreath of hope. For in You we can know that You, our Lord and King, always have one more move.

In Praise of Nazareth

EMANUEL CLEAVER

BASED ON LUKE 4:16

"And Jesus came to Nazareth where he had been brought up . . ."

There is nothing in the Holy Bible, God's Word, that would suggest Christmas is a sacrament to be observed by the body of Christ, or even that it should be celebrated at all. This is somewhat quizzical, considering the musicals, plays, parties, parades, slaughtered evergreen trees, house decorations, and family gatherings that are all a part of the festival of Christmas.

After all of the Christmas merriment, there is very little breathing space for Easter, the celebration of our salvation. Jesus never admonished us, "Remember my birth!" He did, however, at the final meal with His disciples, instruct us to remember His sacrificial death.

During my days of decision while in seminary, I began to believe that it was silly to argue over the authenticity of the Virgin Birth. I have not engaged in debate, nor will I, over what the Catholic Church refers to as the Immaculate Conception. While I do, as a matter of truth, accept the *mysterium tremendum,* or awesome mystery, surrounding the birth of Christ, my faith is not affixed to it. Unfortunately, we seem to have more of a fixation on the birth of

Christ than on the life of Christ. The Virgin Birth is not central to my faith.

And anyway, in all my years, no one has ever asked me about my own conception. No one seems to care. Having served as mayor of a major American city, I attended receptions and political events all over the world, and never did anyone say, "Mr. Mayor, how are things in Kansas City, and by the way, can you give me some information about your conception?"

An examination of most daily newspapers will reveal a full page of death notices, but there is not a single column dedicated to birth notices. That is quite understandable since a life is generally more substantive between birth and death than it is between conception and birth. We enter this world with no teeth, no hair, no history or biographical data, and no job. Why would we be important to a world already suffering from information overload?

Make no mistake. The birth of Jesus was a wondrous event. Christmas is a big deal! It was the point at which the Creator stepped into human flesh in order to make known, through teaching and testing, what God is like. "The Word was made flesh and dwelt among us" (John 1:14, KJV).

When Christ was born in Bethlehem of Judea, God dressed himself in the wardrobe of humankind and allowed the world to see His character. That is Christmas; however, we claim Christ as our Redeemer, not because of His Virgin Birth, but because of His lordly life and sacrificial death. Primarily, it was His death on Calvary.

You see, we are saved by His blood. Nothing could stop the cross. All of the wars could not snuff it out. All of the floods could not wash it out. All of the ice storms could not freeze it out. All of the volcanoes could not burn it out, nor could the hounds of hell scare it out. All the dogs and demons from the pit of darkness could not scare it out. I'm so glad that for my redemption Christ carried a cross.

As had been foretold by the prophet Micah seven hundred

years earlier, Jesus was born in Bethlehem. Therefore, Christians by the tens of thousands flock each year to see and celebrate the Bethlehem birthplace. Christmas, it seems, is preferred over other Christian holy days because a manger is much more palatable than a cross.

To be sure, there are sights, such as Bethlehem's Church of the Nativity, that have significance. It is, for the purposes of this message, important to know that Jesus spent very little time in Bethlehem. Although Joseph was born in Bethlehem, he and his family lived in Nazareth. Therefore, Jesus grew up not in Bethlehem, the second-most-elaborated city in Israel, but rather in the little-known, out-of-the-way village of Nazareth.

Yes, Jesus hailed from Nazareth, where smells from puddles of fetid water abounded. Yes, Jesus hailed from Nazareth, where He played with other Jewish kids over wretchedly paved roadways. Yes, Jesus hailed from Nazareth, where the family of Joseph and Mary raised Him and His siblings in the welter of Galilean poverty.

As a country boy, born in the unessential, unimpressive, and ironclad, segregated town of Waxahachie, Texas, I have often found myself on the receiving end of hick-town wisecracks. One of my college classmates used to say that Waxahachie was so destitute that the residents were issued only one *o* with which to spell the word "poor." Having egressed from a drafty shack in Waxahachie to the people- and problem-packed public housing projects of Wichita Falls, Texas, I must confess that I am tickled brown that my Savior spent all but three years of His life in Nazareth. That suggests that a boy from Waxahachie has a chance to make it.

Located seventy-five miles north of Bethlehem, Nazareth is nestled in the hills of Galilee. The little town where Christ spent His formative years was so historically insignificant that it is never even mentioned in the Old Testament. Josephus, the Jewish historian, didn't deem Nazareth important enough to comment on in his comprehensive history of the nation of Israel.

Nathaniel's crude remark "Can anything good come out of Nazareth?" provides information about how the ancients saw that city. Waxahachie at least hosted the filming of the highly acclaimed movie *Places in the Heart*. As far as history records, nothing hip happened in Nazareth.

The beauty of God is that He ordained that His only begotten Son grow to adulthood in the culturally cryptic and economically lifeless village of Nazareth.

Not only was the town where Jesus grew up insignificant; Joseph and Mary were not influential citizens there—which means that they were even less prominent in Bethlehem. In spite of his new wife's extreme stage of pregnancy, Joseph was unable to secure enclosed housing in or around Bethlehem. He was powerless to pull strings to obtain a room at one of the local inns.

Poor people don't have strings, nor do they know where to acquire them. Most of them have not even seen strings. You see, a person must be a string holder to pull strings. The poor don't get strings; they only get strung along.

The politics of pulling strings is interesting. The string holders don't really want the string pursuers around. String holders respond best to other string holders. For instance, a Nazarene string holder, if one existed, could have gotten a room from a string holder in Bethlehem. A look at the ancient demographics of Nazareth reveals that there were few, if any, string holders. Other than from caravans moving through the village en route to nearby seaports, money rarely found its way to Nazareth.

So why would a Bethlehem innkeeper go out of his way to be helpful to a poor Nazarene couple? It runs counter to common practices for people to prefer the company of beggars. Many people believed then, and accept as fact today, that poverty is contagious; they try to avoid the contamination by keeping a respectful distance from those who are infected. But then, as now, our Savior seeks the sick, the sad, and the segregated.

The God of Abraham, Isaac, and Jacob was not stuck-up or snooty. A snooty God wouldn't have stayed silent and allowed His Son to be born in a barn. A snooty God would have birthed His baby in the plush comfort of a palace, with caregivers in the background, not cattle. A snooty God would never have permitted His Son to be a resident of Nazareth. But then, a snooty God would not have been my God. I am black, and on top of that, I was born in Waxahachie.

All praise and honor to the Almighty God who even loves me—a pigeon-toed and flawed refugee from an unpainted wooden shack in the Waxahachie backwoods—as much as He loves a proper socialite from the mansions of Hollywood. I'm so glad that I serve a "whosoever God!"

That includes whosoever is well and whosoever is weak.

Whosoever can and whosoever can't.

Whosoever is up and whosoever is down.

Whosoever is pretty and whosoever is plain.

Whosoever is poor and whosoever is prosperous.

Whosoever is known and whosoever is nameless.

Whosoever is virtuous and whosoever is vile.

MANY OF US WOULD have been doomed if God's love were based on our education, pigmentation, articulation, reputation, derivation, affiliation, or stock diversification. He loves us simply because we are His divine creation.

When John baptized Jesus in the Jordan River, the heavens opened and a voice from eternity said, "This is my beloved Son, in whom I am well pleased" (Matthew 3:17, KJV). Up to the point of this heavenly announcement, the gospel writers do not provide us with much information about the life and work of Jesus. The only thing known was that Jesus had spent roughly thirty years in the rough little village of Nazareth. Yet the Bible says that God was "well pleased."

It should please us to know that we can please God no matter from where we originate, or with whom we amalgamate, or how much we accumulate.

It might be important here that I assure you that I am not advocating poverty. I am against it. I oppose it. I know poverty well and it knows me. And while we are on a first-name basis, we do not have a good relationship. Poverty is not a sin; but that's the best thing I can say about it. I will never support it. The fact that God loves us even if we are poor does not mean that God wants us poor.

Can any good come out of Nazareth? Thank God and glory hallelujah, the transcendent "yes" is the proper answer to this ancient query!

And at Christmas, it should be applauded and appreciated in every ghetto and in every jailhouse, in every low-achieving schoolhouse, in every storefront-church house, in every drug house, in every gambling house, in every poor house.

The indisputable fact that something good indeed has come out of Nazareth should be celebrated in every sinner's heart and in every unemployment line.

The good news of Christmas is that we can come to Christ in rags and ruin, in tragedy and trepidation, in guilt and guile, and in hurt and in hunger. Knowing this should cause each of us to shout, "Joy to the World!"

God Is with Us

Suzan Johnson Cook

BASED ON MATTHEW 1:20–23

Many times, we reflect on all of the things going on in our families, in our communities, in our nation, and in our world, and we wonder, "Where is God?" We look around and see a rap culture that we don't know or understand. All we know is that it has captured the hearts and attention of our young people.

All around us we see disease, depression, divorce, and devastation overtaking our communities, yet we keep coming to church, wondering if there really is a God. And even those of us who are faithful in our church attendance find ourselves asking, "Is He with us?"

We want so badly to believe that He is, and yet so often we doubt. We want to be sure, but sometimes our faith is shaky. Where is God in all of this?

What's the answer? *God is with us.*

Matthew records, as do the other gospel writers, what the world was like in his day. As he witnessed what was going on around him, he knew there were some people whose families were torn apart. He knew there were people whose hopes and dreams had been deferred or denied. He knew there were people who were helpless and hopeless, yet still waiting on a Word from the Lord. So Matthew and the other gospel writers tried to capture, under the inspiration of God, what life was like at the time of Christ's birth.

But before Matthew offers his words of comfort, our assurance that God is with us, he lets us in on some things that are important to know in order to be with God. It's one thing for God to be with us, but we also have to be with God, so Matthew opens his gospel by giving the genealogy of Jesus Christ.

When I was in seminary, we used to skip over the genealogy part because it had all of those difficult names, and we used to wonder why Matthew had taken the time to include all of those families. What was so important about that? So we would skip over those verses and start reading at verse 18, "unto us a son is born."

But the genealogy of our Savior is important. There are forty-two generations of Jesus Christ recorded for us, and in those generations lie His history, His roots, and His family line, which includes the father of faith, Abraham. Jesus had some royalty in his bloodline, King David, but he also had some real other folk in his life. When you start researching who was hooked up with whom in Jesus' lineage, you will find some harlots, some evildoers, some believers, and some unbelievers.

KNOW WHO YOU ARE

Jesus had in His family tree some ancestors who hooked up with God from the beginning and some who were wholly unfaithful to Him. And so, the first part of knowing that God is with you is to not deny who you are.

You must claim all of who you are—your present and your past, the good and the bad, the proud and the shameful. No life is all pleasure; we've all had some pain in life. Some circumstances are not so pleasant, and there are some we may not want others to know about. We all have some good blood, and we've got some not so good blood in our families. And so we need to acknowledge that, not to hold judgment against those who we think are good or not good. We need to understand that we are connected to a past; we can't escape it.

When we look from where God has brought us, though, maybe the past was shaky. But look what the Lord has done for us! The past is important; we all have a past. Somebody gave birth to you. Your childhood may not have been ideal and life may not have turned out the way you wanted. Your father or mother may not have been at home the way you wanted, but it's still your past.

God calls us to affirm who we are and not deny it. Don't try to be who you are not. Be who you are because, in being who you are, God takes you and makes you and molds you and makes you who He wants you to be.

I HAVE A PAST. My daddy never finished high school, for many reasons, one of them being that he was a black man who grew up in his era without a strong family base. Despite his educational handicap, he took the good things of his past and the bad things of his past and built a family. He gave us love so that the Johnson children could be who we are today. His past made him determined that his own children would not grow up with the same pain he had experienced. But that's my past.

I remember watching an episode of the Arsenio Hall late-night television show. That night, one of his featured guests was Rosie Perez, a young dancer who had completed a starring role in Spike Lee's movie *Do the Right Thing*. She shared with the audience that she disliked being from Brooklyn and couldn't wait to get to Hollywood and forget her past. Well, she finally made it to Hollywood and discovered that a whole lot of people had no identity. She found them pretentious; they did not know who they were. From that experience, she learned that even though she was raised a poor girl from Brooklyn she could be proud of it. She knew who she was and she thanked God for blessing her enough to let her have a strong identity.

You can't deny who you are. God begins with humanness—that we are connected to someone. But not only does God move in Christ through the human situation, Jesus also was divine. God is divine, and He can do more than we can ever dream of or imagine.

Most often, we want to write the scripts of life our way. We want every event in our lives to have a storybook ending. We want to carefully plan our lives and orchestrate everything so that it will end up happily ever after. The problem is that in so doing, we block God out of the picture.

The Jesus story is about God. He told us what He was going to do, and folks kept denying it and ignoring it, and then He did it. People had pictured what God was going to do. They were looking for a great earthly king, probably one who would have all kinds of gold and jewels on, and who was a great warrior.

But God is so good that He said, I am not sending an earthly king as you have imagined. You can't predict how my Spirit is going to move. God decreed, "A virgin shall conceive and be great with child. The Holy Ghost is going to do a great thing. A king is going to come, but not the kind of king you're looking for."

All kinds of things happened in reaction to God's movement. Some people talked about Mary. Some people put it in Joseph's head that she had been unfaithful to him. Kings began plotting to get rid of God's movement inside Mary's womb.

Thankfully, there were some who did not buy into the negative implications building up around God's movement; they chose to listen to God. They sorted out the miracle from the myth.

God came to Joseph in a dream: "All of this is real, Joseph, and it's part of My plan. Others may be saying something different to you now, Joseph. You even may be doubting your fiancée's virginity; but Joseph, this is real. This is the movement of the Holy Ghost."

Joseph heard God and Mary chose to listen to God, even

though everybody around them was saying, "How did you get pregnant when you're supposed to be a virgin engaged to Joseph?" Even though people were messing with Mary, she heard God through an angel saying, "Mary, don't be afraid. Others may not understand it, but this is God's Spirit moving in you."

In this life, not only do you need to know who you are, you also need to know who God is, and that He will do what He has said He will do with you. You need to know God so that no one can make you doubt Him—no matter how many people think you're crazy, no matter how many folks talk about you.

There are times in your journey when only you and the Lord understand what you're going through. Sometimes the Lord places a vision on your heart that no one else can see but you and the Lord. They say, "Where is this thing? God, something's wrong with this woman, I think she's touched!"

But Almighty God tells you, "Don't listen to that stuff! Keep your mind focused on what I've given you to do." That's when you need to be like a tree planted by the rivers of water and not be moved. Don't let rumors move you. Don't let lies move you. Don't let doubt move you. You've got to be still so that you can hear God.

And make sure that you're not listening to your own voice. I know that if I had acted on everything that I've thought of in my life, I'd be in a whole mess right now! When you hear God, however, whether it's through an angel or a dream, like the Wise Men following the star, when you're sure it's God you hold fast to that which is pure and good.

Mary was engaged to a man in a small village, and others there had small expectations of what their life would be like. They had planned to go to the wedding, give them a small gift, and let them live happily ever after in their little town. But God has unlimited mercy. He says, "I have greater plans for Joseph and Mary. I've watched them and I want them to leave this little town and do something great for Me."

God found favor with this unknown couple from a place few had ever heard of. When God loves you and God blesses you, no one can stop what God has for you. So when you're going through whatever it is you're going through—when others don't understand but you know it's God moving in you—God wants you to know that He is with you. That's what "Emmanuel" means: God is with you.

See, Jesus was born from Mary but He had a special mission, to save His people from their sins. That means Jesus is not limited to Mary and Joseph. It means He's the light of the world. It means He's the Savior who saves everyone from sin.

The Word existed before Jesus was born, but folks couldn't understand it. It was the Word that saved Noah and his family on the ark. It was the Word that saved Israel from Pharaoh's domination. God saved so many but they couldn't understand Him because He moved in the Spirit. So God said, "I've got to let them see this."

God turned Himself into Himself and gave us His Son, Jesus, in a way that we would understand. He came as a baby, because He knew that we knew something about babies. He came as a baby, because babies come here helpless, and when we see a helpless baby it tells us not to depend on anyone to help but God.

He came as a baby, who cried just as we cry sometimes, to remind us that God can wipe away all tears from our eyes. Whether it's in the midnight hour or midday, God can wipe away our tears.

He came as a baby, so that we know we have a parent who holds us, God.

He came as a baby—rejected before He was even born, before He started walking—so He would know what it's like when we're rejected. He knows what it's like when we're rejected in a relationship, when we're rejected on our jobs, or when we're rejected by our families. When we're going through it, He wants us to know that He's been through it. And because He's been through it, He can help us in any situation.

Jesus, Emmanuel, "God with us," came to earth as a baby so we would know that everyone starts where he or she starts. We all have some kind of beginning; it may not be a good beginning, but we all start where we start.

Jesus had His start as a baby, but He began to grow. Babies don't stay babies, so God lets us see how Jesus grew in wisdom, stature, and grace so that we would also know how to grow in wisdom, stature, and grace. He let us know that babies don't stay babies, but they become men and women who suffer just as Jesus did.

It is in our identification and connection to Jesus—after we're clear on who we are, after we realize that God has supernatural power, and after we see that He was where we are—that we realize God is with us. His very name translates into "presence." Emmanuel, God with us.

If you call my name, I may or may not hear you; I may not be there when you call my name. But when we call His name, it's music to our ears because it's He who's giving you the strength to call His name.

When you call His name, He heals and He restores your soul. When you call His name, things happen; miracles come when you call His name. The shepherds praised His name and they were blessed to see the Christ Child. In His name, the Wise Men followed the star to see what this name was connected to. His name is a name you can call in the day and in the night. He is with us.

I remember one Christmas season when I went to the hospital to visit a church member. As I was preparing to leave the hospital, I felt the eyes of a young man staring at me. I looked over and saw a pair of beautiful hazel eyes peering out of a handsome young man. I spoke to him and asked him how he was doing. He said that he wasn't feeling very well and asked me to intervene with the nurses because he needed some painkiller and they had been ignoring him.

I went to the nurses' station as he requested, but I felt strongly moved to go back to his room and find out more about him. I asked him if his family would visit him for the holidays. He informed me that he had no family. I felt bad looking at a young man about my age, spending the holidays in the hospital suffering from sickle cell complications with no family.

We talked a while longer and I began to minister to him. I did not leave my name with him before I left the hospital, nor did I leave the name of my church. But there is a name that I left with him. I left him a name that has healing in it. I left him a name that has power in it. I left that sick young man with a name that says "God is with you." I left the name of Jesus.

I didn't leave him my name, because I realized that he may need to talk, but I would not be there. I realized that he may want to pray and I would not be there. He needed to know that in Jesus, God is with him, touching him, healing him, comforting him, and loving him. And even though he didn't have a family that he knew, the name of Jesus hooks him up to a line connected to King David and Father Abraham. The name of Jesus connects him with a God who rules earth and heaven.

That's why we need to tell our children and our loved ones about Jesus, because they will grow up and go to places where we can't be with them. They may be shipped off to war or lying on their sickbed; they may be off seeking adventure like the Prodigal Son. But before they go, they need to know the name that means God is always with them, and His name is Emmanuel.

We like to call Him Jesus but He is Emmanuel, always with us. Boundaries can't keep Him out, wars can't stop Him, rumors don't defeat Him, death couldn't even hold Him.

Jesus has got power! He shocked the rabbis as a teenager. He told the Pharisees and Sadducees, "I'll sit with whomever I want."

Jesus, the one who healed a woman who had been bleeding for twelve years with just a touch from the hem of His garment. Jesus, the man who told Zacchaeus to come out of the tree, stop hiding, and face the facts. Jesus, who walked out on the water when everyone else had given up and told the waves, "Peace. Be still."

And so in the name of Jesus, Emmanuel, we claim victory. In the name of Jesus, we stand like trees planted in the rivers of water and declare that we shall not be moved. In the name of Jesus, we claim that what God has for us shall come and will not be hindered. Call His name; there's power in that name. Say His name; there's healing in that name. Say His name; there's victory in that name.

Jesus is with us, right now. He suffered as we suffer. He cried as we cry. He was wounded because He knew we'd suffer some wounds—physical, emotional, mental, spiritual. Emmanuel: He's with us always, even to the end of the age.

A Night at the Holy Day Inn

KEVIN W. COSBY

BASED ON LUKE 2:1–7

He gets a bum rap. In the words of Malcolm X, he was "had . . . hoodwinked . . . bamboozled." That poor innkeeper who had the misfortune of telling Mary and Joseph, "No room in the inn," has been one of the most vilified and maligned persons in the New Testament. How anyone could be so callous! At his doorstep was a teenage girl, miles from home, frightened and heavy with child, which means her water had just broken and she was about to go into labor. When Joseph asked for lodging for his pregnant wife, the innkeeper's response was, "Sorry, no room in the inn."

What often gets overlooked in the familiar Lukan account of the Christmas story is that, while he turned them away from the inn, at some point the innkeeper must have told them about the stable. Some have even speculated that it was actually the innkeeper's wife who, empathizing with Mary's advanced pregnancy, nudged her husband's entrepreneurial spirit to compassion.

The Savior's birthing room was not the cozy, warm place we've seen depicted on the cover of Hallmark Christmas cards; it was drafty and dirty, with real odor from real animals. Mary gave birth to her first child in a stable. She wrapped her baby boy in swaddling clothes and used a manger for a makeshift crib, because there had been no room for them in the inn. The experience was more than humbling; it was humiliating. The Savior of the world first lay His head in a feeding trough for animals. The innkeeper would not register them at his Bethlehem Hilton, so Jesus, Mary, and Joseph lodged at the Holy Day Inn.

What avaricious qualities would you attribute to the innkeeper? The morality of a pimp? The ethics of a dope dealer? The greed of an ambulance chaser? The coldness of a mafioso? While history has often judged him as sleazy, greedy, and elitist, I maintain that this innkeeper was none of those things.

Do you know why he told them there was no room in the inn? A lawyer might answer, "Well, he must have been afraid for Mary to have that baby in his hotel with no doctor around. If complications arose, they might have sued him."

A businessman might answer, "He was saving those rooms for business clientele who had made reservations."

A socialite might reply, "Those rooms were rightly reserved for the elite, the bluebloods."

Despite all of the speculation, I truly believe that the real reason the innkeeper told them there was no room was that there really was no room in the inn! It all makes sense, really. There was a taxpayers' convention going on. All the inns and rooming houses were filled to capacity. A garrison of Roman soldiers occupied the first floor, and government census workers and tax collectors had taken all of the remaining rooms. The innkeeper was running a business, after all. He meant no ill will by shutting out Jesus and His earthly parents.

And though he meant no harm, the innkeeper's experience is but a microcosmic illustration of the reason why Jesus gets shut out of so many places in life. The experience with the innkeeper is a recurring parable that amplifies the subtle reasons why Jesus gets shut out of so many lives.

PRIORITIES

It happens so often. Jesus comes knocking at the door of our lives. Any room there? Like the innkeeper, many of us have nothing personal against Jesus, but we tell Him, "Sorry, my life is already booked solid with more pressing matters. I have other guests here occupying the various spaces in my life. Work, school, family, and friends are always given priority reservations. But of course, any time Drama wants to come and spend the night, I have to make room." Jesus would later tell a parable about this. A seed fell among thorns and was choked out (Luke 8:5–15). To have flowers, we must first love flowers and, second, hate weeds. Weeds compete with flowers for space, moisture, nourishment, and sunlight. Every time it rains, the flower wants that drop of water, but the weeds say, "Uh-uh," which means there needs to be some weeding out if a person wants to have a healthy, growing garden.

Jesus would later tell a parable about a man who prepared a feast for friends and sent his servants out to invite them (Luke 14). But their lives were booked. One said, "I just purchased a field property." Another said, "I have purchased five yoke of oxen." Another said, "I've just taken a wife." They missed a great feast because of their priorities.

A recent convert was scheduled to be baptized at our church on a particular Sunday morning. However, he called the week before and said that he would have to postpone his baptism. When Sunday arrived, to our surprise the man showed up, ready to be baptized. I remarked, "I thought you couldn't make it." He replied, "I made a mistake. The University of Louisville doesn't play Memphis until next week." Granted, he was a recent convert to the faith, but he saw nothing wrong with postponing his baptism to stay home and watch a basketball game!

PREJUDICE

There's a car wash in Louisville called Karbe's. I get my car washed there regularly, but for several years I didn't know who the owner was. I didn't know his identity because He wasn't behind the cash register or behind a desk. He was out on the line drying cars with his workers, doing menial labor.

Just as I didn't know the identity of the car wash owner, the innkeeper did not know the identity of his would-be guests. He did not know that he had an opportunity to make room for the fourth man in the fiery furnace (Daniel 3), the One who was with Daniel in the lion's den (Daniel 6). The innkeeper had unknowingly turned away the Rose of Sharon, the Lily of the Valley—God Incarnate and Incognito. Had the innkeeper known, he surely would have rearranged some accommodations. But Joseph and Mary were a peasant couple, so they did not appear to associate with a king. Like the Karbe's owner, they didn't look the part.

There is a story about a man who went to a motel looking for a room but it was booked. He argued with the manager. He said, "Be honest with me. If the president of the United States came here and needed a room tonight, would you give him a room?" The manager said, "Yes, of course I would." The man responded, "Well . . . he ain't coming, so give me that room!"

We make accommodations in our lives for certain people based on superficial things—like the way they dress, or the car they drive, or the house they live in. If a man approaches a woman but he's not dressed right or not driving the right kind of car, she won't give him the time of day. If a woman shows interest in a man but she doesn't have the right look, he won't give her the time of day.

Jeff Pierce won the Tour de France in 1987. In order to train, he took a job as a bicycle messenger, transporting messages from office to office. But in order to train properly for the race, he rode his own bicycle, a professional model that cost around $3,000. No one ever stole the bike, however, because Pierce wrapped it in duct tape and spray-painted it black. The bike looked so bad that thieves thought it was a piece of junk; in reality, it was a very expensive piece of equipment.

Some of the greatest blessings we receive in life come wrapped in duct tape. Jesus came to the world wrapped in poverty and helplessness, but underneath lay the King of Kings. Many blessings—a friend, a spouse, a job, or some other opportunity—come in unlikely wrappings.

PRESUMPTION

Since the innkeeper was in Bethlehem, he was a Jew. Like other Jews, he had been awaiting the Messiah's coming. The innkeeper probably never imagined he would turn the Messiah away, but he did. And in so doing, he set a pattern that would follow Jesus throughout His earthly life and throughout history.

In many of His encounters during His earthly ministry, Jesus was presumed to be a nobody. Jesus went to Nazareth wanting to do miracles, but the Nazarenes kicked him out, saying, "He ain't nobody special."

It seems that the only two places on earth where there was room for Jesus was in a manger between animals and on a cross between thieves. That's why the real Christmas tree is the one that was used to hang Jesus on the cross.

Today people are still finding ways to tell Jesus, "There's no room for You here!" But we say it in ways like these:

"When I retire, I'll give more time to the church."

"When I pay off all my bills, I'll tithe."

"When I find a preacher that I like, I'll join a church."

The truth is, there'll never be room for Jesus until some things are rearranged. But powerful things happen to us when we make room for Jesus. The woman at the well made room for Him and it turned her life around. Zacchaeus made room and he repented of all his unscrupulous ways. Mary Magdalene made room and Jesus healed her of seven demons. The centurion made room and the Lord healed his sick servant.

What can happen in your life if you make room for Him?

Jesus said, "Seek ye first God's kingdom and righteousness and all of the things you worry about will be given to you as well" (Matt. 3:33). So if you're worried about how you're going to pay your bills, make room for Him and seek His kingdom first—and what you need will be given to you.

If you're worried about getting ahead in your career, make room for Him and seek His kingdom first—and what you need will be given to you.

If you're worried about getting married and your biological clock is ticking, make room for Him and seek His kingdom first—and what you need will be given to you.

If you're worried that your life will never change for the better, make room for Him and seek His kingdom first—and what you need will be given to you.

During this Christmas season, amid the frenetic holiday festivities, make room for Him. Keep Christ in Christmas.

Make Room for God

Michael Eric Dyson

Based on Matthew 1:18–25; Luke 2:1–7

And she brought forth her firstborn son, and laid him in a manger; because there was no room for them in the inn. (Luke 2:7)

As strange as it may seem, God has a hard time finding room to abide—both in our hearts and in our culture. Most of us who lay claim to being Christians feel that we're already full of God. After all, we pray and politic in God's name; we bless and curse folk in God's name. We preach and posture in God's name.

And we'd like to think that we would never turn God away. We see ourselves with open arms, welcoming God into every nook and cranny of our existence. But the story of Christmas reminds us that it's the very folk who think, "We're in with God," who are the ones who keep God outside—shut out of our identities, our institutions, and our history.

If the Christmas story is about "us," then it's especially about "them"—those poor and powerless folk who are often off our social radar until some controversy or catastrophe draws them sharply into view. As social critic Michael Harrington memorably said, they are indeed "the invisible poor." And when we finally see them, they are often draped in shame and pounded by stigma.

The story of Jesus' birth—the struggles of His parents, and the tough and dramatic circumstances in which He was conceived and delivered—may as well have been ripped from the pages of faith and dropped right into today's social science textbooks.

There's been a great deal of hand-wringing and moralizing about the poor: They don't try hard enough to get an education. They wear their victim status like a badge of honor. They're hopelessly dependent upon government checks and subsidies. They have too many babies out of wedlock. They don't speak with intelligence or eloquence. They spurn moral discipline and are ruled by lust and envy.

Thank God that the biblical account of Jesus' family is free of such harsh judgments of the poor. Joseph and Mary were obviously without means; why else would they have to resort to a manger because there was no room for them in an inn? And yet the Bible doesn't condemn folk for their condition. Instead, the story unfolds in simple eloquence to suggest their purity of heart—that is, their singleness of purpose—even as it captures their struggles for divine direction. They were certain that the finger of God had written on their lives; they were simply trying to figure out what it all meant. They knew it revolved around the special child Mary was carrying in her womb, but they wrestled with inner visions and heavenly warnings to discern His lofty destiny.

Besides those famous "swaddling clothes," Jesus' infant body—and indeed the entire setting of His birth—was wrapped in a great deal of moral distress that is often clouded by romance and mysticism. Of course, the easiest way to fend off questions about Mary's status as a single, unwed mother-to-be is to suggest the holy source of her seed. By insisting that Jesus was born to a virgin, many Christians neatly resolve issues that aren't so easily settled with the rest of us mortals. They don't have to answer how it looks for a young woman who got pregnant before she was married to become the Mother of God.

Saying the Holy Spirit got her that way surely works for those who are already likely to believe that God works that way.

There are plenty of believers in God whose faith doesn't rest upon the idea that God chose to impregnate a young virgin to get God's Son to earth. For them, the regular channels are just as effective, thank you very much. In fact, a great deal of Christian theology is fueled by the belief that God, through Jesus, breathed, suffered, lived, and died the same way we do. And if God could die the way we die, it might not be such a bad thing to be born as we're born. For many Christians, and for those beyond the fold of faith, it makes Jesus' story that much more compelling and believable.

Let's be honest: for many Christians, the insistence on the Virgin Birth is just as much a moral matter as a theological one. The same religious folk who beat up on poor single mothers have to give Mary a pass. The fact that God chose Mary to mother God's Son makes her different; it makes her special. And, thus, she's spared the brutal condemnation that single poor mothers routinely receive in our culture.

But who's to say that God doesn't still choose poor single mothers to deliver another of God's beloved sons or daughters to earth, even if they get here in more conventional fashion? What's more, when those single poor mothers occasionally claim that they, too, became mothers without having intercourse, they are laughed out of the building, or scorned for their contentions.

Listen to the words of Ann Iverson, mother of basketball superstar Allen Iverson, as a case in point:

Allen Iverson was conceived without intercourse. That was 1:00 a.m. on September 22, 1974, at my grandmother's house in Hartford. I'd made up my mind that on my fifteenth birthday I'd have my first sexual encounter with Allen Broughton. We had it all planned. At midnight of my birthday, when everyone was asleep, he tapped on the back door. I was in my PJ's and robe. We went down to the basement and used an old mattress that was down there. He started grindin' against me—he never put it in! And before you know it . . . then I heard the bathroom door upstairs— Grandma was awake! I got him out of the house quick. Eight weeks later I took a physical for basketball, and they told me I was eight weeks pregnant.

I said to the doctor, "You're tellin' a story!" They took the test again, and the doctor called my grandma in and said, "Your granddaughter's gonna have a baby, but she hasn't been penetrated." I'm tellin' ya, I look at Allen and I say God had a plan for him and me.

Now I'm not saying that Allen Iverson became the savior of his people as it was forecast about Jesus in Matthew's telling of His birth. But he sure saved the Philadelphia 76ers from utter disgrace! He even led them to the 2001 NBA finals, where they stole the first game in overtime against the heavily favored Los Angeles Lakers.

As the shortest number one overall draft pick in NBA history, the six-foot Iverson has performed spectacular feats, with legendary toughness, for over a decade. And despite being thrown in jail on trumped-up charges at age seventeen, he overcame a painful and unjust incarceration to become one of the greatest basketball players to ever lace up a pair of sneakers. His rise and performance have been nothing short of miraculous, a tribute to his God-given genius and his determination to succeed against all odds.

Ann Iverson's claims about Allen's virgin birth may strike some as unbelievable. After all, she was a poor black woman living in desperate poverty who eventually looked for a way out through her son. But is she all that different from Jesus' mother, Mary?

Ann Iverson believed that God had a plan for her and her son. That seems true of Mary as well, who, according to Scripture, "pondered . . . in her heart" all the miraculous events around her Son's birth. Of course, Mary's Son would eventually inspire a vision so uplifting that vast numbers of folk outside their tribe and time tapped into Jesus' power to acknowledge Him as their Savior. And millions beyond Ann Iverson's circle have declared her son a messiah of sorts—especially us 76ers fans!

But is Mary's situation, or Ann's for that matter, any more miraculous for never having sex than those who deliver a child under normal circumstances? It is perhaps only when we take note of all the things that can go wrong with the birth process that we are forced to acknowledge how utterly miraculous giving birth is under any conditions.

And is it any more remarkable for Ann, or Mary, to conceive without the hymen being penetrated than it is for single poor mothers to birth and rear their children while the stigma and discouragement hangs above their heads?

This is no praise song to single young teens having babies. We all know too well the social and personal distress that single motherhood can bring for poor black mothers. I do mean, however, to celebrate the feisty, independent spirit of young teen mothers who have children, and who go on to rear wonderful human beings who prosper as adults—all without being able to say that God is their "baby's daddy." However, isn't it fair to say that God is the parent of their children, and the source of their seed's growth? Tragically, too often God is the only Father that many children will ever know.

I am also making a plea that we offer the same sort of guidance to poor single mothers that Mary got—from God, the angels, religious stories, and human beings. Maybe then their children will be able to prosper as Jesus did. We should really hope this is the case for minority mothers who, like Mary, witness decrees sent out to harm their children. Of course, these need not be as explicit as Herod's edict to find and kill the Baby Jesus because the ruler recognized a threat to his kingdom in this child's birth. To be sure, there are some political figures who detect in the birth of black children to poor mothers a threat to their conservative identities and ideologies. The threats are sometimes expressed as moral fears wrapped in political rhetoric—such as the need to regulate poor families choked by "social pathologies" and to wrest vulnerable families from welfare dependency.

On occasion, the potential threat of black children to conservative philosophies comes barreling over the top. That happened when former U.S. Department of Education secretary Bill Bennett pondered aloud the social benefits of aborting black babies. And there is a great deal of danger for black children, engulfed by political and cultural edicts to build more prisons to warehouse young black boys, or to shut down schools in poor neighborhoods, making black youth even more socially isolated and vulnerable. These different disguises worn by political figures invested in black social control makes them little more than Herod in drag.

Of course, as was true for Mary, the shame and disgrace of single motherhood in our day are usually borne by vulnerable young women. At times, righteous men like Joseph seek to save such women from public disgrace. The catch is that too often the best intentions of men to save women only reinforce a culture that unfairly blames them to begin with. Even when men are headed in the right direction, they still exercise too much power in determining how women live.

That's why men's beliefs about female sexuality are written all over women's bodies. In 1973, nine men donned in black robes decided a serious debate in this country over who can legally control a woman's reproductive options. It is also mostly men who determine how women's bodies will be viewed in rap videos. It is men who orchestrated the crass reduction of women to gyrating extensions of male desire. For that matter, the decision to permit women to preach, or to ban them from the pulpit, rests largely in the hands of men in most mainline churches. The way men control women's lives—even if they're well intentioned—is a mark of unjust power.

It's clear that more men must be like Joseph in another regard. His intention to spare Mary public disgrace by leaving her behind was interrupted by a divine vision that lead him instead to provide a space for her. More of us men must make room in our lives for the women God has brought to us. More men must make room for women in the cramped interior of our theological domain. We must be willing to forgo our treasured beliefs and identify with our women in a profoundly empathetic way.

Joseph at first identified with Mary only through the lens of a masculine culture that assigned blame to her for her apparent moral lapse. What he had to do was imagine—make room for—a world where a woman's humanity didn't rest upon her meeting a masculine norm of moral purity. Instead, Joseph's sense of morality was reshaped by yielding to a God whose actions sometimes bring discomfort to those who follow God.

It was uncomfortable for both Mary and Joseph to follow God. Mary had to endure shame and stigma. Joseph had to incinerate his dogma and beliefs in the furnace of obedience to God. Joseph's vision of God finally rose above the limits of his tribe and manhood. He had to yield to God by honoring his woman. More of us men must find the courage and strength to do the same.

It is not hard to see why there was no room for Mary and Joseph in the inn, even though they were carrying the Savior of their people. They were, after all, poor and bereft of the goods of prosperous living. They were not able to command reservations in better dwelling places. We can see how poor they were because they couldn't plan ahead of time to find suitable lodging. The poor often can't plan ahead of time because the crush of financial want makes them live in the moment—and that's not a metaphysical mantra, but rather, a monetary mandate. The poor are forever kept from making plans that make sense.

The poor often can't protect themselves from the elements, and from the withering hand of fate. While it's true that none of us is exempt from destiny's sometimes harsh backhand, the poor are even more vulnerable than those with adequate resources—food, shelter, and clothing—who can fend better for themselves.

It's very difficult for the poor to plan ahead—to save money, invest in stocks and bonds, schedule adequate or affordable housing, plan for retirement, or secure safe conditions for their children's nurture. But it's also tough for the poor to prove that they are worth taking notice of and investing in over the long haul. That was Mary and Joseph's problem as well: very few people beyond sojourning sages and repressive rulers knew the value of their child Jesus.

But like Mary and Joseph, we must insist on our children's worth, and be willing to stick with them in the mess of a manger when the world refuses to make room for them, whether in a motel or a mansion. Few folk found Ann Iverson a person worth protecting and loving, since it was not apparent that her precious bundle—born under difficult circumstances, and reared under a tremendous crisis—would one day repay the world with athletic genius and remarkable performance.

So many high-achieving folk started in humble circumstances. Had society known that they would become stars, though, it might have treated their parents with more kindness and respect.

For the poor, the doors of opportunity are often closed. There is little room for the poor in our hearts or imaginations. We keep them outside—outside economic health, social security, domestic stability, and moral affirmation. The tragedy of such behavior is that we often miss God when we mess with the poor.

If ever there was clear evidence of the biblical warning that "as ye have done it unto one of the least of these my brethren, ye have done it unto me" (Matthew 25:40, KJV), it was when Mary and Joseph were turned away from the inn. When we turn the poor away, we're turning God away. Anytime we keep the poor away from the resources they need to survive, we are turning God away. Anytime we fail to act kindly toward vulnerable strangers, we're turning God away.

We Christians must make room for Jesus by making room for poor mothers, who, like His mother, Mary, carry their children in their wombs and hearts. We must make room for Jesus by making room in our political order for poor single mothers who need protection from social dislocation and poverty. We must make room for fathers in our employment structure who are hounded by low wages that keep them and their families in the poorhouse.

We must make room for poor folk in our health care system who use the emergency ward as their first line of defense against illness and who are made infinitely more vulnerable to curable diseases.

We must make room for the poor in public policies, and in programs that give them a better standard of living. We must stop punishing the poor with mean-spirited rules and regulations.

Finally, we should make room for the poor in theologies that butt them out as we bow to a gospel of wealth and material obsession. We must never forget that Jesus was born amidst dung and despair before He matured into a prophet who threatened religious and political authorities. Jesus' humble birth and revolutionary life are a judgment on the commercialized corruption of His memory.

Jesus' life and teachings are a warning to vicious theological manipulations of His ministry. We've crowded out the poor in our churches with an emphasis on prosperity that blunts the political force of Jesus' challenge to the powerful. Like Joseph, we must awaken from our dreams and do the work of the Lord by embracing the poor as a sign of our humanity—for if there is no room for the poor, there is no room for God.

Sacred Wonder

William S. Epps

BASED ON LUKE 2:8–19

The sacred wonder of Christmas is that we are supposed to become new. Whether you wear new stuff or old, you can still become new. And for your information, you can wear new stuff but still be old.

The sacred wonder of Christmas is the change that results from people discovering the reality of God's presence in Christ.

God's presence in Christ is a reconciling, redeeming, transforming presence that changes our lives, and ultimately our world. That's what makes Christmas special; not the new clothes or other gifts or trinkets. It's not the holiday decorations or traditional foods that make Christmas special. Christmas is special because of what God has done in Christ. If you make the stuff of Christmas more important than the Christ of Christmas, then you have desecrated what is sacred.

The story of Jesus' birth is probably one of the best-known passages in Luke's gospel. At this time of the year, unless we are forced to ignore them, we see Nativity scenes in public places, observing the birth of Jesus. Hopefully, Christians will always use icons like the Nativity to maintain the image of Christmas.

That's very, very important. Some people only want a Christmas tree; I want a manger. Some may want to see thousands of tiny lights at Christmas, and I know what they represent, but I want to see *the* Light.

Luke's gospel makes us aware of the fact that something stupendous happened and that it was a sacred wonder to those who experienced it.

As wondrous as that night was, I find it fascinating that we don't know the names of the people to whom this happened; maybe that's a good thing, because we might think the miracle of Christ's birth was just supposed to be for them.

Their identities remain anonymous but their experience is legendary, and perhaps that's more important than their names anyway. That's a reminder to us that even when we remain anonymous, and our identity is lost in obscurity, we still can be a blessing to others.

In this passage of unnamed characters, there is a sacred wonder for each of us. Ordinary people were doing their ordinary work on an ordinary day, until they were discovered by a sacred wonder. They didn't discover it. It discovered them.

When it found them they were captivated. Isn't it marvelous that while they were doing what they would normally do, a sudden, sacred wonder arrested their attention, causing them to focus on something other than their day-to-day routine?

The appearance of a heavenly messenger would stop any people in their tracks. And that's what happened to this anonymous group of shepherds. An angel appeared, and the glory of the Lord shone brightly around them. The light was so dazzling that it was frightening; they fell to the ground, covering their faces.

The angel spoke to them and said, "Fear not. I bring you good tidings of great joy. Unto you is born in the city of David a Savior, who is Christ the Lord. And this will be a sign unto you. You will find a babe in a manger wrapped in swaddling clothes."

The way Luke described it, we can see the sacred wonder in it all. His words paint such a sharp contrast from one verse to the next. Verse 11 says a Savior, Christ the Lord, is born in the city of David. And then in the very next verse, Luke says that the sign will be a babe wrapped in strips of cloth. What a contrast! How can a baby be a Savior?

The shepherds would find the Christ, the Messiah, wrapped in strips of cloth. That doesn't seem to make sense, does it? How can one who needs meticulous care and attention be a Messiah? How can a helpless infant take on the sins of humanity? What kind of picture is this?

It's an oxymoron, a paradox. We can't figure it out. But Luke explains that there are experiences in life that are inexplicable, and you don't try to explain them. When words fail, energies prevail. So what you do is paint an image of the experience you've had, rather than try to explain so people can understand. You can't convince people about a certain reality; you can only paint an image of the experience that has changed your life.

I can't help but think that the shepherds told Luke about what happened to them; otherwise, he would not have been able to get the detail as straight as he did. Luke did not have the experience; he was going on hearsay. And if the shepherds themselves didn't tell Luke what happened, then they told it with such detail that those who heard it then shared their story with the same kind of exactness, mesmerizing others with news of the experience that left the shepherds awestricken.

Have you ever had an experience that you could not articulate with words? Let me help you: have you ever been in love? Most have had that all-too-familiar experience we call falling in love. You know why we describe it that way? Because we were just overwhelmed, overtaken; it felt as if we didn't have control over what took place. It was as though something or someone invaded our reality, altered our existence, and turned our world upside down. We became like putty in his or her hands. You've been there, haven't you?

That's what Luke, the gospel writer, is describing—out of nowhere, a presence invaded our reality with such light and warmth, and with such poignancy, that it pierced every defense that we had built and left us captivated beyond compare. What has taken place is something that left us feeling that we couldn't help ourselves.

Every time I think about Christmas, I get caught up in the sacred wonder of it all, a sacred wonder that is threefold.

THE SACRED WONDER IS "GOD WITH US"

It's easy for us to think of God as being out there someplace. No one has problems trying to understand the transcendence of God. People understand God as being out there somewhere in heaven. Some people even believe "God is anywhere but where they are."

When difficulty arises, we say like Job, "O, that I knew where I might find him, then I would fill my mouth with arguments and argue my case before him." We respond to difficulty, as if God were lost. You don't need to look for God. The sacred wonder of Christmas is that God has come to you.

We think that we've got to come to the Lord to be saved. No, the Lord has already come to us to save us. All we have to do is acknowledge that it's God; that's the sacred wonder. God has come to you!

We don't have enough understanding to know how to go to God. But God has come to us anyway. Isn't that the story of sacred writ from Genesis all the way to Revelation—that God comes to us?

God to came to us in creation and made us. God came to us in Adam and Eve in the garden to walk in and develop fellowship with us, and God continues to come to us today.

God came to us in Moses, and God came to us in Abraham, Isaac, and Jacob. God has come to us in prophets that God has called to share what God wants us to know about God.

We keep missing it, and then we say that God is silent because, in a period where we are so deaf and we refuse to hear, it seems as though God is not speaking. But the real problem is not whether God is speaking, but whether we are listening.

God says, "Let Me come to you." It's so unmistakably clear. "I'm going to come to where you are. I'm going to come into the world as you come into the world. I'm going to come to you like a baby. I'm going to meet you where you are."

God comes to us; God came to the shepherds. They were minding their business. Have you ever been minding your business and had your reality invaded by a presence, a thought, or an idea, and you attributed it to intuition? Where do you think you got it? That's the sacred wonder of Christmas: God is with us.

God comes to us and all we have to do is reach out and embrace the reality of God's presence. No, God doesn't come to us as we want, or as we think, and or even as we hope; God comes to us in strange but uncompromising ways on God's own terms. We have to open our eyes and become aware.

Have you ever had your attention arrested? I'm not talking about that fine young man who caught your eye. I don't mean that fine young lady who caused your passion to rise. No. Have you had your attention arrested by something noble, something sacred— when you lost yourself and you knew that God had come to you?

God comes to us each and every day in the common experiences of our lives. I'm glad God went to shepherds, people who were ostracized in that day because they were considered unclean. It was all right to use the sheep that they raised for sacrifices on the altar, but the shepherds who raised them could not to come into the Temple to participate in the sacrifice.

I'm glad the Lord appeared to shepherds through an angel, because God wants us to know, "I'll meet you where you are. You don't have to come to the sanctuary; I'll meet you where you are."

God says to us, "I'll meet you at home. I'll meet you on the street. I'll meet you in your despair. I'll meet you in your pain. I'll meet you in your hurt. I'll meet you in your distress. I'll meet you in your losses. I'll meet you where you are. I want you to know where I am, so I've come to you. In the context of the circumstances of your life—that's where you'll find Me. That's where I am; I am with you. That's the sacred wonder of Christmas: Emmanuel, God is with us.

THE SACRED WONDER MOTIVATES YOU

The sacred wonder of Christmas also motivates us to do something. Think about what happened after the shepherds heard the angel's announcement. They said, "Let us go see this thing that the Lord has done."

You have to do something. You just can't bask in the aura of sacred wonder and recline, saying, "Boy, that was some experience." No. You have to do something.

All of life is like that. That's why relationships fail. After the initial period of romance, one or both of the people involved stop doing what they did before. To keep it going, there's some activity that's required of you.

Now notice what the shepherds did. After they got the marvelous news, they got up and they ran; they were in a hurry. They didn't waste any time. Often, we get in a hurry about the wrong things. That's a waste; but it pays to get in a hurry about the right things.

You can get in a hurry about realizing that God is with you and God is working in your life providentially through all the perplexities and problems that you may be experiencing. Get in a hurry about sin. Get in a hurry believing, as you got in a hurry doubting. Get in a hurry about being thankful. Get in a hurry about holding on to what God has revealed to you through the testimony of witnesses. Get in a hurry about it and see if it won't make a difference in your life. We get in a hurry about the wrong things. We hurry to destruction. We hurry to hurt. We hurry to pain. But we don't hurry to help. Get in a hurry to embrace the help that God makes available in our Savior, Jesus Christ.

The shepherds were in a hurry, so they ran, forgetting all about what they were doing before they experienced the sacred wonder.

Forget about what you're doing and get in a hurry about exploring something that's more sublime. We get caught up in the mundane and the ordinary and the monotony of sameness and we miss the beauty that God has available to us. Get in a hurry to embrace the reality of God's presence in the context of your circumstance right now. You have to do that; no one can do it for you. It's as the old folks said, "You got to get this for yourself." There are certain things in life that no one else can get for you; you have to get it for yourself.

I can share my experience with you, but you've got to work at making your own experience. I can't make you see it; you have to help yourself believe it. That's your work to do.

The sacred wonder motivates you to do something. No one who's ever had an experience with God just sat down and did nothing. They all were motivated to do something.

Just ask Moses: "What are you going to do?" He'd tell you, "Well, I'm going down to Egypt with my staff in my hand. I'm going to tell Pharaoh to let God's people go."

What are you going to do, Micah? "Well, I'm going to tell folks what the Lord requires of them. All He wants from them is to do justly, love mercy, and walk humbly with God."

What are you going to do, Isaiah? "Well, I've got to tell the

136

people that though their sins be as scarlet, they can be made white as snow."

And that's how it is. I can't sit and bask in the euphoria of my sacred wonder. I've got to do something; and that's just what the shepherds did. They went to do something with what they had received.

THE SACRED WONDER MAKES YOU TELL IT

After the shepherds saw the babe in the manger wrapped in strips of cloth, you know what they did? They ran someplace to tell what had happened to them. Can't you just see them? They'd started out their evening lying on their backs, looking around and checking their sheep. Suddenly, an angel appeared out of the ethereal blue— lights started shining all around them, and understandably, they were afraid. A voice spoke peace and calm to them. Then they got up and ran. They went from lying around in the pasture to running from place to place telling what had happened to them.

And that's how God works with us. How many testimonies have we heard like that? "I started off just doing what I ordinarily do . . ."

"I started off at home just going about my normal routine . . ."

"I started out getting in my car, going to my job . . ."

We can start out doing what we always do in the way that we always do it. But then God gets hold of us. A divine interruption occurs and diverts our attention, causing us to run someplace. Imagine one of the shepherds' testimonies after encountering the sacred wonder:

> *Go, tell it on the mountain,*
> *Over the hills and everywhere.*
> *Go, tell it on the mountain,*
> *That Jesus Christ is born!*

Go, tell somebody that a Savior is born to save you from the destruction you bring on yourself. He has come to save you from the oppression that others have caused. He has come to save you from the hurt and the pain of life's traumas. He has come to save you from whatever would diminish the quality of your existence. You've got to tell it. Share with everyone the sacred wonder of Christmas.

An Uncomfortable Christmas

KEN FONG

BASED ON LUKE 2:1–7

Mary, Joseph, and Jesus were in an uncomfortable situation, yet they were able to find a way to be quite comfortable in the midst of very trying circumstances. Found in their story is a great lesson for all of us today: life is never going to be perfect. In life there are going to be plenty of reasons for us to feel uncomfortable—over different parts of the world, over different things going on in the church, even over things happening in our very own lives. And yet, one of the signs of Christian maturity is to be able to go beneath our discomfort and find greater reason to trust in God.[1]

The gospel of Luke (NIV) begins with, "In those days Caesar Augustus issued a decree that a census should be taken of the entire Roman world. (This was the first census that took place while Quirinius was governor of Syria.) And everyone went to his own town to register."[2]

You can imagine that Joseph was not looking forward to making the trip; this was not a short or an easy trip. Verse 4 (NIV) reads: "So Joseph also went up from the town of Nazareth [he heard the decree] in Galilee to Judea to Bethlehem, the town of David, because he belonged to the house and the line of David. He went there to register with Mary, who was pledged to be married to him, and was expecting a child." At this point, Joseph and Mary were not officially married, although they had gone through a betrothal ceremony. It was pretty involved.

It you have maps in the back of your Bible, you might want to flip there to the big one that shows Jerusalem and Palestine. If you can locate Jerusalem, kind of near the lower middle half of that, you'll see the Dead Sea. Bethlehem is just above that. If you look more north you'll find the region of Galilee and the town of Nazareth. And if you have those little mileage scales there, it shows that the distance between Nazareth and Bethlehem, which is still south of Jerusalem, is about seventy-five miles. Some of us commute farther than seventy-five miles every day. A piece of cake, no problem. Jump in your car, get on the freeway. If you do it at the right time of day, no rush hour traffic. How long is it going to take you? Maybe an hour, maybe a little bit more. Not much.

Most of us do that without even thinking about it. But going seventy-five miles back then . . . Some of it, topographically, is over some mountains. Walking seventy-five miles alongside a plodding donkey on primitive roads choked with other people on their way back home to register for the census, you figure they may have averaged ten miles a day, and this is with a very pregnant fiancée. Using this calculation, it would have taken Joseph and Mary more than a week to get there. But since this was an official decree from Rome's emperor, people had no option to ignore it.

Some of us wonder, "Well, why couldn't you file an extension? Don't you do that with the IRS if you can't get your taxes in by April 15?" "Ah, man, this is a really bad time for me. My fiancée is about due to have this kid. It's like the worst time to be on the road. Besides, she has the Savior of the world inside her womb. Isn't that enough to get an extension?"

Like any other government, back then or now, when it came to getting taxes from the citizenry, Rome didn't mess around. No extension. So what choice did Joseph have except to pack some provisions, hoist his very pregnant fiancée onto a donkey, and head south on a dusty road to the town of his ancestor, King David?

Now, Mary was very close to delivering. Ever been around a lady in the last couple of weeks of her pregnancy? Those are tense moments when you know that it's been almost nine months now and this baby is ready to come at any moment. So Mary, due to deliver soon, was not looking forward to sitting atop any kind of beast of burden.

The last thing any pregnant woman would want to do is sit on a donkey for over a week, riding on uneven terrain. She'd rather stay home and sleep in her own comfortable bed, do some light activities, stay in close contact with her midwife.

Now, the Bible doesn't tell whether or not Mary had previous knowledge of ancient prophecies that the king of the Jews would be born in Bethlehem of Judea. But even if she did know of those prophecies, being in the last stage of pregnancy, she would be more interested in giving birth to her first child than in prophecy.

I'm sure that Mary, like Joseph, wasn't just thrilled with the notion of going to Bethlehem, and I was trying to imagine what her prayers would have been like if she had talked to God all along on this journey. "God, are you nuts? I let you talk me into this pregnancy because I have great faith in you, and you and I both wholeheartedly agree that the world desperately needs a Savior. But this last week, what I need most of all is to be taking it easy at home. I've never given birth before and I'm already feeling anxious enough as it is. Don't you want your Son to come into this world in a safe and familiar place? I don't understand how us obeying some pagan demigod fits into your plans, especially at this crucial time in this baby's life and mine. What if my water breaks when we're in the middle of nowhere? God, there's plenty of nowhere between here and Bethlehem. What if I can't locate a midwife to help me? Now Joey, he's a carpenter, and I know he's good with his hands, but there's a huge difference between a piece of lumber and a fragile infant straining to come out of me. And even if we get to Bethlehem without incident, what if we can't find a decent place to stay? It's bound to be packed with other pilgrims. Will you promise me that our baby will be born in a four-star hotel? God, are you listening? God, are you there? Now, of course, you don't have to answer me. I know you're there. I know you love me and you intend to deliver your Son to the world through me. Well, I've trusted you with everything this far. I can trust you for the rest. Amen."

Have you ever had one of those prayer sessions that started with, "God, are you nuts?" Or do you even dare to say that? You think that, but by the time you get to the actual praying, it's "O heavenly Father, Thou who art . . ."

I think there's a whole process that Mary went through on this weeklong-or-so journey from Nazareth to Bethlehem. I think maybe this wasn't just a onetime prayer. I think this was like an imagined condensation of the process she went through in starting off where most of us would. The Bible is not a fairy-tale book; this book is about real people who walked with God. You have to step away from those little pictures where you see that glowing circle around Mary's head all the time and see the real people with real-life circumstances.

After making that long and difficult trip, verse 6 (NIV) tells us, "While Mary and Joseph were there [in Bethlehem], the time came for the baby to be born, and she gave birth to her firstborn, a son. She wrapped him in cloths and placed him in a manger, because there was no room for them in the inn."

Apparently arriving in Bethlehem without incident, they were dusty, thirsty, tired, and even more so, they were crestfallen. I'm sure that as they went around town looking for a place to stay, all the inns had those little signs blinking, "No Vacancy." No one left the light on for them. That's probably when the contractions started.

You can imagine she's experiencing these contractions, something she'd never felt, but she pretty much knew what was going on. And there's her fiancé, Joseph, arguing with the umpteenth innkeeper, "What do you mean there's no place for us to stay? Look at my fiancée! She's about to give birth. You just can't tell us we can't stay here. We've got to have a place to stay."

As those contractions increased, Mary must have said, "Joey, just take anything. I gotta get off this donkey. I got to find somewhere to lie down. It doesn't have to be a bed. It's time! He's not waiting for anybody."

Finally, they get to one innkeeper who says, "You know what? It's not great, and I feel bad doing this, but I got a place out back. It's basically a cave where the guests keep their animals, but you're welcome to stay there to get out of my lobby."

So that's where they went, because beggars can't be choosers. There, amid the fetid straw, the manure piles, the assorted bugs and beasts, Mary's water broke. And Joseph, without ever having attended a Lamaze class, did the best to safely deliver God's Son, not even his own son, safely from Mary's womb into the world.[3]

During all of these events, though they were uncomfortable, Joseph and Mary had had to trust God, all this time believing that God knew exactly what He was doing. Even in the moments when they must have wondered if God was paying attention—or if He had taken a coffee break or something—they came back to this believing, despite their uncomfortable circumstances, that God was still running the show.

Even the most faithful, mature Christians have moments of wonder and worry. Some may have been raised in the kind of church setting where they were told that the older you get as a Christian, the more mature you are in your relationship with God through Christ—there comes a point when you don't have any doubts anymore, where you never worry about anything; you always trust immediately, fully, and automatically. And if that's the way someone tells you they really respond to God, they're not telling you the truth, or they're on some kind of medication!

What's really sad is that some of us are under the mistaken impression that the longer you walk with Christ, the more mature you apparently are supposed to be, and the less you are free to express your doubts, anxieties, and worries.

That's the crux of this whole Christmas message. The difference between a mature Christian and someone who's not a Christian or someone who's a very young Christian is not that the mature Christian never ever worries. The difference is, the mature Christian understands what to do with those worries and how to take them to God in a very real and honest way, and be transformed. This is the mystical part—to be transformed in the midst of being honest and angry and real and confused. And somehow, in the midst of bringing that realness of yourself to God, you are transformed into trusting God more.

In Philippians 4, the apostle Paul describes a transformation: "Celebrate God all day, every day. I mean, revel in him! . . . Don't fret or worry. Instead of worrying, pray. Let petitions and praises shape your worries into prayers, letting God know your concerns. Before you know it, a sense of God's wholeness, everything coming together for good, will come and settle you down. It's wonderful what happens when Christ displaces worry at the center of your life" (MSG).[4]

Some of us are still so wrongly respectful of God that we're afraid of getting God mad. We're afraid of God getting bent out of shape or something, so we don't tell God what's really on our heart, what we really want to see happen.[5]

I think I am quite skeptical when people start out praying, "Whatever you want, God, is fine with me." I don't know if that's very real. God wants us to know today that we absolutely have His blessing, His permission to come to Him with our worries and turn them into petitions and prayers, to really lay out to him our hearts' concerns. And before you know it, there's a kind of mystical, transformational moment. It's not all in one moment, but somehow, when you keep going back to God, God doesn't necessarily change the situation, but God begins to change you.

Let me tell you a little bit about how that worked with my wife and myself. A few years ago, we were in a lot of pain; we were very uncomfortable. In 1986, we had been married for five years and my wife and I decided it was time to bring a child into our relationship. We had no idea at the time that this was going to be hard. Seven years later we discovered that we had an undiagnosed problem with infertility. I would have been happier had they diagnosed something, anything.

"Oh, I don't know," was what they kept telling us. "Just keep trying." After about seven years, I was almost forty years old. We decided, "Okay, we're done trying. It's just too hard emotionally." Then God transitioned us into pursuing a child through adoption. We'd seen enough people do it—people in the church, and other friends. They advised that it would take about a year or eighteen months. It took us almost four years. Our adoption agency said that they had never known a couple that had so many failed adoptions. Even they couldn't believe what we had to go through.

About a year and a half into the adoption process, we had been promised a little baby from Japan. We named him Kobe. I'll never forget the day that the picture arrived of Kobe Jamison. My wife, for the first time, allowed herself to get emotionally excited. She had been holding back, holding her breath for a year and a half because we just couldn't believe that it was really going to happen. But when that picture arrived, within an hour we were out of the house walking the aisles of Babies "R" Us. We were really starting to believe that this little boy would be our son.

And about four weeks later, I was in Madison, Wisconsin, on a business trip. I got called out of the meeting. "Ken, your wife is on the phone."

She was crying. "Ken, Japan just called and they said there's something wrong with this baby and the whole adoption's off."

And to experience that is not a great feeling—but to experience that apart from each other, and knowing that we're not going to be together for another couple of days, was really hard. I remember going into Barney Ford's office, and he just let me cathartically rant my prayers to God. It was an outpouring such as I had never even known I was capable of. And Barney had the sense to just let it happen. Some Christian friends try to comfort you, but they're really just trying to shut you up. I thank God that Barney wasn't that kind of friend.

When my wife and I got together, we just bawled; we cried out to God and we were shaking our fists. In the midst of all of that—not overnight, not right away, but over the course of days—as we were allowed to be honest in our petitions and our prayers to God, something very mysterious happened to both of us as we got back into God's presence. God reminded us of two anchor points that we've always had.

Number one is Christmas, and that God loves us so much that He sent His Son. His Son was willing to come into this world and be born into our flesh—and not just leave it at that. Second, we have Easter—His willingness to die on the cross in our place, to take the penalty for our sins and then to rise from the dead. I may not know a lot of things about God, but I do know those two things about God and his love.

As much as that just sounds like doctrine, it was so much more to us then. I came out of that experience thinking, "You know, God, even if we don't get a child, I know that having a child is not the most fulfilling thing in my life. Even if I have a great kid and a great family, ultimately, what we've been created for is to have intimacy with You, God. And so, what you've shown me through this is that life is full of uncontrollable things, but the one thing that is constant is you." And as weird as it sounds, we came out of that experience trusting in God more and being okay if it meant we were not going to have a kid.

Now, I do want you to know that eventually God blessed us with Janessa; she's so precious. I get her ready in the morning when she doesn't want to get up and I forget the eleven years of uncomfortableness. I forget all the pain and suffering we went through, both individually and together. I forget all the times of confusion. I never fail to appreciate the grace of God in giving us, finally, a child. Nevertheless, I believe, after that experience, that we still would have been okay with God even if God didn't give us Janessa.

How do you do that? The answer lies in this Christmas story. You start where you are—as uncomfortable as you are, as uncomfortable as the situation might be. Then you bring all of that in prayers and petitions to God, and you trust God to be able to handle it, and to handle you. And after a time of venting, after you get all of those feelings out—after a while that part's spent and you come to another place that maybe you never even understood before. Then God gives you Himself in a new way.

In such moments, what we come to realize, maybe for the first time, or perhaps for the umpteenth time, is that ultimately what we really want is God. And God has given us Himself in Jesus Christ— the greatest gift that any one of us can receive.

NOTES

1. Take a look again at what Advent is all about. It's time of waiting, of longing, and preparing our hearts to receive Christ. And the four Sundays of Advent help us to appreciate Christ's first coming to us all and to realize why he's still planning on making a second trip. So the Advent season is not just to celebrate and commemorate the first coming of Jesus, but it's to remind us as Christians that we're still wait-

ing for the Second Coming, and that there are things about this world that didn't get all fixed when Jesus came the first time.

2. Wouldn't you like to have the power of Caesar? Do you have enough power and authority to affect other people's lives? Can you say something and make people jump? Does everyone hang on your every word? There are some people who have a lot of power in this world, but most of us do not associate with them.

Several years ago, I was talking to our then executive minister. He was telling me how he got together once a month with other Christian "mucky-mucks" in Los Angeles. He observed that even though all the persons gathered in that room were considered religious authorities, he recognized that there's a big difference between who has a title and who really has power and authority.

He gave his brother as an example. His brother was a medical school professor doing a stint in Nepal. Now, we can't find it on a map, but we know that it's pretty far away. It's where the Himalayan Mountains are. This brother was walking around the streets of Nepal and ran into a Catholic priest he recognized. He says, "Father So-and-So, what a surprise! What a small world to see you here. What are you doing in Nepal?"

The priest explained, "Well, last year I was publicly critical of something Pope John Paul II said, and so Cardinal Mahoney transferred me to Nepal." So my executive minister came back with, "Now that's power!"

The conversation got me to thinking. As a senior pastor, I began wondering, "Well, do I have real power and authority?" No, I really don't. Whatever power and authority I may seem to have comes from the Lord. No one at our church submits to me or any other pastor; rather, they submit to God through the pastoral staff.

So after I realized that I don't really have any power or authority as a senior pastor, I began to wonder, "What about in my home?" I asked myself, "Do I have ultimate power and authority over my wife?" I knew I could find some verses that seem to indicate such, but then when I got back to reality, I realized no, I really don't. Even with the way I understand Scripture about my husbandly role as the head, I'm to serve my wife as Christ served the church, and He gave Himself up for the church. So as a husband I can't speak to my wife like, "Woman, do this!" Instead, I use words like, "Sorry about that. I'll do it."

So by then I was thinking, "There's gotta be somebody in my house that's not a dog that I have ultimate power and authority over." Our-four-year-old. Yeah, there!

I'm bigger, stronger, more educated, smarter, and have more money than you, so therefore I must have ultimate power and authority over you. Yet even with a four-year-old, a parent can order a kid to do stuff, but unless she agrees to do it, the parent really doesn't have any authority over her. She really has to be with the program.

By contrast, Caesar Augustus was a rare person who had the kind of role in the world that allowed him to be one of the most powerful persons on earth. He presided over the entire Roman Empire and in some parts of it was worshiped as a god. Now, you when you have to get everybody to submit to you and do everything you say, right when you say it, it doesn't hurt to have the Roman legions to back you up!

But if you want that kind of power, people almost have to worship you. And when you're running a big empire like that, it takes a lot of money. And in order to get that kind of money, you have to do a lot of taxing. Hence, we have the reason for the census. So Caesar Augustus said, "Hey, it's time to do a census again, folks, because we want to make sure that all of our Roman citizens and all the people who are under the Roman rule are properly accounted for so that we can be sure we get the right amount of taxes from each of you. The requirement is that each of you has to return to your hometown, because that's where they have all the proper records."

The option is that there is no option. You didn't get to ignore this decree unless you enjoyed to be tortured. It's kind of like the IRS.

3. It was probably Joseph who cut the umbilical cord of Jesus and gave him the swat that cleared his little lungs and filled the night air with his first human cry. Then he handed this little baby, still smeared with amniotic fluid, over to Mary. That's when Mary must have tenderly wiped him clean. Then she brought out of her satchel those clean strips of cloth that she had brought along just for this purpose. She wrapped him and swaddled him so that he was warm and snug. Then she started looking for a suitable substitute for a cradle, and this being the stable, there was nothing but a feeding trough. Joseph, being the type A personality that I think he was, had already cleaned out all the old straw and lined the manger with fresh hay. Doing the best that they could, Mary laid him in the manger.

That is the scene that the shepherds came upon when they arrived a little bit later that evening. I'm sure it must have seemed a little weird to them—after having the angels appear and having the whole night sky filled with this majestic glory and this heavenly choir singing, "Glory to God! Peace on earth! A king is born!"—to find Him in a cave, lying on top of a bed of straw in a feeding trough. They must have thought, "Well, I wouldn't have done it this way." But you know, I think those shepherds felt very comfortable in that stable; more so than they would have in a palace. And centuries later, I think there's something very comforting and reassuring to all of us that God chose to send His only Son, the Savior of the world, to such humble surroundings, because we know that God doesn't put on airs and that we can come to Him in a very real sense as our true selves.

4. Notice, Paul's not saying that you reach a point in your spiritual life where you never worry. He's saying where Christ displaces the worry, which is typically at the center of our lives. He's saying, "Okay, you start off by letting your petitions and praises shape your worries into prayers."

5. One of the things that happens when we pastors go to the intensive care wards at hospitals is that we know in our hearts that we can't pray for immortality this side of the grave. But at the same time, we have no qualms with starting with what we want. We trust God, we know God enough to say, "God, we know that we can't pray that someone we love never dies, because that's just not going to happen. But you understand at this moment right now why we're pleading for you to do a miracle here. We want to see this person healed completely and to live many, many more years with us."

There are times when we visit with people who are afraid that we can't pray that. Of course we can. That's doesn't mean that we're telling God what to do; we're being honest with God with what we want.

But, you know what? As you continue to visit in that kind of situation—or if you're the one lying on the bed, and you're asking for the miracle, and you just want to be out of pain—as you keep going to God and you start where you are, something happens many times. Not always, but many times, your prayers begin to change because you begin to change. Ultimately, we yield to God and to who God is and what God knows best. But that isn't necessarily where we start, most of us.

Unto Us a Child Is Born

BILLY GRAHAM

BASED ON Luke 2:11–12

With wars and terrorism, crime at an all-time high, marriages breaking up, drugs—no wonder some people question whether we should say, "Merry Christmas!" Many people ask, "What is there to be merry about?"

Yet it was at such a time that our Lord Jesus Christ came into the world some two thousand years ago. And it will be at such a time that Jesus Christ comes back to this earth.

The angel, on that first Christmas night, said, "For there is born to you this day in the city of David a Savior, who is Christ the Lord" (Luke 2:11, NKJV). If we believe this, then it makes all the difference in the world for us. Life takes on a new dimension.

There is one particular passage of Scripture in the Old Testament to which I often turn, not only at this time of the year, but also at many times other than the Christmas season:

The people who walked in darkness
Have seen a great light.
Those who dwelt in the land of the shadow of death,
Upon them a light has shined. (Isaiah 9:2, NKJV)

Scripture goes on:

For unto us a Child is born,
Unto us a Son is given;
And the government will be upon His shoulder.
And His name will be called Wonderful, Counselor, Mighty God,
Everlasting Father, Prince of Peace.
Of the increase of His government and peace
There will be no end,
Upon the throne of David and over His kingdom,
To order it and establish it with judgment and justice
From that time forward, even forever.
The zeal of the Lord of hosts will perform this. (Isaiah 9:6–7,
  NKJV)

When these words were uttered by the prophet Isaiah, prophetic thunders were heard and the lightning of divine vengeance was seen as the clouds of judgment were gathering. With a trumpetlike voice this great statesman-prophet had declared with certainty the calamity which was soon to fall upon Judah as a judgment from God. Judah's alliance with evil and her departure from God called forth predictions of dreadful disaster. Isaiah had proclaimed with accuracy the Assyrian invasion. All around him were clouds of wrath and desolating darkness.

But Isaiah saw far away at the horizon a rift in the clouds and a clear light shining from heaven. He saw that while the people were walking in darkness, a light also shined upon them. He looked through the next eight hundred years of time and talked about the "garments rolled in blood" (Isaiah 9:5, NKJV). Then he declared, "Unto us a Child is born, unto us a Son is given" (Isaiah 9:6, NKJV).

There is not a shadow of a doubt in our minds as to whom Isaiah refers in the words "A Child is born . . . a Son is given." He is none other than the Lord Jesus Christ. The invasions that Isaiah predicted did take place, but God promised that someday the King would come and set up His Kingdom. The promise given was that God's covenant with David will stand and that someday a King will sit upon that throne.

Centuries later Jesus asked the religious leaders this question: " 'What do you think about the Christ? Whose Son is He?' They said to Him, 'The Son of David' " (Matthew 22:42, NKJV).

Jesus responded: "How then does David in the Spirit call Him 'Lord,' saying: 'The Lord said to my Lord, "Sit at My right hand, till I make Your enemies Your footstool" '? If David then calls Him 'Lord,' how is He his Son?" (Matthew 22:43–45, NKJV). Jesus was quoting from Psalm 110:1.

The religious leaders were baffled, bewildered, and completely silenced. They were not "able to answer him a word" (Matthew 22:46, NKJV). There was a conspiracy to entangle Jesus in this question. But His accusers were frustrated, as they had been many times before. What is the answer to the riddle that the religious leaders could not answer?

A CHILD BORN AND A SON GIVEN

The "Child born" establishes the fact of Christ's humanity. The "Son given" establishes the fact of His deity. Jesus is the God-man.

The "Child born" and the "Son given" is called "Wonderful" because He is wonderful. We must never lose sight of the fact that as a Child He was born, and that as a Son He was given. He is a "Child born" with reference to His human nature and His being born of the Virgin. But He is also a "Son given" with reference to His divine nature and His being God's Son.

The government is to be placed on the shoulders of the infinite Man, not a finite man. We see, therefore, in the "Child born" an infant. But He also is the "Son given." And so we see in the manger at Bethlehem an infinite Infant.

The Bible says, "Christ Jesus, who, being in the form of God, did not consider it robbery to be equal with God, but made Himself of no reputation, taking the form of a servant, and coming in the likeness of men" (Philippians 2:5–7, NKJV).

The two uses of the word translated as "form" in these verses refer to the pre-incarnate and the incarnate existence of the Lord Jesus Christ. The word "form" connotes reality.

For Christ to be equal with God was not a thing to be grasped. We do not have here an independent god of rival power and glory but the Christ of God who is as truly and fully divine as the Father is. Here is the New Testament counterpart of the Old Testament revelation of the Messiah. This is the "Child born" and the "Son given."

"But made Himself of no reputation" (Philippians 2:7, NKJV). The personal pronoun "Himself" is emphatic, bringing before us the voluntary aspect of Jesus' condescension: "He took not on him the nature of angels; but he took on him the seed of Abraham" (Hebrews 2:16, KJV). Christ swept through the realm of angels to lay hold on the nature of man.

He did not empty Himself of His deity, as some people have suggested, but He left the realm of glory and condescended to earth for our salvation. He emptied Himself of the outward manifestation of the glory of His deity.

There is no doubt that He was the "Child born," but with equal certainty we need to declare that He was the "Son given." So when He was here in the flesh, "all the fullness of the Godhead" (Colossians 2:9, NKJV) continued to dwell in Him bodily.

The Bible teaches that "He became poor" (2 Corinthians 8:9, NKJV). Jesus shared in our hunger, thirst, weariness, and pain. In this way He gave evidence to the reality of His manhood.

The Bible also teaches that "He was crucified in weakness"

(2 Corinthians 13:4, NKJV). But we must not think that this weakness implies any incapacity such as ours when we are unable to withstand the onslaught of death. Our weakness is a condition of our frailty. Christ's was the weakness of a voluntarily accepted capacity for suffering. He voluntarily took on His weakness in the self-emptying when He came to that manger in Bethlehem.

"Unto us a Child is born" (Isaiah 9:6, NKJV). He was not born according to the laws and the processes of natural generations. The nature of His birth was supernatural. The "Child born" was born to a virgin: "The virgin shall conceive and bear a Son, and shall call His name Immanuel" (Isaiah 7:14, NKJV).

But "Unto us a Son is given" (Isaiah 9:6, NKJV). Because He is the God-man, He was able to bear our sins on the cross. And God raised Him from the dead as an indication that He had accepted Christ's atoning work on the cross. He was the only One in the entire universe qualified to bear our sins, and He did it voluntarily.

Therefore, at this Christmas season, with our trust and faith in Christ, we hear the angel saying, "Do not be afraid" (Luke 2:10, NKJV). The psalmist said, "The Lord is on my side; I will not fear. What can man do to me?" (Psalm 118:6, NKJV).

This is the Christmas message to you today. You, too, can appropriate the words to believers, words that are used all the way through the Scriptures: "Fear not, for I am with you" (Isaiah 43:5, NKJV).

A Child was born and a Son was given for our salvation. We have complete assurance that Jesus Christ is not only the Son of Man but also that He is the Son of God. And God has accepted what Jesus did on the cross and in the resurrection for our salvation. We trust in Him—and Him alone—for our forgiveness and for eternal life.

Obedience Has Its Consequences

JOEL C. GREGORY

BASED ON MATTHEW 1:18–25

Each Christmas season, one family, just like many others, puts out a Nativity set beneath the tree. Theirs has the obvious cast of characters—the Baby Jesus in the crèche, Mary, with assorted animals, donkeys, sheep, and cows flanking them.

You can tell who the Wise Men are, not because they are wearing halos but because they are carrying gifts. Shepherds of various ages and sizes surround the manger—some older and some younger. But just as it is with most Nativity sets, there are some extra figures, and no one knows exactly who they are.

This particular family of children played a game every Christmas: they ask which one of the characters is Joseph. Some of them said it was the old man leaning on his staff. The more romantic soul in the family said that Mary wouldn't want a crotchety old man like that, so for her Joseph was a young shepherd with broad shoulders. Then they would debate for hours about which one was *really* Joseph.

In reality, Joseph is the forgotten man of Christmas. Surprisingly, Joseph doesn't actually speak a word in Scripture. He is like an extra—a kind of minor character who gets a credit in the cast of characters. Few have ever considered him central to the story of Christmas. He says nothing. He is silent, but he is obedient. Despite historical neglect, Joseph is a significant part of the Christmas story.

The nineteenth-century American poet Ralph Waldo Emerson once said, "What you do speaks so loudly I cannot hear what you say." If that is true, what Joseph did speaks so loudly that it wasn't necessary for him to say anything. He was remarkably simple in his obedience, but he also was simply remarkable in that he was willing to risk everything in immediate obedience on a word from God, which on the surface seemed to be absurd. When you look at this forgotten man of Christmas, you will notice that Joseph models the influence and consequences of immediate, simple obedience to the command of God.

Let's look at Joseph in real life because he shows us obedience to the Word of God—regardless. If we stop romanticizing and idealizing Joseph in Nativity sets or on Christmas cards and look at him as things actually were, we ought to have a great deal of sympathy for him. He was engaged to a young woman who was suddenly and strangely pregnant. An angel had said this was an act of God.

Then this northern Palestinian cabinetmaker had to drop all of his tools and go to Bethlehem for a census. Shortly after that, he received another warning in a dream to flee to Egypt, where he had no network, no connections, no job, and no place to stay. After he escaped from one Herod, he came back and had to run away from another.

AN IMMEDIATE OBEDIENCE

If you look at the life of Joseph, the man who says nothing, you can summarize it in a single, simple word: "obedience." Joseph gave immediate obedience to the Word of God. This forgotten man of

Christmas teaches us that it is possible to obey God with breath-taking, unquestioning immediacy. Once God spoke through the angel Gabriel, Joseph married Mary without hesitation.

In that regard, he acted with an obedience that outran any of the major characters in the story of Jesus' birth. In Luke 1:18, when the announcement came to Zacharias, the aged father-to-be of John the Baptist, he said to the angel, "How shall I know this? For I am an old man and my wife is well-advanced in years," and he was struck silent because he said that. Zacharias met the command of God with a denial.

In Luke 1:34, Mary, the mother of Jesus, met that command with confusion. Mary said to the angel, "How can this thing be, since I do not know a man?"

Interestingly, Joseph did not respond with a recorded denial or doubt, but rather with an immediacy of obedience. He took Mary to be his wife and did not touch her until that holy thing was born which had been conceived within her.

In fact, Joseph had an immediate obedience that outshines many of the luminaries of the Bible. Moses was called as an eighty-year-old shepherd to lead an exodus. What do you hear from him? Four consecutive excuses before he finally submitted to do the will of God.

Isaiah saw God high and lifted up in the Temple of Jerusalem. God called him to be a prophet. What does he say? He gave this excuse: "I am a man of unclean lips."

Jeremiah was called to be a prophet, but he apologetically told God, "I'm too young; I can't speak."

Amos, the keeper of sycamore fruit and keeper of sheep, said when called, "I don't have the credentials to be a prophet."

Joseph, on the other hand, left a record of never having said anything. When God spoke an astonishingly difficult word to him, he responded with an immediacy of obedience. This calls to mind those words in 1 John 2:3, which uses obedience as a proof genuine experience: "By this we know that we have come to know Him, if we keep on habitually cherishing his commandments."

OBEY GOD IN PAINFUL CIRCUMSTANCES

God is not, first of all, interested in our gold or our giftedness, or our guilt-ridden excuses, He wants to be obeyed. According to 1 Samuel 15:22, obedience is better than sacrifice. The forgotten man of Christmas modeled an immediate obedience, but he also shows us that we can obey God in painful circumstances. Joseph did. He was betrothed—or we would say engaged—to Mary.

In ancient Jewish culture, when a girl was only twelve or thirteen years old, her parents signed their consent for her to be betrothed. This was a legally ratified, binding marriage covenant, even though she had to live with her parents for another year. The second phase of that ceremony was the transferral, in which the husband would go get her and take her to his house to be his own.

In Joseph's experience between steps one and two, Mary was with child; she was pregnant. He couldn't deny it because the evidence became clear and brutal. Like most of us in the face of unpleasant circumstances, he wanted to deny it by not even seeing it, but there came a day when it was obvious.

One of the questions that early church historians—who were closer to the event than we—have asked is a very real one: did Joseph suspect Mary of sin, of infidelity? In A.D. 170, Justin Martyr responded "yes." So did Jerome and Chrysostom.

Saint Augustine said that Joseph positively suspected that Mary was guilty of sin. The church father Jerome, however, said, "Joseph knew Mary's holiness, and that it hid in silence a mystery he did not understand."

Actually, Joseph didn't have a legal choice in that culture. One familiar phrase in the gospels said that "he was a just man," which has two meanings. That word, *dikaios*, means that he was a righteous man; under the Law, he had no choice but to put her aside. According to the Law of Moses, she was legally classified as a prostitute for what she had done.

But *dikaios* has another meaning; it refers to being prudent, discreet, magnanimous, or big-hearted. That's what Joseph intended to do—to privately take two other men with him as witnesses to her family and, as was the custom, put her away.

Now, he didn't have to do that. He could have subjected her to the ordeal of bitter waters, a very curious ceremony described in the fifth chapter of Numbers. When a man was jealous of his wife, he would subject her to an ordeal of making her drink water mixed with dust from the floor of the Tabernacle. God would intervene to either validate her guilt or exonerate her.

But Joseph didn't put Mary through that. He intended privately, with magnanimity and a sense of prudence and discretion to end it, when suddenly he had that shattering, intrusive dream from God described in Matthew 1:20: "Joseph, son of David, do not be afraid to take to you Mary your wife, for that which is conceived in her is of the Holy Spirit."

If you look at this practically: Here he was with this dilemma— the obvious was happening to her, and he had a dream. It's likely that he was pacing the floor of that carpenter shop, night and day, dialoguing with himself, "What does this dream mean?" He wanted to go to Mary and ask her, but the words stuck in his mouth, leaving nothing but a question mark in his heart.

At the time, this was not easy. A carpenter's business in Nazareth depended on building up the goodwill of the townspeople over a long period of time. He would be subjected to the backstreet gossip and the malicious slander that characterized any town like Nazareth when Mary was found in that condition without an explanation. And on top of that, she was a betrothed woman.

I have seen men whose family rejected them when they volunteered for the ministry. I spoke with a young woman going to an international mission field whose father turned his back on her because she said yes to the call of God. Some of us have witnessed adults who confessed faith in Christ at a public baptismal service and then lost their world because they did.

Joseph models for us that we can obey God in the midst of painful, difficult, inexplicable circumstances. He was willing to do so, and we too can obey God in spite of fear.

OBEDIENCE IN THE FACE OF FEAR

When the word came to Joseph, it was simply "Fear not." The message that came to him was not "Do not be too proud to obey God," "Do not be too disgusted," "Do not be too angry," "Do not be too hurt," or "Do not be too ashamed." The word that came to him was "Stop being afraid of obedience," for Joseph was terrified by the virginal conception of Mary.

God had come close—very close—and that had created a situation that scalded Joseph with fear and humbled him with awe at the power of God. You see that again in the fifth chapter of Luke, after Jesus provided the miraculous catch of fish. Luke does not say that Peter was overcome with joy or gladness. What does he say? He says that Peter, overcome with fear, got down on his knees and said, "Depart from me for I am a sinful man, O Lord!"

When God draws close and invades our world with His supernatural power, it can create within us a sense of fear. Joseph would much rather have gone back to his carpenter's shop and played with his tools than be the stepfather of the Son of God.

It would have been easier for Peter to go back to the Peter, James, and John enterprise of fishing than to have to become the big fisherman, preacher of Pentecost, so he said, "Depart from me for I am a sinful man."

The truth is that in the face of God's commands, for many of us it would be easier to go back to our comfortable, safe, cozy, predictable little round of activities than to simply obey God in a radical way.

As often, I was deeply moved to tears when I watched the commissioning of twenty-eight international mission appointees. One testimony that particularly arrested me was that given by a young female accountant who had been employed by the fourth-largest accounting firm in the nation and was married to another young accountant. Individually, separately, and simultaneously, God called them to the international mission field. They dropped everything— quit their jobs, enrolled in seminary—and now have gone to serve as missionaries in Yugoslavia, taking their children, a three-year-old and a one-year-old, with them. In that former Eastern bloc country, there was fear, civic unrest, and not even enough food to eat. How will they care for a three-year-old and a one-year-old? Bravely, they said that they were going to obey God, regardless.

Joseph models for us with immediacy that even in spite of painful circumstances and in the face of fear, we can abandon things and obey God, staking everything on His Word alone.

That word came to Joseph in a dream. Have you ever had a dream when you felt certain that God was speaking to you?

The rabbis of that day were divided on the value of dreams. Some of them said they were worthless. Others said that dreams were a mild form of prophecy. And Joseph's was. But even then the rabbis said you had to discriminate between a false dream and a true one.

Most likely, Joseph struggled in prayer over just that, but he didn't have any bishop, or preacher, or counselor to talk with about the matter. He had to discern whether it was a true or false dream. After interpreting that the message was indeed true, he then acted upon it, hanging everything in life on a word from God that came to him in a dream.

Joseph was just like that other dreamer, his namesake Joseph, who hung his life and destiny on the dreams that he had in that Egyptian prison. And because of that, the young carpenter became like Spanish conquistador Hernán Cortés. When he was ready to invade the Yucatan, he ordered his ships to be burned in the bay so that his army would not defect. There was no way to turn back. When Joseph heard those words of command, he burned everything behind him and set out to Bethlehem and Egypt, obedient to the Word of God.

OBEDIENCE HAS IMMEDIATE CONSEQUENCES

From this remarkable, forgotten man of Christmas, we can learn obedience that stakes everything on a single word from God. But is that all? No. We also can learn from Joseph that obedience always has immediate consequences.

There was a president of the United States that a frustrated press nicknamed "the Teflon president." They called him that because nothing negative seemed to stick to him. Regardless of what he was alleged to have said or done by mistake, the public loved him and nothing stuck to him.

It seemed that he had no consequences. But Joseph was not Teflon in his obedience. And there really is no such thing because obedience always has its consequences.

Obedience had a really personal and very immediate consequence for Joseph. In Matthew 1:24–25, he did what the Lord commanded him and took Mary as his wife. That is, he took this woman with child from her parents' home and transferred her to his home, but he did not "know" her. That means he not have sexual relations with her until after she brought forth her firstborn son, and they called his name Jesus. That was the immediate consequence of his obedience to God.

Ancient mythology answered this unthinkable dilemma with

the myth of an older Joseph. That was the viewpoint—that Joseph was much older than Mary—but the biblical evidence does not suggest this. In John's gospel, the people ask, "Is this not Jesus, the son of Joseph? Are not his father and mother with us?" The implication is that if there had been a big age gap between Joseph and Mary, nothing like that would ever have been questioned.

What gives us the idea that Joseph was an old man is a fifth-century apocryphal gospel. The myth claimed that Joseph married when he was forty, was widowed when he was eighty-nine, and then took Mary to be his ward when he was ninety-one. But the Dead Sea scrolls tell us that the usual time of marriage for a young Hebrew man was twenty years of age.

Joseph did not touch Mary—but lived in chastity and restraint with her, honoring the Word of God—not because he was enfeebled; but rather, because he was obedient. This was the real, immediate consequence of obedience for Joseph—the months in which he did not know her until after she brought forth her firstborn son.

OBEDIENCE HAS A LIFETIME OF CONSEQUENCES

But for Joseph, as is true for everyone, obedience also had a lifetime of consequences. No sooner had he married Mary than he had to drop everything and go to Bethlehem in obedience to that Roman census, which arranged the events so that the Son of God would be born where the prophets had said He would be born. Then he had to go to Egypt.

We can understand this story better if we contemporize it; that is, taking it out of Nativity sets and off Christmas cards and putting it in contemporary language. Let's suppose that there is a young man today engaged to a young woman, and suddenly she finds out she is pregnant. One night, he has a dream and God surprises him by saying, "Stay with her. I have to do with this."

After being staggered by that confusion, he has to explain to his parents what is going on. Then, he has to tell her parents what's going on. Then, he has to face the gossip that comes from that kind of circumstance.

As this young man is getting his heart and mind settled down about that, some government bureaucrat says, "Every person in the United States has to go back to his hometown to register for a special tax." So he gets in his old car and drives across country with his very pregnant fiancée. When he gets to his hometown, all the motel rooms are full, and the only place they can stay is in a garage. So he takes this pregnant woman, to whom he is engaged, and in the garage the baby is born. They wrap the baby up in mechanic's rags and lay him down on a workbench.

Just when the young man is wondering what else could happen to him, a group of street people bangs on the garage door, shouting for him to let them in. They fall down on their knees and cry out, "Glory to God in the highest! We've come to worship this baby."

As the young man's eyes grow wider, not long after that, three stretch limos pull up and ambassadors to the United Nations get out bearing gifts—Krugerrands, the finest Oriental silks, and a bottle of Imperial Majesty, the world's most expensive perfume—and they kneel and place them at the baby's feet.

After the young man gets over that shock, the president calls out the national guard to kill all the newborn babies in that region of the country. Then he has another dream. God tells him "You'd better get out of here and go to South America in a hurry."

Can you imagine? By that time he's probably asking himself what outrageous thing can possibly happen next.

If you contemporize this story, you can understand viscerally what happened to Joseph. There weren't any interstates with rest stops for smooth traveling to Egypt. There were no McDonald's, no hotels, and no restaurants. There wasn't a branch outlet of the carpenter shop in Egypt. Joseph didn't have a job or any network of support. He found himself there out of obedience to God, and he accepted the consequences.

Joseph models to us that when you obey God, the highest joy always follows; but immediately and for a lifetime, there are consequences to that kind of response.

When I was sixteen years old, I was sitting in a teenage vacation Bible school in Connell Baptist Church of Fort Worth, Texas, and a word from God came to me. The word simply said, "Preach!" And for forty-two years now, I have lived with the consequences of that word that so surprised me.

You may have decided recently to keep a pledge even after you've lost your job or it looks like your company may close down. Your obedience then has consequences.

I've watched theology students for years quit jobs, move across the country, and go to seminary, divinity school, or Bible school. When they got there, it seemed everything turned against them because obedience has its consequences. This biblical story that leaves us wide-eyed shows us that when we say yes to God, obedience has immediate and ultimate consequences.

THE INFLUENCE OF OBEDIENCE

Another positive word is this: the forgotten man of Christmas reminds us of the influence of obedience, for Joseph was the father figure in the home of Jesus. All of those old clichés about fathers and sons must be true. In the relationship between Jesus and his stepfather, Joseph, the twig did grow in the direction that it was bent. The apple didn't fall far from the tree.

When Jesus started preaching, what did he call God? He didn't call Him "Emperor." He didn't call him "Sister." He didn't call him

"Brother." He didn't call him "Camel Driver." He called him "Abba," the Aramaic word for "Papa," or "Daddy," a word of hearth and home. In all of Jewish literature, no one had ever called God that before, not in the Talmud or the Mishnah. Only Jesus called God "Abba"—Dad, Papa. Why?

It was said of Martin Luther, the great reformer, that the relationship between Martin and his father was so terrible that all of his life he had difficulty calling God "Father."

Not so with Yeshua—Jesus, the son of Joseph. Perhaps because of the remarkable, simple obedience that he saw in the life of Joseph, he was able to take that example, look at it, and then use the familiar word for His heavenly Father.

An article in *Psychology Today* reported that the most difficult relationship of the four between adult parents and children is that of fathers and sons—more so than the relationship between adult mothers and adult sons, adult mothers and adult daughters, and adult fathers and adult daughters. That was just not true of Jesus and Joseph.

One of my favorite paintings in the Louvre is one by Georges de La Tour titled, *Christ and Saint Joseph in the Carpenter's Shop.* Every time I've been there, I've looked at it with admiration. It's a great picture of a carpenter's shop, with an older and sturdy Joseph and a ten-year-old Jesus watching his father and helping him. Jesus appears to be holding a candle behind his hand. As you look at the painting, the hand looks translucent and you can actually see the light coming through the hand. De La Tour had an incredible ability to paint light. I'm dumbfounded that he could paint something that looks so real.

The two are working on some intractable material on the floor. By the look of it, Joseph is trying to meet a deadline. When you look at the shadows illumined by the candle in the hand of the boy Jesus, you see that what's on the floor is really two pieces of wood in a cross shape. In de La Tour's painting, Jesus and Joseph are putting together a cross.

Our Lord, who saw that remarkably simple obedience in his earthly father, learned obedience Himself, even to the cross. That obedience started at the carpenter's shop of Nazareth, watching the forgotten man of Christmas.

Living with Deferred Hope

FORREST E. HARRIS SR.

The words of Isaiah 11 are simply incredible and captivating. The prophet articulates possibilities that we long to see fulfilled. In this chapter, Isaiah's hopes and dreams unfold to center stage of the human struggle:

> *The wolf will live with the lamb,*
> *the leopard will lie down with the goat,*
> *the calf and the lion and the yearling together;*
> *and a little child will lead them.*
> *(11:6, NIV)*

We are drawn into the prophet's dream of utopia—the possible living in creative tension with the impossible.

Isaiah's proclamation declares the establishment of a peaceful reign of love, justice, and community on earth. He announces a dramatic transformation where natural enemies live in peace, and where justice, mercy, harmony, and safety define human relations in every corner of the world.

Embracing Isaiah's dream draws us to the anchoring place of the tried faith of our Christian forbears—possibilities and promises of hope yet unseen.

Advent is a season of hope, expectation, longing, and anticipation for the newness of God; yet Advent traps us in a paradox. Against the heap of human despair, sickness, poverty, and grief, how can we continue to live with the deferred hope that has spanned centuries of delay and human disappointment?

What does it mean to live in a world where hope is deferred? Poet and playwright Lorraine Hansberry described it as being "like a raisin in the sun; it dries up and turns hard."

Has hope hardened in our world, where genocide, disease, and violence stand against human flourishing?

Has hope calcified in our world, where faith seems to consecrate the privileged in society?

How do we live with deferred hope in a world that has demonstrated resistance to God's future?

How do we live with deferred hope in a world where legions of people suffer social incarceration as well as institutional incarceration?

How can we continue to hope when widening gaps of disparity between rich and poor continue to expand?

To avoid an honest confrontation with hope during Advent, the season of hope, we could simply opt for cheap Christmas optimism. But Isaiah's prophecy is not an appeal for anemic possibility thinking, glibly promising that things will get better.

The Christian world lights Advent candles in a dark world that defers hope, dashes dreams, and distorts our reality.

But Advent hope is a sobering antidote to artificial Christmas cheer. Advent hope is all we have. But what kind of hope is it?

Advent hope has endured through the best and worst times of human history. It has outlasted empires that stood against its promise. It has given oppressed people the inspiration of marching feet toward the dream of God. It has marshaled faith against human failure.

Hope may be deferred or even delayed, but the ultimate end of its work cannot be defeated. Hope deferred, denied, or even derailed is not hope defeated. This is why the hope of God holds us captive.

The fact that hope cannot be defeated is why our ancestors of the Christian faith never allowed false optimism to rob them of hope.

This is why, in the black Christian tradition, James Weldon Johnson's "Lift Every Voice and Sing" can be appropriately sung during the season of Advent:

> *Stony the road we trod,*
> *Bitter the chast'ning rod*
> *Felt in the days when hope unborn had died;*
>
> *Yet with a steady beat,*
> *Have not our weary feet*
> *Come to the place for which our fathers signed?*[1]

The ancients lived with deferred hope. With a steady beat of hopefulness they believed that the dream of God shall come to pass.

Advent hope takes imagination and courage. In spite of hard circumstances, the hope of Advent inspires living before the presence of God. This hope never allows us to take for granted who we are or trivialize the reality of another human being.

Advent hope inspires us to live as agents of the possible—of what is to become. This hope gives us a holy and righteous discontent that can never be satisfied until life is what God intended it to be; until we are doing what we were created to do. This hope will not be satisfied until the wolf and lamb lie down together.

This is what the Hebrew term *shalom* means—dwelling in peace with God, with self, with neighbors, and with all of creation. *Shalom* is both God's cause in the world and our human calling and vocation.

Looking within the confines of his own social circumstance, Isaiah saw this hope far into the future, farther than his own time and context would allow. "A shoot shall come out from the stump of Jesse, and a branch shall grow out of his roots," the prophet declares.

Jesus appeared on the scene of human history, giving this hope eternal vigor and power that none previously had been able to provide. Christ is the Prince of Peace who beat the sword of a brutal cross into the plowshares of resurrection.

Jesus was one upon whom the Spirit of God rested; one who shouldered the promise of everlasting peace; one whose suffering healed and made the promises of God real. Jesus is God's eternal gift, bringing *shalom* to us.

I shall always remember the now famous phrase of Dick Ebersol's fourteen-year-old son. The boy died in an airplane crash, which his brother and father survived. For some reason this boy had begun writing his life story, even at age fourteen. They found his incomplete autobiography a few days after the tragic crash. In it the family found these profound words: "In life the finish line is only the beginning of a new race."

Advent is about beginning a new race of courage and imagination to hope for possibilities that will be left for future generations to fulfill.

"I may not get there with you," Martin Luther King Jr. said, "but we as a people will get to the Promised Land."

Knowing that one day we as a people will get to the Promised

Land, despite any and all obstacles—this is living with hope deferred, and this is our testimony at Advent.

NOTE

1. "Lift Every Voice and Sing" ("Negro National Anthem"), lyrics by James W. Johnson. Copyright © 1927, Edward B. Marks Music Corporation.

Unwrap the Gift of Righteousness

MARILYN HICKEY

BASED ON ROMANS 5:17

> How much more will those who receive God's abundant provision of grace and of the GIFT OF RIGHTEOUSNESS REIGN IN LIFE through the one man, Jesus Christ. (NIV)

During this Christmas season, discover your greatest gift from God—*righteousness*. It can change your life!

At sixteen years old, I was born again. Yet, after more than fifty years of serving God—reading through the Bible countless times, memorizing whole books of the Bible, and ministering around the world—I've become no more righteous than I was on the day of my salvation. Righteousness isn't earned or even developed—it's a gift that we receive. This gift—righteousness through Jesus Christ—gives us the power to rule and reign over the situations of our lives

CONFESSION BRINGS POSSESSION

"With the heart one believes unto RIGHTEOUSNESS, *and with the mouth confession is made unto salvation"* (Romans 10:10, NKJV).

Have you noticed that you must "believe" and "confess" salvation before you *receive* it? When you confess Jesus as Savior, something happens inside—you receive a nature of righteousness.

When people ask, "How are you?" don't make the mistake of confessing your "old nature." Rather, believe and confess your new one. Instead of saying, "I'm weak, stupid, always blowing it, poor, and sick," say, "I am the righteousness of God in Christ Jesus. Because of righteousness, I rule and reign over every circumstance of my life." If questioned about your weaknesses, say, "I have God's righteousness to overcome all things!"

Don't say—and never believe—that sickness, poverty, bondages, or any other negative things rule your life. Instead, declare that you reign over every obstacle because of His righteousness at work in you! Your confession will bring possession!

RIGHTEOUSNESS CONSCIOUSNESS

Have you heard the story of the man who bought a beautiful, powerful new car? The man loved his car, but never had it serviced. After a couple of years, it would hardly make it up a hill. Finally, he took the car in to be checked and discovered that he was driving on only half the cylinders!

Some Christians remember the "good old days" when they were first saved. Like the man with the new car, things were great and God worked powerfully in their lives. Yet, today their every problem is like a mountain. They're trying to travel through life using only half their cylinders. They've forgotten that through *"the gift of righteousness [they can] reign in life"* (Romans 5:17, NIV).

Recognize your righteousness, and *"be renewed in the spirit of your mind . . . put on the new man which was created according to God, in true righteousness and holiness"* (Ephesians 4:23, 24, NKJV). When your righteousness becomes a literal truth to you, feelings of inferiority fade away, fear of failure flees, and faith for victory arises.

Righteousness protects you from emotional wounds. Your heart is a favorite target of the enemy. The devil knows that if he can discourage you, he can steal your blessing, stop your ministry, and spoil your peace.

THE "BULLETPROOF VEST" OF RIGHTEOUSNESS

When you want to "dress for success," you probably take a shower, fix your hair, and put on your best clothing. As a Christian, you should always dress for spiritual success. Each morning, prepare yourself for victory by putting on the full armor of God. One piece of that armor is your righteousness. Ephesians 6:13, 14 reads, *"Therefore put on the full armor of God, so that when the day of evil comes, you may be able to stand your ground . . . with the breastplate of righteousness in place."* (NIV). Did you notice? Righteousness is like a breastplate that covers your heart.

Without the protection of righteousness, your heart can be wounded by the thoughtless or deliberately negative things people say and do. However, when you surround your emotions with righteousness, the devil's arrows will crash against your armor and bounce harmlessly away. Arrows that target your heart and emotions can't stand up to God's gift of righteousness to born-again Christians and His promise that *"all things work together for good to those who love God"* (Romans 8:28, NKJV).

RIGHTEOUSNESS PRODUCES POWER

When you walk in righteousness, you tread in the power and authority of your all-powerful Father, God. You may not look to others as if you are in control. You may not even feel that you are in control. Yet, when you really believe that you *are* the righteousness of God in Christ, no sickness or disease can cling to you, no financial setback can keep you down, no bondage can imprison you, and no demon from hell can remain between you and your God-given blessing.

This Christmas, remember that tucked into your gift of salvation is another powerful gift—righteousness. Speak it, wear it, and walk in the power that makes you rule and reign in this life!

Power to the People

Donald Hilliard Jr.

BASED ON PSALM 113:7–9; LUKE 1:46–53; 2:1–4
Like many people, I enjoy the Christmas season—even the carnal trappings of the tree, the mall, the lights, and the throngs of people doing last-minute gift shopping! It's easy to become submerged in holiday cheer and the hustle and bustle of the season. Amid the celebration and merriment, however, the Lord's church must not overlook the multitudes for whom Christmas, and life in general, holds no cheer.

Regrettably, a dangerous slant has infiltrated the theology of the contemporary church. We have easily bought into, taught, and preached a gospel that is clearly partial to the "haves." As a result, our messages have lost their balance, because too much emphasis has been placed on a God who dispenses prosperity rather than on a God who advocates for the poor and the powerless.

This is not to put down prosperity or to advocate poverty as a more noble state of being. God wants to give power to the people and He wants us to prosper. It is not the will of God that we live from hand to mouth or be in constant want and need. God gets little glory when we make a lifestyle out of being "a day late and a

dollar short"! Jesus has come that you might have life, and life more abundantly.

Third John 1:2 (NKJV) reads, "I pray that you may prosper in all things and be in health, just as your soul prospers." All of this is true, and all of this we do believe. Nevertheless, I also believe that in the midst of all the preaching and praising about prosperity, God's people must never forget that the poor—whether economically poor or poor in spirit—are still very present among us.

Many of us can relate to being poor—when we placed cardboard in our shoes because we could not afford to have them resoled. Standing in line to receive government cheese, bread, food stamps, and public assistance is all too familiar to many who now rank among today's middle class. Despite this, we rarely hear sermons that address those among us who are not well coiffed, well heeled, or well educated. Perhaps we've become so blessed that our years of lack are too painful for us to remember.

As we read the account of Jesus' genealogy, we are reminded of just how painful the circumstances of life can be for some. The gospel of Matthew takes us through forty-two generations that includes forebears whose lives were muddled with pain—adultery, incest, rape, and murder.

But the fact that God chose to use this lineage through which to send the Savior of the world demonstrates that God is concerned about the poor and those of lowly estate—because all have come from some kind of mess and some kind of insanity! There's no such thing as someone who's fully pedigreed. All of us have a mixture—a little bit of good, a little bit of bad. There are some things in our lineage that we're embarrassed about and some things we wish we did not know. Yet by the grace and mercy of God, we are who we are and we are where we are. And it is a miracle that some of us, having come down through what we have come down through, still know our names and know enough about God to still wave our hands and tell God, "Thank You!"

While the first chapter of Matthew emphasizes the genealogy of Jesus, the first chapter of Luke emphasizes the poverty of Mary. In the second chapter, Luke emphasizes the location where Jesus was born. In the first chapter he talks about Mary and quotes her as giving praise to God in verses 46–55 (NRSV), known as the Magnificat: "My soul magnifies the Lord, and my spirit rejoices in God my Savior, for He has looked with favor on the lowliness of His servant. Surely, from now on all generations will call me blessed . . ." The Scripture says God has regarded the lowly state (the poor state) of His maidservant. God had mercy on her poverty.

Jesus was born from a poor woman's womb, and He is still concerned about poor people. He still raises up the poor. God is so concerned about the poor and powerless that He chose the unassuming city of Bethlehem as the place where His Son would be born. The prophet Micah records, "But you O Bethlehem of Ephrathah who are one of the little clans of Judah, from you shall come forth for me one who is to rule Israel" (Micah 5:2, NRSV).

Bethlehem, least of the nations; Bethlehem, so unassuming, so lowly. "Out of Bethlehem there shall come the root of the tree of Jesse, even out of Bethlehem, I have called my Son" (see Matthew 2:6). Bethlehem, which means "the City of Bread," was situated on a hill twenty miles north of Jerusalem. The houses were limestone and they were in high places. Underneath the houses it was common to have a cave of sorts, where animals were kept, and it was here that Jesus Christ was born.

God chose the town and the timing and used Caesar Augustus, the first Roman emperor, who didn't even know that he was being used. When he called for a census, Joseph and Mary had to go back to the city of David to register to pay the tax. God used Caesar Augustus to call them back. God has everything in order and under control. Even the things that you don't think—the things that you think are fate, the things you think are karma, the things you think are coincidence—are indeed planned by the hand of God! All things really do work together for good, for those who love God (Romans 8:28).

Joseph and Mary had to go back home. And when they got there, she gave birth to Jesus, the Son of the living God. He was born God! He did not become God at baptism, but was born God. And God has highly exalted Him, giving Him a name that is above every name, and "at the name of Jesus every knee should bow" (see Philippians 2:10).[1]

Joseph and Mary were in the City of Bread when Jesus was born. A humble, lowly, poor place that was full of lowly, poor, unassuming peasant people. Jesus was not born in a palace and He was not born among the pompous. Do you know what it means to be pompous! Pompous means to be proud and arrogant. It means to be showy and stiff. It means that you think more highly of yourself than you ought to think (see Romans 12:3).

Jesus was not born among these people; He was born among the poor. He was born among people who knew that they didn't have anything. And God chose this location for the Son of God to be born—to give power to this people who had none; to give recognition to this people who had none; to give a name to this place, Bethlehem, which had no name. And God is still using the least likely situations to show up and do amazing things.

That's why Mary says, "My soul rejoices in the Lord because He has scattered the proud. . . . He has put down the mighty from their thrones and exalted the lowly. He has filled the hungry with good things, and the rich He has sent away empty" (NKJV). It behooves us to be careful how we treat people, because God raises up one today and puts down another tomorrow. God sent the rich away with nothing, but God is concerned about poor people, lowly people, broken people, people who have fallen through the cracks of society, people who have lost their hope and have lost their song, people who have been disinherited and disenfranchised. God is concerned about the indigent and the homeless. God is concerned about the working poor earning minimal wages and unable to make ends meet.

Each year, our family takes a trip into New York City to see the Christmas show. We enjoy the feel of the city during the holiday season. But while we are there, it is important to us to show our children how other people live. Once, as we drove down Avenue of the Americas, we noticed a man picking garbage out of the trash and placing it right in his mouth! Jesus is concerned about those who have no power to change their condition. He's concerned about those who can't keep food on the table and those with no health insurance. He's concerned about those who can't afford car insurance, hoping to slip under the watchful eye of the law as they illegally drive their "hoopty" to work!

Yes, many of the poor have gone from welfare to work, but they have dead-end jobs that offer no benefits, and their children are falling through the cracks. Many of us blame the poor for their condition. We tend to look down on the poor. The greatest challenge for many of us today is being prosperous and needing to remember those who are poor.

God is concerned about the poor. He challenges us to remember the poor. "Blessed are the poor in spirit" (Matthew 5:3). Throughout Scripture, Jesus addresses the poor. Yes, you should prosper, but that prosperity was never intended just for you! Deuteronomy speaks of God giving us riches so that we would establish the kingdom, and establishing the kingdom means putting God first. Being part of the kingdom means taking care of the poor who are among us—with a hand out, but more important, with a hand up!

Jesus said, "The spirit of the Lord is upon me, because He has anointed me to preach the gospel to the poor. To heal the brokenhearted, to proclaim liberty to the captive and the recovering of sight to the blind. To set at liberty those who are oppressed and to proclaim the acceptable year of the Lord" (Luke 4:18–19, quoting Isaiah 61:1–2).

He has anointed us to preach the gospel and minister to the poor. Proverbs 14:21 says that God has mercy on the poor. Proverbs 22:22 says, "Do not rob the poor."

Next door to our church is the Timothy House, a facility we opened to help troubled men coming out of alcohol addiction. No, we don't have a string of success stories, and half of the men we've helped have slipped back into their addiction. But thanks be to God, some of them have remained clean and sober and are going on in the Name of the Lord!

The Lord directed us to purchase the house adjacent to the Timothy House to feed the hungry on one floor and provide clothing for the needy on another floor. While sharing in our food-and-clothing outreach, I was approached by a woman who said, "Reverend, I'm just so blessed that a pastor would come out here for us! With all of those buildings you have and all of those people—to think that you would come out here in dungarees and a baseball cap for us!" Her words shamed me as a pastor. In her attempt to compliment me, she indicated that she never saw pastors doing "that kind of thing." For the record, I've been doing "that kind of thing" for twenty years, because it's what we should be doing. Along with preaching, praying, blessing babies, and healing the sick, we ought to be feeding the hungry and clothing the naked!

When people come to our outreach ministry, I want them to feel a sense of dignity. I want them to know that Jesus Christ is concerned about them and that He has given them power! John 1:12 says, "To those who received Him, He gave them power to become the sons and daughters of God!" Jesus gives power to recognize that while they may be poor today, they don't have to die poor and powerless. His power enables persons to know that while they may live in the projects today, they can become home owners. His power enables persons to know that while they may live in bondage to addiction today, through Him they can live whole and addiction free.

That's the kind of power the Lord has sent us, through Jesus of Bethlehem! Joy to the world, the Lord has come! Let earth receive her King and let every heart prepare Him room! When you prepare room for Him, you prepare room in your heart to receive those for whom He cares—widows, orphans, the hungry, and the homeless.

Throughout Scripture, God challenges us to remember the poor. Yes, we should prosper, but prosperity was never intended to be a goal, but rather, a means. Proverbs 19:17 reads, "He who has pity on the poor lends to the Lord."

So at Christmas, rather than charging $1,000 on a credit card to buy gifts for children who have already become self-absorbed, why not find someone who does not have what you have and share with them? Why not make room in your heart this holiday season for the poor who are among you? Allow the Holy Spirit to saturate your being, and become the true "salt of the earth and light of the world." That's what we're all about as believers.

God sent us a Savior in the person of Jesus Christ. If our greatest need had been information, God would have sent us an educator. If our greatest need had been technology, God would have sent us a scientist. If our greatest need had been money, God would have sent us an economist. But our greatest need was forgiveness, so God sent us a Savior, to give power to the people!

NOTE

1. 1 Immanuel means "God with us"! That means all the time—"God with us" in our pain, "God with us" in our poverty, "God with us" in our shame, "God with us" in our embarrassment, "God with us" in our mess, "God with us" in our disappointments, "God with us" in our hurts, "God with us" in our helplessness, and yes, "God with us" when we are pathetic. "God with us" means that He is always available to take us through, to pull us up and out. God is with us!

Christ in You

Barbara King

BASED ON COLOSSIANS 1:25–28

During this Christmas season, meditate on Christ in you and unveil the mystery that has been hidden, not only by the world, but by yourself as well. In Colossians 1:25–28 (KJV), the apostle Paul says:

> *Whereof I am made a minister, according to the dispensation of God which is given to me for you, to fulfil the word of God; Even the mystery which hath been hid from ages and from generations, but now is made manifest to his saints: To whom God would make known what is the riches of the glory of this mystery among the Gentiles; which is Christ in you, the hope of glory: Whom we preach, warning every man, and teaching every man in all wisdom; that we may present every man perfect in Christ Jesus: Whereunto I also labour, striving according to his working, which worketh in me mightily.*

Jesus solved the mystery for all ages when He said, "I can of mine own self do nothing. . . . If I speak of myself, I bear witness to a lie. It is not I but the Father in me, who doeth the works." He said, "This message is not mine, but the Father's who sent me."[1]

In giving us this revelation, Jesus showed that His human identity was the same as yours and mine. Then He said, "I am the way, the Truth, and the life; no man cometh unto the Father but by me" (John 14:6, KJV). "I am the resurrection, the bread, the vine, and the water."[2]

Through Him we are connected to the Father. What a wonderful and blessed gift from our heavenly Father!

Jesus helps us to understand more of the significance of His indwelling in these words: "I am a man as you are, yet I am not subject to human failures because I know the 'I' of me is God and the 'I' of you is God." So, knowing this, you can receive healings, supply, peace, love, order and freedom; it's up to you.

In Matthew 23:9, Jesus spoke these words: "Call no man your father on earth" (RSV). Through telling us to declare no man as father but God above, Jesus does not declare that He alone is divine; but rather, all are sons and daughters of God. Since He is our Father, we are heirs and joint-heirs with Christ.

So the Messiah, or Savior, that humanity is searching for is found with the self, and it is called "I-Christ." What dwells in the midst of you is Mighty: "I will never leave you, nor forsake you. The kingdom of God is within you and it is the Father's good pleasure to give it to you."

Take time daily to be still and realize that "I-Christ in the midst of me is my life; the Source of my integrity, my peace, my expressions of love, kindness, intelligence; all that I am." It may take a long time to get it completely, but keep relaxing and meditating on "I am."

Think about the "I" (Christ) within you; abide in it and let it abide in you. This is the real celebration of the birth of Christ. The Christ spirit has always been in you, but you want it to be born into your human consciousness; that is, *revealed* to your human consciousness.

It is important to realize that even though Christ is in the individual, it is of no avail until it is recognized by the individual. Until then, there is murder, rape, sin, disease, and lack because Christ does not dwell within.

Yes, the real celebration of Christmas is an inner experience, a communion in the soul of humanity—an electrifying contact and encounter with the indwelling Christ.

During this season of rejoicing, affirm these words: "This Christmas, I celebrate Christ in me, my hope and guarantee of glory!

NOTES

1. Based on John 5:30, 31; John 14:10.

2. Based on John 11:25; 6:35; 15:1; 4:14.

The Greatest Christmas Gift

JACQUELINE E. McCULLOUGH

BASED ON ISAIAH 9:1–7
You probably receive several gifts during the Christmas season, but let me share with you the greatest Christmas gift.

The prophecy of Isaiah centers around the life, person, and ministry of a man whose name means *God is salvation.* Prophesying at a time when God's people were in rebellion, Isaiah saw these salvific events seven hundred years before they came to pass.

Even in the middle of your gloom, you have the ability to see. Isn't that marvelous? That's why we celebrate Christmas. Isaiah said, "I see a Son coming, but not an ordinary son. This Son is not coming just for any and everybody; He's coming to us."

Seven hundred years later that child came. Luke 2:11 (NIV) reads: "Today in the town of David a Savior has been born to you; he is Christ the Lord."

But before all of that happened, as recorded in Luke, Isaiah prophesied (7:14–16, NIV): "Therefore the Lord himself will give you a sign: The virgin will be with child and will give birth to a son, and will call him Immanuel. He will eat curds and honey when he knows enough to reject the wrong and choose the right. But before the boy knows enough to reject the wrong and choose the right, the land of the two kings you dread will be laid waste."

Isaiah was saying, "The stuff you're worrying about, God has already taken care of." Isaiah had seen the future; his eyes were fixed. He saw it coming down the timeline of history seven hundred years later and he didn't waver.

That's the only way to live; otherwise, you're going to be depressed, morose, and indecisive. You're going to be bound for the rest of your life if you are tossed by every wind of change. That's not living!

Seven hundred years after Isaiah spoke words of hope to a hopeless people, the angel Gabriel visited Mary, announcing the fulfillment of Isaiah's prophecy (Luke 2).

This Christmas, even if nobody gives you a gift, you already have a gift. Now this is no cheap gift. This gift didn't come from JCPenney. This didn't come from T.J.Maxx or Target. This gift came straight out of heaven.

THE GIFT COMES WITH HEALING

Acts 4:12 says that not only is He given as a child, He's given as a Messiah. Salvation can be found in no other. No healing can be found apart from Him, whether for the body or the soul. So when this gift comes, He comes with healing.

What is locked into this gift? Healing—the spirit of life, the spirit of power, the spirit of healing (Matthew 1:21). The Bible stays there is no other name under the heavens whereby persons can be saved. So Jesus comes with healing and salvation.

Some of us walk around with scars and use them as scarves: "See, I was wounded. See, I was abused." God takes away the scars so you can't even remember. You are a new creature in Christ Jesus. All things pass away.

THE GIFT COMES WITH SUPREMACY

The gift is the Lamb that takes away the sins of the world. And not only does He come with healing and salvation, He comes with supremacy. Ephesians 1:22 tells us that God placed all things under His feet and appointed Him to be the head over everything for the church.

So He's in charge. He comes with healing, he comes with salvation, and he's in charge. Your gift in the person of Jesus Christ does not take orders from anyone on earth. So why worry about who says what? Why worry about a supervisor with a pink slip? Why worry about somebody who says you can't get the house because you don't have enough money? You have a Gift who says, "All things are under my feet."

John 17:4 (NIV) says, "I brought You glory on the earth by completing the work that You gave me to do." He finished the work and is sitting at the right hand of the Father. Everything that you need is already accomplished. Jesus came to earth and accomplished it, so everything you need is in Him and through Him.

Now what was His assignment? Isaiah says that the government shall be upon his shoulders. Soldiers, leaders, or heads of state usually wore in those days a certain kind of insignia or logo on their shoulder to show that they were in charge.

When you understand that He is your leader, that He is in charge, what you hear shouldn't bother you, because you know He has the last say.

THE GIFT IS WONDERFUL

We know who He is. What is His name? He came as a son, a child. But Isaiah said that His name shall be called "Wonderful."

The word "wonderful" means distinguished or great; it also means miraculous. But "wonderful" literally means that He is exalted above the ordinary. You can't box Him in. Whatever He does creates excitement, amazement, and admiration.

This wonderful God is doing things beyond our comprehension. We will never be able to understand why He brought us the way He did. Who can fathom Him? He's too high to climb to find Him and He's too low to get down and find Him. If it's easy to trace, then it's not a miracle. When you trust God, and He uses the unexpected, it's called wonderful.

THE GIFT IS COUNSELOR

He is Counselor. Sometimes we put that name together— Wonderful Counselor. But Counselor stands on its own; it means He's of an honorable rank. When you're a counselor of an honorable rank, you advise the king. Kings in the Old Testament always had private counselors.

Why Counselor? Because you need advice. You need to know whether you are taking the right road. In the multitude of counselors, there's safety, so He's called Counselor. That means He has divine wisdom. He is qualified to guide and direct the human race. Read Psalm 23.

If you're saying, "I don't know, I don't know, I don't know," it's because you don't know who you have. He's a guiding light. His Word is a lamp unto my feet and a light unto my path (Psalm 119:105). The Lord does not desire that you hit your head against the wall. No. He has a path for you.

THE GIFT IS A MIGHTY GOD

The word "mighty" used in Isaiah refers to a hero, a warrior, an undefeated champion.

But look at Jesus. He's your undefeated champion even when He was a baby. He was a warrior God, and a baby. He's our battle-ax and our real God. If God is for you, who can be against you? He that is with you is mightier than all that is against.

He said they'll come against you one way and I'll make them flee before your face in seven ways (Deuteronomy 28). He said I'll even turn around and make your enemies your footstool (Psalm 110). Joy to the world! Your Warrior is here! You don't have to fight. You don't have to get ugly. You don't have to curse anybody out. All you have to do is trust Him. That's your gift today.

THE GIFT IS EVERLASTING FATHER

He's an Everlasting Father. He's a child, yet He's a Father. That is confusing to the human mind. How could He be both child and a Father?

He was from the beginning. The gospel of John opens, revealing to us that in the beginning was the Word, and the Word was with God. He has the luxury of being anything that He wants to be. He can be a child and He can be a Father—at the same time! But He's not just a temporary Father. He's an Everlasting Father! Once He puts His mark on you, even when you act ugly, He says, "You're mine."

Not only is He an everlasting daddy in name, He's an everlasting daddy in provision. He's the Father of the age—the age now and the age to come. You're part of His kingdom. He's the author and the finisher. And even when you're in trouble, He says, "I cannot deny you. I have you etched in the palm of my hand."

He says, "Wherever you go, you're my child. Even when you're down and out, you're still my child; even when you don't want Me to be your daddy."

When your earthly father rejects you, He steps in. When you can't find your biological daddy or you don't know what your own daddy looks like, when your own daddy doesn't want you, He says, "I am your daddy."

THE GIFT IS THE PRINCE OF PEACE

The word "peace" used by Isaiah is *shalom*, meaning tranquilizer. We all think that if we take something, go somewhere, or become someone else, we'll have peace. The world tells us that a body rub, a face-lift, weight loss, or a lavender candle will grant us peace. But there is no peace, except in Him. He is the peacemaker; He is the peace giver.

You can be in a storm and still be peaceful. I think what makes Christians so indomitable is that things are happening around us and yet we can be at peace. That's peace money can't buy. It's peace that the world didn't give and the world can't take away. He's your gift of peace. Take your peace. Take what God has given you.

Jesus came to balance your emotions so that the enemy won't take you from one extreme to the other; so you can live with yourself and you can be an example of the glory of God. He came to make a testimony in your life that "I can give you peace."

But this word *shalom* not only means tranquility or harmony, it means He is the prince of prosperity, the giver of all blessings. What kind of gift are you expecting? Whatever your wish is, look at what you already have. You're no longer looking at a child in a manger, but a mediator, an intercessor, and a conquering king.

Hebrews 4:15–16 (NIV) says, "For we do not have a high priest who is unable to sympathize with our weaknesses, but we have one who has been tempted in every way, just as we are, yet was without sin. Let us then approach the throne of grace with confidence that we may receive mercy and find grace to help us in our time of need."

In Jesus we have a miracle worker, one who does the impossible. Mark 10:20 (NIV) says, "Jesus looked at them and said, 'With man this is impossible, but not with God. All things are possible with God.'"

. . .

WHAT DO YOU HAVE TODAY? A Wonderful Counselor, one who gives directions that keep us from harm and death.

What do you have today? A Mighty God who fights for you and protects you, even when you are clueless.

What do you have today? A Prince of Peace. You don't have to go under a Christmas tree; you're already loaded. Luke 2:14 (NIV) says, "Glory to God in the highest and on earth peace to men on whom His favor rests."

This Christmas, call on His name. When you call His name, things happen in ways you can't even conceive. Let go of your plan this Christmas and walk into the miraculous. Believe He's miraculous.

This Christmas, rely on the Counselor. Stop looking to people and leaving your ears open to all kinds of suggestions. Just trust Him.

What do you want this Christmas? You already have everything you'll ever need. You have Him who sits on the throne. Appreciate Him, love Him, and respond to Him. If you have Him, you have possibility, you have healing, you have salvation, you have protection, you have guidance, and you have peace. You already have the greatest Christmas Gift of all.

No Longer Business as Usual

VASHTI MURPHY MCKENZIE

BASED ON LUKE 1:17–19

If we are not careful, we may give permission to the vast spectrum of our twenty-first-century cultural environment to cheapen Christmas—to devalue its significance and make it less than it really can be, a celebration of God's love manifested in human flesh.

If we are not careful, we may denigrate the fulfillment of God's promise—the evidence of God's grace and this proof of God's intention to reconcile heaven and earth. God fixed the fall of Adam and Eve in the fullness of time and now it is a reality that the church has decided to remember at this time of the year.

If we are not careful, we will secularize this sacred event in human history. People disrespect the Christ Child's coming by replacing the Christ with an *X*. Many people spend their whole lives replacing Christ with things from their X-files. Instead of Christ, they celebrate Rudolph the Red-Nosed Reindeer, Frosty the Snowman, or a Charlie Brown Christmas. Instead of Christ, they celebrate the Grinch who stole Christmas. Instead of visions of the Christ event, there are visions of sugar plums dancing, ten lords a-leaping, and five golden rings purchased on layaway from the mall. Instead of focusing on God's gift to the world, we focus on

196

what we want the world to give to us. Christ gets confused with Santa as some think Jesus is making a list and checking it twice, trying to find out who is naughty or nice.

This is a good time for a hasty retreat to examine in God's Word the first Advent, recorded in the gospel of Luke to help us spiritually prepare for the coming of the Christ Child again.

Luke includes what the other synoptic gospels, Mark and Matthew, leave out. Luke the physician is a scientist whom you would expect to gather the details of the life and ministry of Jesus Christ and carefully present his diagnosis. Luke includes the birth of John, the preparer of the way of the Lord, as does Mark.

Matthew's infancy narrative traces the genealogy of Jesus to show that He is the long-expected Messiah. It is in Luke, however, that the role of the two women Elizabeth and Mary are elevated.

Luke employs a Greco-Roman literary methodology as he begins to elucidate the events surrounding the first Advent. This method, according to some scholars, was a means to give evidence of the coming greatness of a personality through the events surrounding his or her birth. In that context, it was typical for an author to hint at extraordinary greatness by revealing some sign that was present at the birth of a great leader. Luke reveals that this child is destined for greatness because of the circumstances of his birth.

Luke gives clues to the roles that both John and Jesus will play through the prophecies given at the birth of each. The angel Gabriel appeared to Zachariah to announce the miraculous birth of John the Baptist, the one who would prepare the people for the coming Messiah. His would be an extraordinary birth because he was born to a couple beyond the normal childbearing age.

Gabriel also appeared to Mary to announce the miraculous birth of Jesus, the promised Messiah sent to take away the sins of the whole world. She was a woman of appropriate age but not in an appropriate relationship.

One birth was to a woman whose biological equipment had naturally deteriorated over time. The other birth was to woman whose hymen was intact as she had not engaged in activity that would disrupt her virginity.

One baby was born to a woman in a covenant relationship, and the other to a woman betrothed.

One baby was born to a woman who had prayed and given up hope. The other was born to a woman who had not prayed a pregnant prayer.

One child was miraculously given to a woman with a mature track record. The other was given to a woman with no distinguishing characteristics on her résumé.

One woman bore the marks that time leaves on the folds of the skin, while the other woman was emerging out of adolescence.

One woman was too old, and the other was too young.

One woman was in her retiring years of life, and the other was a rookie.

Here were two women living different lives and in different locations, both pregnant with possibilities that converged and changed the world forever. They were two unlikely candidates who would never have been picked out of a lineup of those most likely to be used in God's plan of salvation.

They were two women who lived traditional lives according to the Hebrew culture of their time. They exercised no power or authority beyond their tent doors. They sat in no seats of decision in their community.

Yet God chose these ordinary women to be a part of an extraordinary event. It is often incredible how many times God does what we least expect, and with those whom we suspect. There are times we are certain that our options and alternatives are clear, only to find out that God is moving in a different direction.

There are times in our lives when we expect God to be silent, and God speaks. Ask Elizabeth.

There are times when we are sure about the road ahead, and God changes both our direction and destination. Ask Mary.

There are times when you know you don't deserve another chance, and God gives it anyway. Ask Peter.

There are times when you fear that things will never get better, and they do. Ask the woman with the issue of blood.

There are times when you think you have seen everything life has to offer, and God shows you the impossible. Ask Moses.

There are times when the opposition has outnumbered you, but God showed up and changed the odds in your favor. Ask Gideon.

There are times when all you wanted was to be a spectator, and God enlists you to help carry the load. Ask Simon of Cyrene.

These two women, Elizabeth and Mary, were relatives; cousins perhaps. Both received divine messages through Gabriel, the angel of the Lord, that God was about to do the impossible.

Both women would give birth to male children, and the name of each of their sons, John and Jesus, was divinely given. They were told the future roles of the children and were encouraged not to be afraid.

Mary responded to her revelation with, "Be it unto me as the Lord wills." However, Luke records that Zechariah, the husband of Elizabeth, who received the message, responded differently.

Zechariah was in the temple, face-to-face with Gabriel. He was told that the prophecies that had been heard generation after generation were being fulfilled. His wife would give birth to a son who would be a messenger to prepare the way for the coming Messiah. He would be a prophet after the spirit and quality of Elijah.

Luke is clear about the definitive roles of each. John would be the messenger and Jesus the Messiah.

Upon hearing the news, the priest questioned how it could be possible for an elderly couple to have a child.

How do you respond when God finally answers your prayer?

Sometimes we pray so long that when God shows up and promises fulfillment, we can hardly believe it! Are you humbly submissive, like Mary, or do you fall into disbelief, like Zechariah?

Sometimes when God answers our prayers we don't know what to do with it. We give it back, fall into a season of denial, fail to act, or stifle the praise. Thanksgiving gets caught in our throat. Instead of shouting for joy, we sit pouting and pondering.

> *Lord, help us to receive the answers we have been awaiting with joy and gladness. Help us to run with Your promises fulfilled. Help us to tell the testimony of how You did the impossible, fixed what was broken, solved what was problematic, straightened what was disfigured, and restored what had been taken away!*

Zechariah was in the Temple performing priestly duties when Gabriel appeared. The proclamation was made and the revelation given. God not only answered the priest's prayer, God supersized the answer. As Paul wrote to the church at Ephesus, God is able to do more abundantly above all that we ask or think (Ephesians 3:20).

Zechariah and Elizabeth's prayer was for a son, perhaps to carry on the family name, manage the family possessions, and lead the family affairs into the next generation. God, however, not only gave them a son, but a prophet who would be great before the Lord, filled with the Holy Ghost from birth. This elderly couple not only received a son but a prophet who would return the sons of Israel back to the Lord. Zechariah the priest's private prayer rendered universal blessing. His personal answer became a part of the answer to the sin problem for all of humanity.

Zechariah then asked for a sign. He wanted evidence of the future foretold as an omen and tangible witness to God's revelation. (When Christ was born, the manner of infant wrapping was a sign to the shepherds regarding the birth of the Messiah.)

There have been other times when divine signs were given. God put a rainbow in the sky after forty days and nights of rain. It was a sign, not of more water, but of fire the next time.

Elijah's wet sacrifice was consumed by fire before the four hundred prophets of Baal. It was a sign that God is almighty, the one and only true God.

Gideon's fleece was a sign that victory was assured over an opponent that was more powerful in numbers.

This good news was given, but it was rejected. The judgment was swift. For his doubt, Zechariah would not be able to speak until the day these things were manifest. Perhaps Zechariah saw the answer to his prayer in the light of its seeming impossibility rather than in the light of the God for whom nothing is too hard.

Outside the Temple, people waited for Zechariah to emerge from prayer and pronounce the traditional Aaronic blessing: "The Lord bless you and keep you . . ." (Numbers 6:24, NKJV). They had come for the blessing, but the priest emerged silent. Silence removed him from his priestly responsibilities. Silence removed him from communication with his family and community. Silence became a wall between him and his world.

Questions hung in the air. How can the priest perform priestly duties without words? How can he preach, pontificate, and pray? He can pray without words. He prays out of his heart, but how can he proclaim, "Thus saith the Lord," to others without words?

Wordless Zechariah went home to wait. Psychologist William Marston once asked three thousand people, "What do you have to live for?" He was shocked to discover that 94 percent were merely enduring the present while they waited for the future. They lived waiting for something to happen: waiting for next year; waiting for someone to die; waiting for tomorrow, unable to see that all anyone has is today. Yesterday is gone and tomorrow exists only in hope.

So what shall we say to these things?

God does His best work when the odds are against Him. Zechariah and Elizabeth were beyond the age to procreate. Mary and Joseph had yet to consummate their relationship. God was greater than the circumstance of their physical and biological conditions.

This helps us remember that just because it looks like everything is against us doesn't mean that we're not going to make it. Impossibility and improbability require faith to believe that God is greater than our circumstances—faith that is not satisfied simply to know God, but to really know God in new ways, as revealed through what appears to be unachievable.

Although it didn't look like it, the Lord had been working behind the scenes in the lives of this ministry couple. Many times, the unseen hand of God is moving across the landscape of our lives, out of view and undetected until the fullness of time. This requires us to trust in God and lean not unto our own understanding. Trusting without seeing means we totally believe that God has our best interests at heart.

Our confidence is not in ourselves, but in a Christ who is infinite above our finite human idiosyncrasies. Our confidence is in this Messiah, whose birth we celebrate, and who is interested in who we are and what we can become through a new relationship with Him. Our confidence is steadfast in Christ, who wrapped Himself in human flesh to save us from sin and self.

Zechariah may have given up on his prayer, but God had not given up on His answer! God loves us so much that even when we have doubts or even when we give up, His love gives us another chance. All of us need another chance—whether now or in the future. *Lord, give us another chance to say yes to Your will and Your way!*

The best gift you can give yourself this Christmas cannot be purchased at the mall. It cannot be put on layaway at your favorite boutique or electronics store. The best gift isn't available online or through luxury catalogs.

Forgiveness is above earthly valuation. Grace is not for sale. Mercy is priceless. Healing from the hem of His garment doesn't come in a bottle or a pill. Deliverance cannot be gift-wrapped and placed under the Christmas tree. Happiness cannot be bought. If that were so, rich people would have cornered the market on happiness and there would be nothing left to purchase!

The best gift to give yourself is your "yes" to Jesus Christ! Stop trying to live a Home Depot life where you think you can fix everything yourself. God does not expect you to live a do-it-yourself existence.

God can do more for us than we could ever do for ourselves, because greater is He who is within us than he that is in the world.

The announcement of the angel tells us, then and now, that we have waited long enough. Jesus is here. Our waiting period is over. God is beginning a new thing in the world and we have a part to play in it, because the best gift we can give our friends and our family is Jesus Christ.

God is breaking into the world with the best gift that could be given—His only begotten Son, Jesus Christ. The expected and the ordinary have been overcome. It is no longer business as usual!

An old woman will give birth! It's no longer business as usual!

A virgin will be with child! It's no longer business as usual!

The lame will walk! It's no longer business as usual!

The blind will see! It's no longer business as usual!

Withered hands will extend! It's no longer business as usual!

The sore oozing blood will dry up! It's no longer business as usual!

Leprous skin will become smooth! It's no longer business as usual!

The dead will rise again! It's no longer business as usual!

The tables will be turned! It's no longer business as usual!

The first will be last and the last first! It's no longer business as usual!

It is no longer business as usual! Demons will tremble! Hell shakes. The keys to the kingdom have been snatched. Satan has been declawed. Sin is washed away by the blood of Jesus Christ. The grave will empty and death has given up!

This Christmas, celebrate this extraordinary event, because it is no longer business as usual!

O come let us adore Him.
O come let us adore Him;
O come let us adore Him, Christ the Lord!

He alone is worthy.

The Journey of Joy

BERTRAM MELBOURNE

Nearly three hundred years ago, Isaac Watts penned "Joy to the World." Watts heralds the coming of the Lord to a world in need of joy. The Lord has come; joy to the world!

But what exactly is joy? Dictionaries define it as "the passion or emotion excited by the acquisition or expectation of good; pleasurable feelings or emotions caused by success, good fortune, and the like or by a rational prospect of possessing what we love or desire."

Joy is "an intense awareness of life." To have joy means to have "enchantment and rapture."

Since the advent of sin, humanity has awaited the joy promised to come in the seed of a woman. Human beings and the whole of creation have longed for reunion with the divine, for in God's "presence there is fullness of joy (Psalm 16:11).

Sin has caused us to suffer and to weep. The psalmist experienced the anguish of sin that causes us to suffer and weep. He wrote, "Weeping may endure for a night, but joy comes in the morning" (Psalm 30:5).

Jeremiah, describing the desolation of famine, wrote, "Joy has gone from the orchards and the fields. There is no sound of singing in the fields anymore" (48:3).

The joy that we know as Christians does not come as a onetime event. It is not a once-and-for-all happening. This joy that we have is a journey that began the night that Jesus was born. But humanity had waited for His arrival surrounded by oppression and sorrow.

Anticipating the coming of the Messiah, Isaiah spoke of a time when gloom would be no more, when the people who walked in darkness would see a great light, and when joy would increase. It is in this context that he wrote, "For unto us a child is born, unto us a son is given . . . and he is named Wonderful Counselor, Mighty God, Everlasting Father, the Prince of Peace" (9:6, NRSV).

Can you imagine the indescribable joy of the shepherds attending their flock on the Bethlehem hillsides two thousand years ago, when the angel told them, "Fear not, for, behold, I bring you good tidings of great joy which shall be for all people" (Luke 2:10, KJV)?

The angel's announcement made it official; God had fulfilled His promise: The seed of the woman had come! The Messiah had arrived! Yet, how sad that He came to His own—the world that He created—and His own did not receive Him (see John 1:11).

The journey of joy was inaugurated by the Messiah's coming to a people in desperate need of liberation from sin. Their longing for the restoration of joy had blinded them. They were obsessed with deliverance from Roman bondage and the reestablishment of their political supremacy. Their need was different from their desire.

The people Christ came to save allowed their political urgency to crowd out something that was of far greater importance. Thus, the very ones He came to heal and to set free did not recognize Him; He did not come the way they expected.

Christ's coming was not told to the religious leaders; instead, it was announced to a group of common laborers. The shepherds who first heard the good news were living along the margins of society, in need of justice, equity, liberation, and fair play.

He came to bring joy to the despised and the oppressed, but

His contemporaries did not recognize Him. They had no room in their inn for Him and had no musicians to welcome Him.

Have you made room for Him? Or is it possible that history will repeat itself upon His return? Is it conceivable that we could miss Him if He does not return in a way that we anticipate? Would you recognize and be ready to meet your Redeemer should the Advent come right now?

Just as there were then, there are people today on the margins of society who need liberation and equity. There are lonely faces in the streets and longing hearts all around us who need to experience the wonders of His joy so that

sin and sorrow will no longer grow nor thorns infest the ground.
His blessings must flow, far as the curse is found,

as Isaac Watts so eloquently wrote almost three centuries ago.

Because there are people living in hopelessness—always have been, always will be—the expression "joy to the world" has a missionary tone. It promises something to us and requires something of us. To spread the good news of Jesus is to experience the journey of joy.

There are endless possibilities and opportunities to bring joy to the world and let God's blessings flow: we can feed the hungry; visit the sick and shut-in; provide cheer to those in need; visit the incarcerated; smile with those who need a smile; educate those who cannot afford education; and pray for and with those in need of prayer.

Pursue the journey of joy. We can spread God's joy daily, but what better time than Christmastide, when the world is singing "Joy to the World"?

The journey of joy is not experiences of happiness and warm fuzzies. It is a journey of doing, spreading the message of joy to others with our deeds, not just with symbols like Christmas trees and lights, beautifully wrapped presents, and mistletoe. The accouterment of Christmas can camouflage the true meaning of the celebration. In our quest to experience the joy and good feelings of the season, we may not recognize the one who initiated the journey of joy.

Christmas celebrates the journey of joy, signaled by the coming of Christ. It is the journey of a lifetime, but at Christmas we celebrate the day when God Himself came down to begin this journey with us.

WHAT IS CHRISTMAS?

Christmas brings joy once a year,
When we give gifts to those we hold dear.
You ask the origin of this custom revered,
Hush and we'll tell you the story as revealed.

No! Christmas isn't about Santa and toys;
Jolly ol' Saint Nick can't bring peace and joy!
What, then, is the story of this custom revered?
Hush and we'll tell you the story as revealed.

Long, long ago when the earth was still very young,
Eden's pair was deceived by a plan that was devil sung,
Doomed to death, as promised, were they until that day,
When God to give them assurance of a coming seed
       did say.

Long, long ago in Nazareth, on a very fair day,
An angel to a maiden fair did appear to say:
Favored of God are you, my dear, so you shall bear
The promised Seed that all who believe shall hold dear.

So once upon a time as joyful shepherds watched their
    flock,
Angels to them did appear with joyful news that earth did
    rock.
For to them was revealed the coming of God's promised
    One,
Who would bring peace and cause sin's reign to be done.

Christmas, my friend, reminds us of the best news earth
    ever got;
It tells of the joy that came to the world that would change
    our lot;
A joy that came in the form of a babe who said with a new
    voice,
"God to the world has come, thus humankind can once
    again rejoice."

Jesus, the real reason for the season, came from heaven
Bringing love, light, life, salvation, and joy as leaven
To set free a fallen world lost in sin, despair, and woe
So joy would make them glow and unafraid of any foe.

But how do you respond, my friend, to Jesus, God's great
    gift of joy?
Is He your gift to hoard or One to share with even a girl or
    a boy?
This is a gift that must be shared with others so God's joy
    is spread,
For Christ His life did sacrifice and God's only Son was
    not spared.

My friends, you have an obligation as Christians to accept
This gift divine and its principles in your daily life inject;

For, share the joy of this blessed redemption you must,
With a world gone mad, and in need of salvation from
    lust.

There are lonely faces in the city, and on the streets
With whom we must share a smile or give some treat;
To this joyless multitude who daily walk the streets,
We must tell of God's gift to them, even joy so sweet.

Perhaps, my friend, yours may be the task to give a cup,
So some lonely, helpless, forlorn soul may have a sup;
Perhaps, you may be the angel bringing mercy and justice
To those crying for deliverance from all kinds of injustice.

Will your lips be the ones to tell those who doubt that,
    indeed,
God is the God of the oppressed and downtrodden who
    can feed
Their hungry souls with food that human funds cannot
    buy, and
Who can truly satisfy their every need with God's very
    own hand?

Will you share the Christ-like spirit with a needy soul, my
    friend?
Will His light shine through you to dispel the darkness of
    some fiend?
Will you illuminate the path of some perishing soul with
    the light?
Will someone be saved from perdition's path by your light
    so bright?

Yes, friends, there is joy for a world that is seeking for
   delight;
There is a Ruler, whose reign is marked by truth, grace,
   and light,
Who can truly unite the nations and their rulers with His
   might!
Who will study war no more and will bring in love, peace,
   and right.

God will no longer allow sin, injustice, and sorrow to
   grow;
Sin will be known no more; no thorns will infest the
   ground;
God will come and will truly make God's blessings flow,
Far as the curse is found; yes, as far as the curse is found!

So, enjoy the journey of joy Christmas, and joy to your world is
my wish, dear friend; but this you must understand. A decision
about God's gift to the world you must make so Christ's sacrifice
will not be in vain.

So, is there room in your inn this Christmas for God's gift divine? Room you must make to travel the journey of joy.

A Testimony at Christmas

ELLA PEARSON MITCHELL

BASED ON LUKE 2:13–14; MATTHEW 2:11

And suddenly there was with the angel a multitude of the heavenly host praising God, and saying, Glory to God in the highest, and on earth, peace, good will towards men.

And when they were come into the house, they saw the young child with Mary his mother, and fell down, and worshipped him: and when they had opened their treasures, they presented unto him gifts; gold, and frankincense, and myrrh.

In the midst of one more Advent, what do I, a nearly ninety-year-old grandma, have to say that hasn't been said untold times before?

Well, in the first place, it isn't just one more Advent.

What, then, is the meaning of Christmas? I found the answer in the song of the angels (Luke 2:13–14) and the gifts of the Wise Men (Matthew 2:11); in other words, the answer lay in worshipful songs and generous giving.

The typical rat race of Christmas has somehow overlaid these two passages, in terms of time and energy expended at Christmas.

The reason for the season has been pushed to the periphery. We seem driven to encourage "I want" petitions, presumably addressed to a jolly old man residing at the North Pole.

Ironically, our mature years tend to follow the same "I want / gimme" pattern between parents and others who are dear to us.

Reflecting on the meaning of Christmas, it has dawned on me that my family has never conformed to the conventional Christmas of our day. Our celebrations have been somewhat different and nontraditional.

We have majored in music and in giving, but not like most people. In our inventory of the observance of Christmas, we have tried to sift out the "I want," seriously seeking to emphasize "I give," meanwhile enjoying praising God in song.

My words probably seem strange and radically countercultural, so perhaps I had better testify in more concrete terms and images. Early in our marriage, more than sixty years ago, my husband and I decided to affirm Christmas as Jesus' birthday.

We don't know exactly when our children took ownership of this decision, but the conviction was in our very bones; and it was contagious. Within our family's self-sufficient cultural community, there were no "I want's" heard as Christmas approached. Our children had full freedom to do their "I want's" in the days leading up to their individual birthdays, however. Thankfully, these occurred one in each of the four seasons—winter, spring, summer, and fall. We watched the sales and lavished on them as much as our budget would afford.

They were usually quite happy with the arrangement, although there was one serious matter. Of course there were Christmas gifts, but there was a rule we followed, and it was extremely important and well remembered: no gifts except to Jesus. This was our way of saying that the gifts we gave had to be to persons who could not give gifts in return. Every year, as we voted on a birthday gift for Jesus, we found some new and interesting, even exciting, way to give to Jesus. We took seriously Jesus' saying in Matthew 25, "Inasmuch as ye did it unto the least of these, ye did it unto me."

We enjoyed sending breeder rabbits to children in Ecuador one year. Another year we sent breeder chicks to another country, and blankets to yet another. We bought a heater for a missionary's car, ice cream for children in an orphanage, and Braille storybooks for blind children. Then there was the unforgettable Christmas when we kept a teenage boy from the Indian reservation for three weeks. The whole youth group helped us lavish him with love and gifts; and could he ever eat!

One year, our Christmas cards contained a picture trumpeting our adoption of a Korean "war orphan." We printed Isaiah 9:6 with it: "For unto us a son is given. . . ." Kim (now Ken) was four and a half years old at the time. He is now past fifty, with one of his three daughters having finished Purdue University. As our children grew older, we undertook another major project: we helped a mother of three to escape eviction and move into a home of her own.

Now, of course, some people said, "It was a great thought, but didn't your children feel deprived when others were bragging about their presents, and asking them what they got for Christmas?" Yes, and they did arrive, finally, at a vote to try other people's approach to celebrating Christmas. So we voted to set aside $200, a huge sum at the time, for presents for the six of us. Dad was to take the girls, and Mom the boys, on the shopping trips.

The decisions regarding presents were fairly easy, but the shopping trips were disastrous! The crowds, the crush, and the rush were not only unbearable but utterly incongruous and out of keeping with what we believed Christmas to be. The prices were terrible, and the children found themselves buying things they did not need with money they could have used to better advantage at a different time. The whole shopping experiment turned out to be an exercise in futility; thankfully, one never to be repeated.

In later years, our older daughter, Muriel, was the only black student enrolled at her Ivy League–type women's college. She became depressed and frustrated. Her counselor suggested that it was due to her having been denied Christmas presents. Her vehement reply was, "If I ever had anything I cherished, it was those Christmases I had growing up!"

Our whole testimony revolves around the fact that our family of six learned to remember Christmas as Jesus' birthday and not to make it about ourselves. Making a crèche and the cookie tree for the neighborhood children was a gift for Jesus' birthday, and the sacred Christmas music on the hi-fi we had assembled was all a part of a Mitchell family Christmas.

We parents always sang with some church's choir or some community chorus at Christmas. In later years, the whole family would sit around the hi-fi and sing in four parts from complete scores of Handel's *Messiah*. Liz was our gifted soprano soloist. The joy was indescribable! However, our four-part family choir ended all too shortly with Hank's untimely passing from leukemia at age twenty-six.

Since then we still sing, as a duet, in the empty nest. We love to sing that stanza of "In the Bleak Midwinter" that spells out so well the meaning of Christmas:

What shall I give Him, poor as I am?
If I were a shepherd, I would bring a lamb;
If I were a wise man, I would do my part;
Yet what I can I give Him: give my heart.

A View from the Bottom

HENRY H. MITCHELL

BASED ON LUKE 2:7
With this Christmas season, let's start from zero and gain some new understandings.[1] Let's do away with all sentimentality. In other words, let's not have any more of that "po' little Jesus Boy" stuff this time. And another thing: let's get off the innkeeper's back.

Everybody and their sisters and brothers were in town. With no prior reservation at the Bethlehem Holiday Inn, one simply could not get a room. This night manager was only doing what he had to do, following company policy. Mary and Joseph didn't get a room because the desk clerk simply didn't *have* a room to give.

Now, of course, I must admit that when I worked in the old Deshler-Wallick Hotel in Columbus, Ohio, over a half century ago, every now and then I would hear of an important person who had arrived at the desk with no reservation. When that happened, the alarm would go out, and we would have to "make" a room in minutes. But that's a horse of another color.

The people we "built" a room for had money, and they were regular customers. It was the clerk's job to find rooms for people like that. But that clerk in Jesus' day wasn't running an obstetrics ward: and the fact that he turned Mary down is not to be construed as meaning that he was a coldhearted, cruel fellow. We've got to stop this business of giving the innkeeper a bad time.

To tell you the truth, I have no problem with the stable and the manger: a feed box differs very little from a cradle, except for maybe the rocker on the bottom. The hay in the manger is a form of grass; and it's clean and soft and sweet-smelling and comfortable. When I was a kid, I *ate* it and enjoyed it. That is, I walked through fields and pulled up stalks of hay and ate the bottom inch or so. It was sweet and very nourishing. So why do we worry about the hay that Jesus slept on?

In fact, while we're at it, why worry about the swaddling clothes? Rich or poor, all any baby ever really needs is a diaper. Even in this age of designer labels, there are no high-fashion diapers, so far as I know. Have you ever heard of a Versace or Vera Wang diaper? If today the only choice is between paper disposables and soft cotton diapers, I'll take the cotton every time; that's swaddling cloth. Besides, a baby couldn't use any more than that even if the baby had it.

What I'm saying is that Baby Jesus is not to be pitied. At birth, He had five fingers and five toes, all His faculties, two loving parents, and His good health. The cattle weren't going to bother Him, and the Wise Men and shepherds had no problem finding Him. So what is there to pity? Let's quit pitying Jesus for the circumstances surrounding His birth. He may have looked as if He was down, but He really had everything He needed.

Furthermore, I have a strong notion that God even preferred it this way. And, quiet as it's kept, there are many, many advantages to a manger birth.

STRATEGIC ADVANTAGE

The Savior of the world had to be accessible to everybody. It was no problem for a king to come down to visit at the lower echelon of humanity, but there would have been great protocol problems had the wretched of the earth sought audience in royal circles in order to pay homage to Jesus. No matter how poor we are, or what class we have been designated, we can get to Jesus, the child in the manger.

Even at His birth, Jesus demonstrated that He is a Savior for all people. Picture the first Christmas: There were shepherds who had come straight from the fields, having no time to bathe and shave. They were dressed for the field, and they had been sleeping there for days. I know of no other place where two such diverse groups—royalty and rough-hewn shepherds—could find common ground. So the manger had some strategic advantages. The manger proved to be a convenient place for the visitors and worshipers to get together.

PHILOSOPHICAL ADVANTAGE

But the manger had other advantages as well, such as the clarity of perspective that the view from the bottom provides. It's a philosophical advantage. The existentialist philosophers say that if you want to understand a civilization, ask the slave, don't ask the sovereign. There are two reasons for this. One reason is that the slave is at the bottom; therefore, he can look in one upward direction and see the whole situation in perspective.

The other reason is that the slave has nothing to lose by telling the truth. If the report comes from halfway up, there may be advantages to protect. And it may cost too much to tell the truth if one is at the top. But if the report comes from the bottom, there is nothing to lose because there is nowhere to drop down to. Being accustomed to the lower ranks, the one reporting is apt to say, "I've been down so long that it don't bother me. I'm just gonna tell it like it is." God wanted the Savior of the world to be born in this position of lower ranking, yet of superior wisdom and objectivity.

Since everything God allows eventually can be used for some good purpose, when I look at the manger, I see God witnessing. The manger speaks to the issue of God's omnipotence and providence. In the manger, God says that all the power to establish the leadership of the earth is finally God's.

God is saying, "If I so desire, I can renew the world's leadership from the most unexpected and lowly of places. No dynasty or tribe or class of people can have a monopoly on the high places of state."

Through the manger, God is reminding the powerful people of the earth that they cannot give their gifts and power to their children unless the Giver of every good and perfect gift permits it. And any child, no matter how illiterate or debauched his or her parents, just may be used by God as a strategic contributor to the welfare of humanity.

ORIGINS DO NOT DETERMINE ENDINGS

Manger kids can go all the way to the top. In *Black Preaching*,[2] Gardner C. Taylor recalls reacquainting with a friend from childhood. The man had come from poor, illiterate sharecropper parents, and he had many times come close to leaving college and medical school because of a series of financial crises. But he had never given up, and God had given him great gifts and provided for his needs. When Taylor met up with him this time, he was a professor at a medical school.

Through experiences like the professor's, God is giving witness that origins do not determine endings. The author of the world's intelligence can raise up whomever—from mangers and from all sorts of unlikely places.

The crowning detail in Jesus' unlikelihood can be seen in His family tree. The manger baby's genealogical chart in the first chapter of Matthew offers some interesting family history. The genealogical documentation of Jesus' day did not usually record mothers, only fathers. But there are four women named in Matthew 1, and they are an unusual group, to say the least. Some scholars say God wanted them listed because they all were non-Jews, which establishes Jesus' ancestry as multiethnic. Jesus has blood ties outside the Hebrew race and in this sense He is all the more the Savior of the world.

But there is something even more remarkable in this story than Jesus' non-Hebrew ancestry. Thamar/Tamar (verse 3) had to resort to strange tactics to guarantee an heir for her late husband. She played the part of a prostitute.

Next, in verse 5, comes Rachab/Rahab, the ally of the scouts of Israel, who was elected to the Hebrews' Hall of Spiritual Fame in chapter 11. She actually was a prostitute, yet she was also David's great-great-grandmother. Her daughter-in-law was Ruth, the mother of Obed and grandmother of Jesse. Ruth's technique for securing a husband would raise some eyebrows amongst dignified church folk.

Then there is this mention of Solomon's mother, Bathsheba, an adultress. Whatever scholars may think of this genealogical report, it is clear that Matthew the evangelist wants it known that the manger baby had what many would consider a less than socially or religiously acceptable family tree.

And as unacceptable as some may find Jesus' ancestry, it has the opposite effect on me. I feel close to Jesus, because His roots are like my roots and the roots of so many I know.

I hear what God is saying to me and the likes of me with the manger where Jesus began His earthly sojourn: "If the world was saved by a baby born in a manger, you can be proud of your own manger-class background. And you can go as high as any man or woman in the kingdom of God."

NOTES

1. Originally published as "Bethlehem Revisited or On Starting from the Bottom," in Henry H. Mitchell, *Celebration and Experience in Preaching*, published by Abingdon Press, copyright © 1990. Used by permission.

2. Henry H. Mitchell, *Black Preaching: The Recovery of a Powerful Art* (Nashville: Abingdon Press, 1990), 131–32.

Raising Another Man's Baby

OTIS B. MOSS III

BASED ON MATTHEW 1:18–35

Her name is not important. For the purposes of this dialogue, we'll just call her Jane, not her real name. Jane's story is not like many of the other stories that we have heard growing up listening to all of the negative news that swirls around our community and our children.

Jane's story sheds light on the dusty damp corner of nagging truths sitting to the far east of our spiritual peripheral vision. Jane is a middle-aged woman living in a middle-class dream—the generic, homogeneous suburb, safe from the mythic terrors that are presented on television about the inner city. Jane was worshiping, working, and raising her family with 2.5 kids and a dog in quiet Generic Suburb, U.S.A.

Jane spent time helping disadvantaged youth in the inner city, about fifteen miles from her home. She felt it was her duty to pass on knowledge and faith to children who were cut off from the elusive American dream.

But one night Jane told me a story that will be etched in my memory forever. She said her life was changed one night almost ten years prior, at two o'clock in the morning.

She'd heard a noise at the front door. Her husband woke up and discovered that three young men brandishing shotguns had broken into their home. They put the guns in her face, in her husband's face, and in her daughter's face. Their suburban dream life had been invaded by a nightmare. All the stories that they had seen on the news were now their reality.

And before the night was over, Jane's husband was dead and her daughter violated—all of this at the hands of young men no more than seventeen years old. All three of these young men had been kissed by nature's sun; Jane did not look like them. It would seem as if her life was broken, and never would she be able to gather the shards and the shattered pieces of her life again.

But somehow Jane pulled herself and what was left of her life together. When the young men were on trial, she put on her clothes and went down to the courthouse to hear their sentences. The prosecutor was prepared to push for the death penalty; for in the state where Jane lived, that was the common response when young men who had been kissed by nature's sun invaded the home of someone who did not look like them.

While Jane sat in the courtroom at the hearing that would determine their fate, the Spirit of God spoke to her, and she demanded that the prosecutor allow her to speak. The prosecutor, thinking that he had in Jane a witness who would drive home the point that these young men should be executed, petitioned to let her speak.

Jane slowly moved toward the judge and faced the jury. She said, "You would think that I would agree with the prosecutor that these three young men should be sentenced to death. But I've got to tell you about the God I serve." She went on, "Yes, they took my husband's life. Yes, they violated my daughter. But I'm here to tell you that I serve a God of redemption, grace, and mercy. I do not want to see them die because that would be vengeance. I want the cycle to stop."

The three young men who had been kissed by nature's sun were there, clad in their orange jumpsuits. They could not believe the words that had come from this woman whom they had violated in the worst ways imaginable. The judge did not give them the death penalty, but sentenced them to twenty-five years to life.

But Jane couldn't stop there. She visited each of the young men in prison and talked with them. She looked in the eyes of one young man, expecting to see someone who was evil, but all she saw was a scared sixteen-year-old boy. And she looked in his face and uttered three words that would change his life forever: "I forgive you."

At her words the young man began to cry uncontrollably. He cried and doubled over, and then began to share his story. He said, "My father walked out on my mother when I was five. My mother was hooked on crack by the time I was seven. I walked around the streets of Oakland, California, trying to find a man to raise me. All I could find were pimps and ballers and shot-callers. They are the ones who took an interest in me and I got hooked up with the wrong crowd. I just wanted to belong. I didn't even want to be there that night."

In the decade following that terrible night, Jane and the one who inflicted the harm have developed a relationship. They spend time going from prison to prison, telling young men and women the dangers of crime. But as she was telling her story, Jane stopped and looked at me and said, "You know, Rev, the problem here is not just poverty and racism. The problem is not just one of resources and opportunity." She looked me dead in the eye and said, "If somebody had raised another man's baby, then my husband would still be alive."

And maybe that is the question for us today. Do we have the courage to raise someone else's baby? This particular message is not just for those who are raising their children by themselves. It's not just for you who have raised your children already. This message is for all of us, because we would not be here if somebody who was blood-related hadn't taken an interest in us.

In order to save the world, Joseph had to raise someone else's baby. He had to raise the baby of God. I just have to say in the words of Johnny Youngblood, I thank God for Joseph. Not much is written about the brother because he disappears from the biblical canon just after the beginning of Jesus' ministry.

There is no fanfare. We have no great songs written about Joseph. We don't talk much about Joseph. But I like Joseph, because Joseph had enough courage and integrity to raise someone else's baby.

Don't look at this wrong. You may be thinking, "No, but it's Jesus, it's the Holy Spirit." That is true, but understand that Joseph was a man, and if any man finds out the woman he loves is pregnant by somebody else, there's going to be hell to pay!

I can imagine that they were planning to get married at the synagogue. They knew exactly what songs would be played, and where the reception would be. I can imagine that Mary called up Joseph one day and said, "Joe, I've got to talk to you about something."

And Joe said, "Sure, baby. You can tell me anything. Don't you know I love you? Ain't no mountain high enough, ain't no valley low enough, ain't no river wide enough to keep me away from you."

At that, Mary proceeded, "Well, I've got to tell you something."

"Baby, you know I love you. You know you're my boo. You know I love you, girl. Just tell me."

"Well, Joe, could you come over? I've got to talk with you."

When Joseph got over to Mary's house, Mary answered the door, and he said, "What's up? What's going on?"

And Mary says, "I think you need to sit down for this. I've got something to tell you."

"Well, come on with it. You can tell me anything."

"Before I tell you, would you like a piece of cake? Would you . . . I've got some sweet potato pie in the kitchen. Would you like anything to drink?"

And Joe says, "No, no. Just tell me what's going on."

"Well, Joe, do you love me?"

"Girl, you know I love you. Now tell me what's going on."

Mary began to tell Joseph about her dream. "Oh, Joe, I had this dream the other night. This angel came to me and started telling me all these wonderful things about how God would bless me in a wonderful way. And I'm pregnant, and I want you to know that God is going to move—"

"Wait, wait, wait! What you say, girl?"

"I had a dream?"

"Yeah, I heard that part. Now fast-forward."

"I'm blessed?"

"No. Rewind, girl."

"That the Lord spoke to me?"

"Keep on . . ."

"I'm pregnant?"

"That's the part. You're what?"

"I'm pregnant, Joe. The Holy Spirit made me pregnant. I am going to bear salvation in my belly."

"Don't lie to me. Mary. Now, now, come on. We've been dating for a while. I've dealt with your crazy parents. I've done all the . . . Now, come on. Tell me the truth. Who's the daddy?"

"The Holy Spirit."

"Now, as long as I've been living, I ain't never heard of the Holy Spirit getting anybody pregnant."

"No, no, no, Joe. It's true. The Holy Spirit got me pregnant and I'm gonna have a baby. That baby will be salvation. Remember, in Isaiah it says, 'For unto us a child is born'? Well, that child will come through my belly."

"Mary, I loved you, and you're going to sit here and lie to me after all the mess we've been through? The wedding is off! I'll deal with you later!"

The Bible says that Joe was going to quietly dismiss Mary. But when Joe fell asleep the same angel that came to see Mary had a visit with Joe.

When you are involved in a relationship, if the two of you are on the same wavelength, if you serve the same God, bad news won't destroy the relationship. Bad news will be just a hurdle in the relationship. After the angel talked to Joseph, he had to go back and apologize and say, "Yes, I've got to raise another man's baby."

Why did he do this? How did he do this? Why did he do this? Joe had a commitment to the Creator. He didn't let his ego get in the way of doing God's will. The word "ego" simply means Edging God Out. Let's be honest: all of us have egos and often we listen to the ego instead of listening to God.

But Joe said, "Wait a minute, ego. My ego will say that brothers will be laughing at me because I am taking care of somebody else's baby. But I'm not going to listen to the fellas. I'm going to listen to God, because God gave me a directive."

When you have a commitment to the Creator, God will put you in a difficult position, but one that you definitely can handle. Joe was in a difficult position, but he knew he could handle it because God said, "Take Mary home as your wife and raise this child as your own. Don't let your ego get in the way."

Too many people let their ego get in the way. Some people let what they're thinking get in the way. But if you move the ego out and let God move in, God will step in and take you places you never imagined. I'm so glad that God can break through your ego and step in and do something that you never thought possible.

All of us have an ego. There probably have been times when you didn't want to do what God called you to do because you were worried about what people would say to you. You thought that they would look at you crazy. Stop worrying about everybody else and about your ego and start worrying about what God says.

The Bible says that Joe was a righteous man. That means that he was a man who was willing to consult God before he consulted his ego. But there's another thing revealed in this text: not only does Joe have a commitment to the Creator, he has a commitment to commitment before he has consummation.

Let me flip it. Some of us have consummation before we have commitment. Joe had intimacy before he had sex. It is possible to have intimacy without having sex because sex is a physical act; intimacy is a spiritual act.

Joe had intimacy with Mary before he had sex with Mary. If he'd had consummation before commitment, his ego would have won out over the Word of God. Because his ego would have told him, "Hold up, man. Do you mean that somebody else impregnated your woman? Oh, man! You can't allow that! You are going to have to displace her and disgrace her." But since Joe had commitment to commitment before consummation, Joe could hear the word of God.

Part of our problem is that we have confused sex and intimacy, thinking that just because you are physically involved with somebody there is intimacy happening. Just because you lie down with somebody doesn't mean they're going to stand up next to you when you stand at the altar. Sex is just a physical act. Joe said, "I'm committed to commitment before consummation."

The Bible reveals that Joe did not connect with Mary until after she had the baby. When the baby came, Joe was so glad that he waited because he then realized, "Wait a minute! I have a great responsibility. I'm holding my son, but I'm also holding salvation at the same time. I'm holding my little boy, but also I'm holding the Prince of Peace. I'm going to teach him how to stand right. I'm the one who's going to teach him how to speak right. I'm going to be an influence in his life."

Understand that God chose Joseph. God said, "I need a man's man to raise Me. I need a man with integrity to raise Me. I need a man who loves Me to raise Me."

Too many women have been looking for the wrong kind of man. You need somebody with a Joseph spirit, somebody who loves the Lord.

Joseph was committed to commitment before consummation, and so he waited. He understood that there could be intimacy without sex.

But he was also committed to consideration. He considered Mary. He considered the Word of God. He pondered; he thought about it. Instead of allowing his emotions to rule, instead of cursing everybody out, Joe said, "Let me think about this for a minute because I'm a man of God. I was raised right, so therefore let me take a few moments before I fly off the handle."

Joe was committed to contemplation. You have to learn how to contemplate before you act. That's part of our problem: we're always flying off the handle, doing what we feel we need to do. "I got so-and-so told." "I cussed so-and-so out! You should have seen me." Well, you looked like a fool. You should have considered what God wanted you to do.

We understand the principles under which Joe operated, but the question for us is, how do we raise another man's baby? How do you allow your spirit to influence the life of another child? I'm talking about spiritual influence.

To give spiritual influence, here's the first thing you have to learn: you can't do it all by yourself. To every person who thinks he or she is raising a baby alone, understand that you can't do it by yourself. There is no special award for saying you did it by yourself. As a matter of fact, you will catch hell if you try to do it by yourself. You need to have enough sense to say, "Look here. I can't do this thing by myself. I know things didn't work out the way I wanted, but I'm telling you right now, I can't do it by myself."

Don't try keeping all your pain to yourself, keeping all your issues to yourself. You've got to let somebody know, "I can't do this by myself. I need some help raising this child."[1]

We also must understand that we have to be open to the Word. Joe was open to the Word. When the angel stopped by in his dream, Joe said, "God said it; therefore, I've got to do it because God spoke to me."

The only way Joe was open to God's Word is that he had parents who raised him on God's Word. So when the angel stopped by, Joe didn't say, "I think it was some type of apparition. I really don't know what it was. Some psychological malformation in my mind." No, he understood that he was hearing the voice of God.

I know sometimes it doesn't seem like your children listen. But if you keep on pouring enough into them, some of what you're telling them eventually will get on the inside. There will come a Joseph moment when they will hear the voice of God and say, "I remember when Momma said . . . ," or, "I remember what Daddy said . . . It took me a few bumps and bruises to get where I am right now, but they put something in my spirit and now I am open to the Word of God."

Why should you raise another man's baby? There is just one simple answer: because someone else raised you. No, not your uncle or your grandmother; you see, God raised you. When everybody else walked out, Jesus was still there. When no one else was around, God was there. And if God can do all of these things for you, then it's time to return the favor.

It's time for us to return the favor with the spirit of Joseph. Your momma didn't raise you; it was the Spirit of God. Your daddy didn't raise you; it was the Spirit of God. Your momma couldn't go everywhere with you. Your daddy couldn't go everywhere with you. All of us have been in some places that Momma and Daddy didn't know about. But God was there when nobody else was there.

God was there to protect you and keep you, and hold you, and lift you. God raised you when everyone else stepped out. When you were crying your eyes out, and couldn't tell anybody about what was happening in your life, God showed up and said, "Your weeping may endure for a night, but joy comes in the morning."

Do you know that God raised you? That God picked you up? That God healed you? Blessed you? And if God has done all of that, then it is our responsibility to return the favor with the spirit of Joseph and raise someone else's baby.

NOTE

1. And there is something that I've got to say to every single parent: once you are raising a child by yourself, if the mother walked out, if the father walked out, you lose the right to be critical in front of your children. Just because things didn't work out between the two of you doesn't give you the right to mess up the spirit of your child, talking about how no good the other parent is. Children don't need to hear that; they weren't there in the first place. Keep it to yourself!

It's not your role. And if the children say something out of line, you say, "Don't speak that way about your daddy," or, "You don't speak that way about your momma, because otherwise you would not be here." We have to learn that when we put the spirit of criticism into a child, the child will develop all kinds of issues. The child will develop the same issue you had with your momma or daddy. And when the child is old enough, they will have that baggage with them, stuff that you passed on to them.

So once you have a child and things don't work out between you and Daddy or Momma, you give up your right to criticize. They don't need to know all your business. They don't need to know he ran up and down the street with everybody. They don't need to know what she did. It's not their business. Raise them to love the Lord. Raise them to trust in God with all their heart. Raise them to know that God is able, that "even if Daddy ain't here, I've got a Daddy in heaven who will take care of my needs."

The Glory of Christmas

MYLES MUNROE

BASED ON ISAIAH 7:14

During the Christmas season, people around the world are addressing the issue of the greatest miracle of all time—that is, the Incarnation of God. God becoming man is what Christmas is all about. This is the essence of the greatest birth celebration throughout the world today.

The celebration we know as Christmas has many different concerns. Many people say that Jesus was not born in December; that's probably true. Some say that He was not born of a Virgin Birth; that is definitely not true. Despite these controversies, the celebration of His birth has had more global impact than any celebration in the world. At Christmas, even people who don't believe in Jesus suddenly begin to talk about peace, goodwill, and the prospect of hope for a better world.

While the celebration of the birth of Jesus transcends the faith itself, only the Christian celebrates the birth of its founder. The other major faiths of the world—including Islam, Buddhism, Confucianism, and Hinduism—never claim a miraculous birth for their founders.

Some complain that the celebration of Christmas is contaminated by paganism and should not be embraced as a legitimate part of the Christian faith. They say that the practice of the Yuletide celebration and the Yuletide log find its roots in the pagan practice of the Norsemen of the ancient European days.

However, we must not confuse the incarnational mystery with the empty idol worship of paganism. There's a difference between Jesus and Santa Claus. I believe that Christmas should be seen as the redemption and reclamation of God's earth, and all that is in it belongs to Him.

Was Jesus born in December? Probably not. Some scholars put His birth in April, others in September, and some even in August. But it really doesn't matter where or when; what is important is that He was born.

The fact of Jesus' birth is without question or controversy. Yet no one has caused more controversy in history than the person of Jesus Christ.

The world does not try to stop people from preaching in the name of Muhammad. No one tries to prevent people from preaching in the name of Buddha. The world has nothing to say against Confucius. But if you call the name Jesus anywhere in the world, it irritates people. That means there's something about this man that sets Him above Muhammad, Buddha, and Confucius, and *that* unbelievers cannot deal with.

I once read a statement that said, "If Jesus Christ was not the Messiah, He deserves an Oscar." In other words, Jesus put on such a perfect messianic act that He deserves to win all the Oscars in Hollywood, because He really did mess up everybody's mind. Someone said Jesus was either a liar or a lunatic, or He was Lord. I accept Him as Lord and He has changed my life.

Christmas is the result of God's faithfulness to Himself. God had to become man.

I want to offer three questions that must be examined with regard to Jesus:

1. If God became man, what would he be like?
2. Did Jesus possess the attributes of God?
3. Why would God become a man?

If we accept that God became a man, we would expect Him to fulfill at least eight requirements of a Messiah:

1. If God became a man, He would have to have an utterly unique entrance into human history. The mode of Christ's birth has been the subject of controversy for two thousand years, yet it has stood the test of time. The Virgin Birth of Christ is not only a miracle, it is God's personal declaration to King Ahaz as a sign to all that He would deliver humankind from bondage. The Virgin Birth is the most important sign of God's declaration of His power to deliver.
2. If God became a man, He would have to be without sin, because God is holy.
3. If God became a man, He would have to manifest His supernatural presence in the form of supernatural acts, or miracles. He would have to manifest His supernatural presence by acts that no human being could do.
4. If God became a man, He would have to live more perfectly than any other human who ever lived. Have you noticed that nowhere in the Bible does Jesus ever apologize? Everything Jesus ever did was so perfect that He never had to apologize.
5. If God became a man, He would have to speak the greatest words ever spoken, words that could not be ignored.
6. If God became a man, He would have a lasting influence on humanity for all of history.
7. If God became a man, then He would have to satisfy the spiritual hunger in humanity.

8. If God became a man, He would have to overcome humanity's most pervasive and feared enemy—death.

In giving humanity a sign of His power to deliver, God told Ahaz through the prophet Isaiah, "Therefore, the Lord himself" would give a sign (Isaiah 7:14, KJV). God didn't send an angel to do the job. He did not promise to send a prophet to accomplish the task. God would give a sign that could not be ignored.

The Virgin Birth is not just a miracle; it's God's sign that God can deliver. God's sign would put into nature that which is above nature. When God gives a sign, no one on earth can match it.

So Christmas is not just a celebration; it's a revelation. If God could impregnate a woman who had never had intercourse, he can save you. This is a serious statement. This means if you have financial problems, God says, "I have given you a sign." Whatever is going on in your life—if you have emotional difficulty; if your marriage is falling apart; if your home is in disarray; if your business isn't working; if you can't get your vision to work—to these things God says, "Remember, I gave you a sign. If I did that, I'll bring you out of whatever situation you're in."

Christmas is one of the greatest promises of faith in God. If the Virgin Mary could get pregnant, you can be delivered. The Virgin Birth is our sign that God can do the impossible in us and through us.

Christmas was purposed by God, evidenced by His declaration through the prophet Isaiah. God was prepared for Christmas long before we were ready to receive it from Him.

The Bible says that the Lord cares for us. "Care" means anticipating a need and meeting it. God had already anticipated our need. Sometimes we think God is not in control of the circumstances of our lives. But in every situation, God has everything set up and under control. God is not wondering whether you will be redeemed. He's got the whole world in His hands.

The word "virgin" in Isaiah 7:14 is a strange Hebrew word. There were three types of virgins in the ancient Hebrew culture. One was a virgin who had never been married. Another was a virgin who had decided to remain a virgin for life. And the third type was *almah*, a virgin who was married but had not consummated her marriage. The word *almah* is used here. The prophet said an *almah*, a young virgin, or unmarried girl, would bring forth a son.

The way people got married in the ancient Hebrew culture is very important to understanding Mary's situation. When a guy wanted to marry a girl, he went to his own father and told him he would like a particular girl's hand in marriage. The boy's father then would go to the girl's father and say, "My son would like to marry your daughter."

If the girl agreed, the girl's father would establish a dowry and a contract. That contract would include provisions and all kinds of stipulations. And if the guy's father agreed with the contract, both fathers would sign. That would be called the dowry.

Then they would have a ceremony. The two fathers would then bless the kids, they would sign the contract officially before witnesses, and then each father would go back home with his child. But after the ceremony, the two children would be pledged to marry. So even though she was already married, the girl couldn't go to her husband, nor he to her, because she was too young. In those days girls were betrothed when they were about thirteen or fourteen years old. So while the young woman was married but not yet with her husband, she was called an *almah*.

So, when you read in the Christmas story that there was a young virgin named Mary who was espoused to Joseph, she was already married in contract, but they had not yet consummated their relationship. And to this *almah*, the angel of the Lord says, "You are highly favored. The Lord has looked upon you as in perfect condition."

Mary was submitting to the law of God and so she attracted God. You want to attract God? Live right.

The word "conceive" in this verse is another strange term that God uses. The word for "conceive" is not a verb, as it reads there, and it's not a participle. Rather, it is a feminine adjective. "A virgin shall conceive"—the word actually means "bearing," so, "The virgin will come bearing a child."

Let me explain why this is important in the Hebrew. The way God said it to Isaiah sounded like this: "Behold, the virgin is with child." In other words, she's already bearing a child and is giving birth to a son. God spoke in a tense that indicates it was already happening.

In other words, the event was already finished before God even announced it! It was spoken as if the scene was present to the prophet's view. Isaiah was actually seeing a pregnant virgin giving birth to a child. The great miracle of Christmas is the fact that God had already given birth to His Son long before we needed Him.

Isaiah 9:6–7 (KJV) reads: "For unto us a child is born, unto us a son is given: and the government shall be upon his shoulder: and his name shall be called Wonderful, Counsellor, The mighty God, the everlasting Father, the Prince of Peace. Of the increase of his government and peace there shall be no end, upon the throne of David, and upon his kingdom, to order it, and to establish it with judgment and with justice from henceforth even for ever. The zeal of the Lord of hosts will perform this."

The zeal of the Lord God almighty will accomplish this. "Almighty" is a powerful word. Whenever you see the word "almighty" it means that the Lord is getting ready to do something that no one can stop. In the Bible, "almighty" is God's emphasis that He is taking charge.

"Almighty" is two words put together. "Al" is many; the word "mighty" is translated "hosts" in the King James Version. The word "hosts" means all powers. So when the word "almighty" is used it means that God is about to do something in which He controls all the players. When God doesn't use the word "almighty," that means He allows things to happen. Whenever the Lord uses the word "purpose," He uses the word "almighty" next to it. In Isaiah 14:27, what the Lord has purposed, Almighty God will do.

In the birth of Jesus and the Incarnation miracle, God said, "I am controlling all power. I'm controlling the devil. I'm controlling demons. I'm controlling angels—seraphim, cherubim. I'm controlling the governments—Pilate, Herod, everybody is under my control when it comes to this thing!"

God said, "Look, I'm going to use Wise Men to bring gifts. I'm going to use camels to get them there. I'm going to use the stable to make sure He has a place to sleep. I'm going to use Herod—everything. I'm in control of everything."

God controls everything to make sure prophecy is fulfilled. So when God is committed to doing something, you don't need to worry about anybody getting in your way because God controls them, too. He's almighty.

If you want to use a word to get God excited, just call Him "Almighty." He gets excited and starts doing things when you call Him "Almighty": He's in charge of the bank; He's in charge of the real estate agencies; He's in charge of the whole economy.

God will make everything work for your good if you follow His almighty power. But why would an almighty God become man?

1. God became a man because of His faithfulness to Himself.
2. God became a man because of His faithfulness to His word.
3. God became a man because of His commitment to His own purpose.

4. God became a man because of His love for His own creation.

5. God became a man because of His integrity. He wanted to keep true to Himself.

6. God became a man because of His nature, what He's like.

7. God became a man in order to fulfill His original purpose.

That may not seem like an important list, but it's probably the key to the whole Bible. Christmas was necessary because God had to be faithful to Himself. He had to keep His own word.

Genesis 1:26 reads, "And God said, let us make man in our own image, in our likeness, and let them rule over the fish of the sea, and the birds of the air, over the livestock, over all the earth, and over everything that creeps upon the ground."

The key to Christmas was established by these words: "Let them rule." That statement made Christmas necessary. If God had not said, "Let them rule," Christmas would not have been necessary. When God says, "Let them rule," he established five things:

1. The official authority on earth was transferred to man. The official authority on earth is in those words.

2. "Let them rule" established the limitation of heaven.

3. "Let them rule" established the rights to power on earth.

4. "Let them rule" establishes the priority and the purpose of your body.

5. "Let them rule" established the need for the physical body.

When God created the heavens and the earth, God established how they function; He does it with everything. I think it's important to read this verse. There are many other verses that affirm this statement, including Psalm 115:14–15 and Hebrews 10:8–10.

Whatever God promises, He will bring it to pass. God sent

forth His Son, born of a woman, under the law to redeem those who have been cursed. When that angel showed up to Mary, all hell woke up. In Luke 2, Gabriel came with another message and said, "Mary, guess what?" According to the watch of heaven, it's time. It's Christmastime!

Mary responded, "How will this be?

The angel said, "Don't worry about that, just say yes."

And Mary said, "Be it unto me just as you have spoken it."

As soon as she consented, that seed of the Word dropped into her womb and she began to build a casing for that Word. It's a miracle: the Virgin has a child.

Mary bore the child, but God gave the Son. Mary bore Jesus, but God gave Christ. Mary bore the body, but God gave the Spirit. Mary is the mother of Jesus, but not the Mother of God. That's why when Jesus was twelve years old and they went to the Temple for Him to be bar mitzvahed, or to become a man, He stayed afterward and was there for three days, until his parents came back and found Him.

You'll always find God right where you left Him. Some people wander off from Him, but you'll find God wherever you left Him. God doesn't go anywhere. He never leaves us; we are always the ones who are like sheep gone astray.

When Jesus' parents found Him at Temple, they asked, "Son, what are you doing here? What are you doing to us?" His answer was, "Wist ye not that I must be about my Father's business?" (Luke 2:49, KJV).

They didn't understand what Jesus was talking about. But Jesus was saying, "I created you and I used you to come into the world legally."

Because His conception did not come from the sperm of a man, but out of the Word of God Himself, He is without genealogy. He's the Ancient of Days. He is the God without beginning or end. And Mary gave birth to that awesome gift, a pure baby.

Christmas is really about God becoming legal so we all can be delivered. He had to put on a human body to keep His word so He could come into the earth and die for us.

Hebrews 10:10 tells us that "we are sanctified through the offering of the body of Jesus Christ once for all." And we have been made holy once and for all through the blood of Jesus Christ.

How can one man's blood, shed two thousand years ago, still cleanse my sins and yours? The answer is that it was not a man's blood. It was the most holy, precious, wonderful, efficacious thing on earth—the blood of Jesus. And today we celebrate Christmas because He was born so that He could die for us.

Joy to the World

WILLIAM (BILL) E. PANNELL

BASED ON MALACHI 1:1; LUKE 1:5–16; 2:1–20

Advent begins out of silence—when for four hundred years God seemed to have taken leave, gone on sabbatical, when God did not release His voice into the nations through the prophets. For four centuries there were no miracles such as those that had occasioned the lives of Abraham, Isaac, and Jacob.

It would have been easy for a Jew living during that time to feel abandoned by God. Foreigners were in their land and they had become captives in their own society, and God was silent. Greek culture threatened to overrun their whole way of life. And as if to add insult to injury, that horrible horde of pagan Romans had swept across with military might, threatening, once again, to rob them of all that was sacred and blessed in their own country.

Yet through all of this, God seemed to be silent. So, for them, the announcement that too many of us take with casual observance once a year, the announcement that came to a select few, initially was not simply one of joy, but was also a message of confusion, amazement, and wonder.

Zacharias was an old man, certainly a man far beyond his years of optimum physical productivity. As Zacharias was participating with the rest of the cohort in serving God before the altar, he heard the voice of an angel announcing to him that his prayer had been heard. That was the first time in a long time that Zacharias knew for certain that God, who had been silent, had not been inactive in his behalf.

The angel said to him, "Your prayer has been heard." And oh, what a prayer that had been! He and his wife Elisabeth had prayed that prayer lots of times. They had prayed it so much that the angel was able to compress all of those prayers into two words: "your prayer."

That prayer that had gone unanswered all of those years—that prayer which, humanly speaking, wasn't even close to being possible—that prayer has been answered.

Life emerges out of barrenness; life and well-being come out of silence. The coming of God into human life and history sometimes comes stealthily, but not always simplistically. The coming of God doesn't solve all your problems—just ask Elisabeth and Zacharias. God coming into your life may bring joy, but it may also bring a sword. It complicates things. Good news is good news, but the *basso ostinato* of that melody can be almost overwhelming.

So Luke tells us that in that region, there were shepherds living in the fields keeping watch over their flock by night. Then an angel of the Lord stood before them, and the glory of the Lord shone round about them. The poor shepherds were terrified. The angel said to them, "Do not be afraid, for see, I am bringing you good news of great joy for all the people. To you is born this day in the city of David a savior, who is the Messiah. This will be a sign for you. You will find the child wrapped in bands of cloth and lying in a manger." And suddenly there was with the angel a multitude of the heavenly hosts praising God and saying, "Glory to God in the highest heaven, on earth peace among those whom he favors."

"In that region ..." I thought about that phrase one Sunday

morning as I was preparing to preach. As I was getting dressed, I was looking in the mirror and thinking about those who are "in that region," as my thoughts rummaged through the text. My thoughts then wandered to the back side of Phoenix, Arizona, where the people of God are engaged in ministry in that region. I saw the poor there, those far removed from the palatial estates where professional athletes and World Series champions hang out, where money is exchanged, and all the hoopla that's associated with all such activity occurs. People of Latino extraction are there on the back side of this great metropolitan complex; they're on the back side of nowhere, a community that history has bypassed. All that has stayed with them is the rubble, dashed hopes, and hopes yet a-borning, struggling to be free.

I thought of them there because it is to such people that the angels had come that first Christmas night. And it is to these people that God comes again and again and again and again, because that's the neighborhood in which God seems most comfortable.

The angels came to the shepherds, a group of common laborers. They had nothing going for them—no power, no clout, no representatives in high places. And they had nothing to offer except a bit of faithfulness on behalf of some sheep. Yet God came to them.

When the angels set up shop, they arrayed themselves as choirs are wont to do, and as that marvelous tone of God began—that downbeat exploded with joy and they filled the heavens and the earth with sounds never before heard. They announced the birth of a Savior: "For to you is born—to you, to you is born—this day in the city of David, a Savior, Christ the Lord." Aina that good news?

Consider the words again from the pen of Malachi: "Behold, I am sending my messenger to prepare the way before me, and the Lord whom you seek will suddenly come to his temple. The messenger of the covenant in whom you delight—indeed, he is coming, says the Lord of hosts. But who can endure the day of his coming, and who can stand when he appears? For he is like a refiner's fire and like fullers' soap; he will sit as a refiner and purifier of silver, and he will purify the descendants of Levi and refine them like gold and silver, until they present offerings to the Lord in righteousness. Then the offering of Judah and Jerusalem will be pleasing to the Lord as in the days of old and as in former years. Then I will draw near to you for judgment; I will be swift to bear witness against the sorcerers, against the adulterers, against those who swear falsely, against those who oppress the hired workers in their wages, the widow and the orphan, against those who thrust aside the alien, and do not fear me, says the Lord of hosts" (Malachi 3:1–5, NRSV).

I can assure you that in the midst of our celebrations of the Messiah's birth, that passage in Malachi is not usually dealt with. To be sure, we rejoice when Handel discovered it and set it to music, "Who shall abide His coming?" It's marvelous stuff.

But the rest of that text is associated with the unfolding of God, the cadence of God, the rhythm of redemption that includes the alien, the stranger, the workers that have been oppressed by the fat cats in every community around the world for all of time—those people. It is to them that justice and righteousness will come to earth.

We won't usually dance to that music; it's too uncomfortable in many ways. It's the back side of every town and village in America that needs to hear the Word. It's the folks out at the country club who need to recognize that they might think that they have been chosen by dint of their own devices; but God reckons differently.

I struggled with this passage that morning when I was preparing to preach. While I was working on it, it was working on me. I didn't know quite what to do. There's so much in the text, and as you get into it, it gets into you. It begins to germinate and bubble up within you. Then you find yourself conflicted a bit because there is joy here.

Joy suffuses this whole Christmas story. It's a celebration of triumph, of joy, and of rejoicing. Think of the laughter. Think of that curious joy, that gripped the old woman who had been praying to become pregnant—and now it was about to happen. They didn't even know how to do that anymore! I can just hear Elisabeth: "Give me a break! You must have been drinking that wine instead of offering it, Zack."

Zack: "No, no, no. The angels said we've got to get at this." And it happened. But then, you know the story of John the Baptist. He was faithful to God and it cost him his head. He was the fulfillment of the prophecy. The advent of the prophecy came—and to be sure he was a delight and a joy—but the sword would take his head.

The teenager who heard the message was filled with joy as well, but the other prophecy she received from the angel was "a sword will pierce your own soul too" (Luke 2:35, NRSV). It's all there— joy and grief, joy and sorrow, joy and hope, and all of that. Yet, there is reality, too, because all of this joy was taking place in the kind of world that is no friend to grace.

As I reflected on all of this, I realized that I must put a question mark behind the title of this message, "Joy to the World?"

Joy to this world? Joy to your world and my world? This world, with all of its brittleness and violence? This world, with all of its greed and gluttony and self-centeredness? This world? This world that one writer called this "McWorld that comes reluctantly together and is falling precipitously apart at the same time"? Joy to this world?

Well, yes and no. No, because joy issues out of life, and life issues out of barrenness; and, metaphorically, this is about a willingness on the part of persons to come to terms with their emptiness, with their inadequacies, and with their powerlessness.

It is about the willingness of the people to come to terms with their pride and arrogance and turn it all over to God—to confess it, repent it, and allow God to be God in their lives. It's out of that rubble of brokenness that life is birthed.

It's a biblical principle: "unless a grain of wheat falls into the ground and dies, it remains alone; but if it dies, it produces much grain" (John 12:24, NKJV). If it dies, it produces life.

So save yourself, if you will. Wrap yourself in tinsel, if you can. Enjoy the festivities, if you please. Stuff yourself with all the goodies of the holiday, if you want. But know this: that might be fun, and that might be the fulfillment of the state that guarantees you the right to pursue happiness. But that's not necessarily joy—for joy issues from God, who brings life out of barrenness and well-being out of the ashes of repentance and faith. Joy comes from God, who fulfills hope among His faithful servants.

Grab a copy of Malachi and take it to the beach or to the mountains or wherever you relax. Get Malachi, the charming, devastating prophet of God who begins his prophecy from the Lord with thus saith the Lord: "I love you" (Malachi 1:2). Isn't that great? "I love you," God tells us; I'm going to mess with you, but I want you to get this straight, "I love you."

It's sensational! It's so simple, so artless, so unencumbered, so straightforward and pure: "I love you. Now let's talk."

What did God want to talk about before He would wax silent for four hundred years? God wanted to talk to them about their lack of reverence for the things of God. They had become so enmeshed in their times and their circumstance that they had gotten sloppy in their worship. Their priests were offering God unclean animals—diseased animals, products of violence—on the altar.

The people had deduced that it was not of great value to be pious, to be righteous. Can you blame them? After all, the people who are driving BMWs and such don't seem to be particularly pious or righteous all the time. The people's sentiment was, "We're paying our dues to be righteous before God and we're getting kicked in the chops all the time. For crying out loud!"

They went to the synagogue. They kept coming to church, as we would say, but their hearts weren't in it.

One of the reasons why the story of Zacharias attracts us—and one of the reasons why God was pleased with Zacharias and his wife Elisabeth—is because of their faithfulness.

When Elisabeth married Zacharias, he was a priest. But coming from a long line of priests herself, Elisabeth was expected to marry a priest, and so she did. So the two partners were yoked together in faithfulness, but they had no children.

And to them God came and said, "I love you. Your prayer has been answered and you shall bear a son." Faithfulness to God is never done in vain.

Every once in a while I go over to the golf course and practice my ugly swing. Invariably, someone comes alongside of me and says, "You ought to keep your head behind the ball. Keep your head still." The guy keeps messing with my swing, and by the time it's all over I'm worse off than when I started.

And then we sit over coffee and begin to talk. He's about my age, and we begin to talk about what he's doing, how he's spent his life, and all that jazz. Almost always, what emerges out of the conversation is a story of faithfulness: commitment, reverence, respect, a certain sense of sacred duty—might be to the corporation, or it might be to a family business: "I spent x number of years . . . I retired . . . they gave me the gold watch . . . I have this little Evinrude on the back end of my boat . . . that little A-frame in the woods . . . I earned it."

Faithfulness seems to have disappeared these days. The corporation doesn't expect you to be loyal because it knows it's not going to be loyal to you. Most of you are old enough to remember when loyalty was a virtue in the society; when faithfulness was a simple expectation.

Reverence, respect, commitment, a willingness day by day, to slug it out come hell or high water, lighting the candle, igniting the flames, making sure the incense rises into the nostrils of God at the appointed time—God comes to people with these experiences and fills them with inexpressible joy, knowing they have honored God.

I suspect that joy is really not for the world, generally speaking. Wouldn't you like to slip into a side door and walk across the platform at the United Nations and preach or sing this?

Joy to the world, the Lord is come,
Let earth receive her king,
Let every heart prepare him room,
and heaven and nature sing . . .

In that world? Come on. In that world?

Could we have gotten the ear of Sadam Hussein and sung "Joy to the World"? In that world?

Can you sing "Joy to the world . . ." at the White House? Well, you can get the ear of our president and he'll sing it along with you, even if he doesn't necessarily know what it means.

There's nothing sentimental, nothing sappy, nothing American about the fact that we can do this in America. We're included, but it's not our personal, private province. Jesus was not born in a log cabin on the hillsides of Georgia someplace. He was born in a stable, on the back side of nowhere, in a community that the rest of the world looked down upon.

"Does any good thing come out of Nazareth? Come on, give

me a break!" But that's where God makes Advent. That's where God enters the scene. That's where God always enters the scene—always—from the back side of your life that you've ignored, perhaps have given so little attention to that you don't think it's worthwhile.

Maybe God comes at you off of somebody's experience in the congregation that you've looked down upon: they're not particularly sophisticated, and they didn't graduate from a prestigious school.

Maybe they're "cursed" with a bit of charisma. Maybe they've been sanctified. Maybe they're from a different religious tradition, one that is a bit more expressive in their praise and worship. And you just don't do that, do you?

But then you hear the voice of God, the shepherd's voice coming from unexpected sources into the barren part of your life that has been ignored for too long. All of a sudden, the Holy Spirit says, "Deal with it."

Joy issues out from God, and it moves into the lives of men and women who are prepared to allow God to be God.

Listen to the voices of this passage, and you're thrilled to hear people say, "Bless the Lord! God triumphs over the enemies of Jehovah. The Lord reigns! God is about to step out onto the human scene again and fulfill all of His promises to humankind; being delivered from our enemies, having political liberation again, being established as a nation under our own terms as God determines; we'll be free to honor God in holiness all the days of our lives."

The politics of God breaking through into human history, setting a captive people free, and they explode with joyful expectation. Now it's going to take God a little while to set that up. It doesn't happen the first Tuesday of the week, but it will happen. It is settled.

God says, "I have set my king up on my holy hill."

Jesus shall reign where 'er the sun
Does his successive journeys run;
His kingdom stretch from shore to shore,
Till moons shall wax and wane no more.[1]

And that is fixed in heaven. No tainted elections there. No political payoffs there. No questionable characters parading as leaders among the people.

This king is way beyond the taint of anything. God has raised Him from the dead, seated Him at His right hand, and Jesus Christ is Lord, to the glory of God the Father. Aina that good news?

If Jesus were to come tomorrow, would that be okay with you? Would it be okay for Jesus to come to fulfill this ancient promise? Be careful before you answer, for His coming is about judgment, purification, justice for the oppressed workers of the world. He doesn't have to ask permission of the United Nations or the White House. Would that be okay if the leaders of the free world weren't contacted first?

Well, it's true anyhow, even if it wouldn't be okay. God has got this thing set up, and God is running it on His own timetable. God has the whole world in His hands. And for those who are prepared to trust Him, to allow God to be God, they shall receive joy, life, and goodwill.

❧ PRAYER ❧

Dear Lord, we thank You that You are with us. We really do struggle with this, Father, because there's so much about this that isn't neat, it isn't manageable, it doesn't comport with our expectation, nor does it throb with our timetable. There's a lot about this that's disappointing to us. And so we ask You to catch us up in the cadence of redemption and grant us grace to believe You and to trust You and to revere and respect You—to honor You in all of our doings. Fill us with the spirit of joy so that in going into all the world others may know that Jesus has indeed come and that joy is available to all of humankind.

NOTES

1. "Jesus Shall Reign." Lyrics, Isaac Watts, 1719.

Draw Near

Victor D. Pentz

Based on Hebrews 4:14–16

Occasionally, I go to a shopping mall with my wife and our three daughters. Invariably, one of them says, "Let's go in here."

I'll quickly say, "No way."

They'll say, "Dad, you are such a chicken."

I'll reply, "Fine, but I'm not going in there. I'll meet you in a half hour." Then they walk into Victoria's Secret. From the time I was a little boy I have had lingerie department phobia. I do not belong in those places. Even the mannequins freak me out.

Believe it or not, there are people who feel the same way about walking into church. The building gives them the creeps, and the ministers freak them out. Otherwise strong, confident people who are successful in government, business, or academics will do anything to avoid walking into a place associated with the presence of God.

I met a man at a party, and when I was introduced as a pastor he became flustered. He said, "I won't tell you the last time I was in church, but I think I was wearing bell-bottoms."

Friends, entering into the presence of God can be scary even for Christians. Dr. Tom Long, now a professor at Emory University's Candler School of Theology, tells of a time when he was an active pastor. He was in his study at church when there was a knock at the door. He opened the door to find a woman who was one of his most active members. She said, "Pastor, do you have a minute?" He moved some papers off a chair in his office and invited her in.

She said to him, "I know I shouldn't feel this way, but I just don't think God can ever forgive me."

Caught off guard, Tom asked what she meant. The woman said she wasn't sure, only that she had an overwhelming sense of unworthiness before God. The "just a minute" visit quickly became an hour.

At one point he asked the woman, "What have you done that you think God can't forgive?" He knew her to be a devoted wife, model citizen, and faithful church member. She said she had no shameful secrets or hidden addictions.

"I just feel guilty," she said.

Tom resorted to the classic spiritual sound bites. "God loves you." "Jesus died for you."

She said, "I know God loves me. I know Jesus died for me. I know all that. I still feel judged by God."

Tom says he almost wished the woman had done something awful for which could be forgiven. Instead, she left that day with an unnamed, nagging sense of feeling not good enough before God.[1]

The book of Hebrews was written to people like this woman. They were a group of Christians who knew a lot of things in their heads that they didn't feel in their hearts. They did not feel like Jesus loved them. They did not feel like God had really forgiven them for their failures and mistakes. They did not feel God's concern for their heartaches and struggles in life. So the author of Hebrews puts together and sends off a huge package of pastoral encouragement.

In words that seem archaic to us today, the author goes into mind-numbing detail about the ancient Jewish penitential system of sacrifices. He discusses how the high priest would enter the Holy of Holies once a year on behalf of the people, but how that whole clunky system was just a stopgap measure because now a cosmic Savior has soared through the heavens and become our new great high priest. Christ enters the heavenly tabernacle to sprinkle his own blood, to make a perfect sacrifice, and to wash every stain and blemish from our lives before God.

God is saying two words to us. There are two words that summarize the book of Hebrews. Those two words are the meaning of Christmas and are a divine invitation. God is saying, "Draw near."

Draw near. By coming as a helpless baby, God was saying to the world, "Draw near." Here is a look at two of the great "draw near" passages in Hebrews. The first is Hebrews 4:14–16:

> *Therefore, since we have a great high priest who has gone through the heavens, Jesus the Son of God, let us hold firmly to the faith we profess. For we do not have a high priest who is unable to sympathize with our weaknesses, but we have one who has been tempted in every way, just as we are—yet was without sin. [Here is the "draw near" invitation.] Let us then approach the throne of grace with confidence, so that we may receive mercy and find grace to help us in our time of need.*

People who are discouraged need that reassurance more than once, which can be found six chapters later in Hebrews 10:19:

> *Therefore, brothers, since we have confidence to enter the Most Holy Place by the blood of Jesus, by a new and living way opened for us through the curtain, that is, his body, and since we have a great priest over the house of God, let us draw near to God with a sincere heart in full assurance of faith*

[this is the message the lady who visited Dr. Long needed to hear], having our hearts sprinkled to cleanse us from a guilty conscience and having our bodies washed with pure water. Let us hold unswervingly to the hope we profess, for he who promised is faithful. And let us consider how we may spur one another on toward love and good deeds. Let us not give up meeting together, as some are in the habit of doing, but let us encourage one another—and all the more as you see the Day approaching.

The readers of this letter may have thought that drawing near was something the priest would do in the ancient Tabernacle. First, the priest would enter the outer court, where he offered a blood sacrifice on the brazen altar. Using water from the basin he would wash himself and then pass through the veil into the holy place, where no natural light could come. Only the golden candlestick would cast its glow.

Inside the holy place was the sacred "showbread," representing the manna in the wilderness (Exodus 16), and the altar of incense with its fire of unceasing prayer (Exodus 30). Yet still beyond was the final veil into the Holy of Holies. Above the mercy seat, in the empty space between the wings of the golden cherubim, was enthroned the glorious and terrible presence of the Most High God. Once a year, the high priest could enter to make atonement for his sins and for the sins of his people (see Hebrews 9:1–7).

What the author of Hebrews was saying is that those days are over when only the high priest could enter the Holy of Holies. When Jesus died, the final veil into the Holy of Holies was *"rent in twain"* (Mattew 27:51, KJV). I love the way Matthew puts it: *"beginning from the top."* God ripped that curtain from top to bottom. So all we see now is Jesus standing with his arms out, saying, "What are you waiting for? Y'all come."

We all have an invitation to a life beyond the veil. Christmas, more than anything else, is an invitation to intimacy with God. Jesus was born in the flesh to be our bridge between humanity and divinity. In fact, the Latin word for priest, *pontifex,* means "bridge builder." Hebrews 4:14 says Jesus is our high priest—our high bridge—who has passed "through the heavens" to span the chasm between God and us.

In road construction, the wider the chasm, the more elaborate, complex, and costly is the bridge construction.[2] The Incarnation was God's ultimate engineering feat. God arranged all of world history for that one moment when that one baby would be born to that one woman in that one time in that one place. Think of all the pieces that had to come together for God to build His bridge. This is what Paul had in mind when he wrote the Galatians, "When the time had fully come, God sent forth his son born of woman" (4:4, NIV).

Now there was no way for the humans involved in this pivotal moment in time to grasp the magnitude of God's construction project or the role they were playing. To Mary, the situation would have seemed like the worst possible scenario. "God, I'm not married yet. This is no time for me to have a baby." Second, the country was under the rule of a brutal occupying army. What hope is there for a child born into such a mess? Third, there was a census going on.

When it came time to deliver the baby, Mary wasn't at home surrounded by her mother and sisters; instead, she was in a strange town with a new husband. And what did Joseph know about delivering babies? Not only that, all the hotels were full. "Lord, this is no time and no place for me to be having a baby, especially my first baby."

One day I was talking to a father who had small children. I asked him, "How's it going?" He replied, "Here I am flying to London almost every week for my job. If our kids were older it would be wonderful. My wife could travel with me. As it is now it's just lonely. It's the wrong time. It's just not the right time."

As finite beings, all we can see is one tiny piece of the eternal puzzle. We look at our lives and just shake our heads. None of this makes one bit of sense to us; but never forget that what felt like chaos to Mary was God firmly in control of her life. He meticulously orchestrated every last detail of the birth of that baby, perhaps even down to a quota on the number of fleas on the cows in the stable!

Centuries before Jesus' birth, Micah prophesied, "From you Bethlehem . . . shall come forth for me one who is to be ruler" (5:2, RSV). The problem was that Mary and Joseph lived in Nazareth while the prophecy said the mighty ruler would come from Bethlehem. Well, it turns out the bureaucracy in Rome was contemplating a tax increase at the time. You can just hear an ancient Rush Limbaugh saying, "See, I told you so—a tax increase!"

God used the massive wheels of Rome's bureaucracy to move Mary and Joseph from Nazareth to Bethlehem at the exact time to coincide with the end of her nine-month term in order to fulfill Micah's words. The baby was born in Bethlehem and the prophecy was fulfilled. God orchestrated a series of human events in order to fulfill prophecy.[3] The divine engineer was building His bridge through the heavens. His word to us today, and to every generation, is "Draw near."

What are you waiting for? Draw near. Y'all come. Not only should we draw near, but He assures us we can cross that bridge with confidence.

Hebrews 4:16 (RSV) says, "Let us then with confidence draw near to the throne of grace." And even more in Hebrews 10:19, 22 (NIV): "Therefore, brothers, since we have confidence to enter the Most Holy Place by the blood of Jesus . . . let us draw near to God with a sincere heart in full assurance of faith."

In my early years of ministry, I knew a very wealthy family who lived in a gated estate on a point jutting out into the Pacific Ocean. After having three daughters born to them, this wonderful Christian family adopted a nine-year-old orphan boy from a boys' home in a nearby city. Up to this point Christopher had spent his life bouncing from foster home to foster home. Then he found himself in the loving embrace of a terrific family in a magnificent home with a breathtaking view of the Pacific Ocean.

As their pastor I was making weekly visits to the family because Christopher could not bring himself to believe that he belonged in that house with that family. He'd do the slightest thing wrong, such as let the dog in with muddy feet or spill his milk, and he would go into a hysterical fit. "You're going to send me back to the boys' home. Please don't send me away!" They'd say, "Christopher, this is your home. We are your parents and you're our son! These are your sisters. We love you. You belong here." Then he did some really inappropriate things all because of his profound insecurity.

Finally, everything changed for this young man on one particular night. In one of the most beautiful moments I've ever known, after a special dinner, the family went into the living room for a ceremony wherein Christopher changed his name. The three daughters in that family were Jeralyn, Jana, and Joanne. That night, Christopher became Jay. It was the beginning of an almost miraculous turnaround in that young man's life. At last he belonged.

That's what happens to us in our baptism. We are given a name and come to belong in God's family.

Several years ago I officiated at the wedding of one of those daughters. There was Jay in uniform as a naval officer and as fine a young Christian man as you have ever met.

Friends, for too long some of us have been living like Christopher, out there on the fringes. We're a bundle of insecurities before God, like the woman Tom Long spoke with. God says, "You are no longer Christopher. You come to me as Jay. Approach with confidence the throne of grace."

The verb in Hebrews 10:22 is in the present tense. "Be continually drawing near." It is speaking of a life lived in the presence of

God. God wants us to go day by day beyond the veil into that quiet place where we focus on the flame.

Ironically, the Christmas season may be the most difficult time of year to do that because of all the distractions. Remember the story of how the Grinch stole Christmas? The plot backfired. The grumpy old Grinch had decided to steal Christmas to get the Whos down in Whoville to cut down on the singing and rejoicing. He turned his dog into a fake reindeer and the Grinch became a sort of reverse Santa Claus. He went down every chimney in Whoville and stole all the presents, decorations, and holiday foods. With everything gone, he thought, "There'll be no Christmas now." But the exact opposite occurred. He had only succeeding in stealing the accouterments of Christmas. When he looked down in the valley he saw all the Whovillians in a big circle singing Christmas carols. At this sight, the Grinch had a epiphany and his tiny heart grew three sizes.

Christmas is not about parties, punch bowls, presents, and poinsettias—as lovely and enjoyable as they are—it's about drawing near and staring at the flame. As John 1:9 tells us, the true light who enlightens every man was coming to the world.

Take time at Christmas—and each day—to be "continually drawing near." Go through the curtain into the quiet place. You may even want to light a Christmas candle and stare at the flame. Draw near and praise God. Read His Word. If you do, heaven will fill your soul and the peace of God will surround you. You'll walk with God.

PRAYER

Holy God, we thank you for Jesus, who has opened a new and living way into your presence. Lord, we know we have no business being in your presence except for the fact that you really want us there. You have given your very self in the birth of Jesus to bridge the chasm. The author of Hebrews says it so well: How dare we neglect so great a salvation? Some of us have been afraid to set even one foot on the bridge. Others of us are halfway across and filled with anxieties of what we'll find beyond the veil. Help us walk with confidence into your presence. Let us draw near. Be with us, we pray. In Jesus' name. Amen.

NOTES

1. Tom Long.

2. I'm a big fan of highway bridges. I don't know why, but I always try to position myself in a lane where I can glance over the edge. Driving north from Mobile, Alabama, on I-65 there is a bridge that goes for miles over swamps and wetlands. At one point the bridge comes way up and then it goes down. The workers who built that bridge spanned a chasm of miles, and did so in swamps, while up to their posteriors in alligators and snakes! The wider the chasm, the greater the complexity and the resources required to build the bridge.

3. That was only the beginning. The message of the baby's birth needed to go to the whole world. But how could that happen when the ancient world was a crazy patchwork of different languages? To resolve the problem, along came Alexander the Great. He was so arrogant he wouldn't let local business be conducted in the local language. Everyone had to speak his language—Greek. Bingo! A common language emerged.

So there's a language and there's a message, but how will the message get out to the far reaches of the world? What was Rome famous for? Remember History 101? Roads! For the first time, paved roads were crossing the world. Why? Because God wanted the story of His Son to go forth to the all world, a feat made easier on paved roads!

But there also had to be stability in the world so travel could take place. Up until this point in history there had been an unending succession of small kingdoms rising and falling. But with Rome came the famed *Pax Romana*—stability—which made travel possible.

Now the language, the message, the roads, and the stability are in place, but what would be the distribution points for getting the word out? At this time there was the Diaspora of the Jews. They were dispersed throughout the world, thus there was a synagogue in every town. So wherever Paul traveled, there was a pulpit waiting where he proclaimed the good news of Jesus' birth, ministry, death, and resurrection.

Mere coincidences? No.

Emmanuel: God with Us

W. Franklyn Richardson

BASED ON MATTHEW 1:23

At holiday time, there are things that most of us like to do, things that define the holiday for us. For some of us it is being around the dinner table that defines a particular holiday. Some look forward to a particular dish on the table, like Momma's sweet potato pie, some Virginia corn pudding, turkey, ham, and homemade rolls. Still others may look to some other object or event to define the holiday, like singing carols around the piano or the annual Christmas play at church. All year long we look forward to that occasion when we can partake of that special delicacy, object, or event that signals the holiday season has arrived.

One of those events for me, other than eating those great special dishes, is the ability to preach from a particular text. On average, I preach about two hundred sermons a year, but I always look to Christmas for a particular text that I have been preaching for over thirty-five years. I draw from this particular text every Christmas because for me it is the whole gospel of Jesus Christ.

The text is found in Matthew 1:23. It is a powerful, hope-filled verse. It is actually the resuscitation of Isaiah 7:14, and Matthew's attempt to put forth prophetic credentials on the Messiah. By bringing in the prophecy of Isaiah as an Old Testament credential, Matthew is authenticating his understanding of Jesus: "Behold a virgin shall be with a child, and shall bring forth a son, and they shall call his name Emmanuel, which being interpreted, is God with us" (KJV). What a powerful notion: God with us. Emmanuel, God with us—God electing to participate in the creation that he made.

It is the gospel in a single word—Emmanuel.

Emmanuel is the Incarnation—the love of God, the grace of God, the Holy Spirit, the existential and eschatological, all wrapped up in one. Emmanuel.

Emmanuel traverses the scape—from the cradle to the cross, and the resurrection. Emmanuel defines the relationship between the human and the divine. This one word makes clear the accessibility of God to each one of us. What a marvelous notion! If there wasn't already such a word as "Emmanuel," one would have to be invented because it so clearly describes what it means to have a God who has selected to participate in the creation.

That is what's so marvelous about Emmanuel. God has chosen to participate in the creation that He made. He could have made that creation and turned it fully over to the custodianship of those he had created. But He wanted to be a part of the creation He made. I don't know another religion where the creator deity has chosen to participate intimately in that creation.

God left the throne of glory and participates in humanity, coming where we are. What a marvelous, comforting notion that, as we make our way through this veil of tears, the One who made us is available and accessible to us because He has chosen to be where we are. God is with us.

Sometimes that's all we need to know to keep going forward— God is with us. Against the odds, against the assaults of the human circumstance, we can make it if we know that God is with us.

In the face of failing health and frailing bodies, departing loved ones, challenging financial circumstances, and emotional depression, we can make it. We can stand the storm if we know that God is with us.

Is there a more important word? Is there a more important announcement to make to humankind than that: "The God who made you has not abandoned you; God is with us"? Is there a more encouraging word, is there a more hopeful notion that we can embrace and celebrate? "God is with us."

That means that I can grab His hand because He's with us. That means I can speak to Him because He's with us. Because He's with us, I can hear His voice. Because God is with us, there is cause for celebration.

In light of the Incarnation, we can pray and talk to Him. But what does it mean in the light of the message of Advent? What does "God with us" mean in the light of the message of Christ? We may have our own abstract notions about what it means that God is with us. Let's unpackage what it means for God to be with us.

GOD WITH US FOR US

That God is with us for us means that God is not driven because God needs to be where we are; for God does not need anything. If God needed something, He would not be who God is—*El Shaddai,* God Almighty. The very characteristic of the eternal is that God is self-sufficient.

Have you ever thought about that? God doesn't need you. He doesn't need me. How can the Eternal One need anybody? The One who has all creation, the ground of our being, the source of our strength. He who has all wisdom doesn't need anything.

God doesn't need your real estate holdings, because the cattle on a thousand hills belong to Him (Psalm 50:10); the hills belong to him, too. He doesn't need your intellectual capacity because He already has all knowledge. He's omniscient and omnipresent.

Since God is self-sufficient, what drove God to come and participate in the creation is that God loves us. God is with us for us, for our sake. It is on our behalf that He has come down from the margins of glory and dwelt in our midst.

He came because He cares so much for us. Read John 3:16: "For God so loved the world, that he gave his only begotten Son, that whosoever believeth in him should not perish, but have everlasting life" (KJV). God came in Jesus Christ for us because we needed reconciliation. He understood that we need Him. We needed to be forgiven and put right with Him, and so He came for us.

God is with us for us; love drove Him to us. Even in the face of disobedience, God was driven by God's love for us. And each one of us can reduce God's love to its least common denominator, "God loves me."

GOD WITH US AS US

The Bible says that He was made flesh and dwelled among us, so He is with us as us. The first chapter of the gospel of John begins: "In the beginning was the Word, and the Word was with God, and the Word was God," and further explains in verse 14: "The Word was made flesh, and dwelt among us (and we beheld his glory, the glory as of the only begotten of the Father), full of grace and truth." God is with us as us.

God had options; that's what it means to be God. Being God means He can do what He wants anytime he wants. Nobody can be like that but God. I don't care how well off you are, no one has options the way God has.

Since God has options, that means God did not have to save us as us. He could have spoken to the birds and put salvation in their wings so that when they flapped against the molecules of the air, the vibrations would cause stirring recurrences in our hearts, and we would surrender to His grace.

God could have caused the mountains to bubble over like a volcano, and the lava to run to down the hillsides. When the lava took the land, all humanity would open up themselves and surrender to the fact that there was but one almighty source and in that moment surrender to Him. But He did not choose the mountains.

He could have put Himself in the aroma of the flowers and let their fragrance become the manifestation of eternal grace. The aroma spilt throughout the air could have reached out and grabbed those who found themselves in the dismal disgorge of the human circumstance, and because of the profound impact of that aroma they would confess, "I know the Lord and I love Him." God could have done that.

God could have chosen any way to come, but the Bible says that God came as us. There needed to be somebody who would pour Himself into the human frame, and God did. Jesus Christ surrendered His eternal capacity, His passport to heaven, to be with us, as us. Before the days of dual citizenships, when you wanted to become a citizen of another country, you had to give up your passport in order to become a citizen of that other country. That's what Jesus did.

Jesus was a citizen of heaven, but because He loves us so, he gave up heaven's passport and took on the restrictions of the human circumstance. Jesus came down through forty-two generations and dwelled among us. God lived in the mortal frame of humanity, participating on our behalf—God with us as us.

Because He was with us as us, His voice was amplified by human lips. God with us as us could see our plight through human eyes. No other religion has a deity who so intimately knows humans' circumstance. The eternal God, the abstract God, the intangible God has put on human form, which makes it possible for us to relate to Him as a person. Because God took on the amorphousness of humanity we can say, "He walks with me, and talks with me, and tells me I am His own. And the joy we share, no other has ever known."[1]

Because He came as us, He knows our pain. He knows our tears and He knows our plight. He knows where our hurts lie. We can relate to Him and He can relate to us. He came for us as us.

GOD WITH US HAS NEVER LEFT US

God is with us for us, and as us. But that's not all. Jesus said, "And I shall leave you a Comforter. And it will be with you." God with us has never left us. You see, if God only had been with us as us, and dwelled in the limited restrictions of humanity, when He left, our relationship with God simply would have been a nostalgic encounter. We would always be going down the road looking back instead of looking ahead. If God had not fixed it so that His earthly sojourn was not just a visit, but a permanent engagement in the human drama, we would always be looking back, saying, "Do you remember Bethlehem?" or, "Do you remember Calvary, when God was with us?"

But thanks be to God that God fixed it so that when He came in Jesus Christ, He never left. The Bible says that He left us the Holy Spirit, the Third Person of the Trinity. The Spirit would comfort us, and guide us, and teach us, and direct us, so He never left us. Hallelujah!

That's why we can feel Him, because He never left. He's not just a historical Jesus; he's not just a Nazarean and a carpenter's son. He's the continuing reality of God who, every now and then, causes me to feel something down on the inside of my soul.

He's that something within me that holds the reins. I can go to Him in the midnight hour because He never left.

He's still healing because He never left.

He's still making a way because He never left.

He's still calling the dead from death because He never left.

GOD WITH US IS COMING BACK FOR US

I live in the tense of the already and not yet—He's already coming. Hallelujah! He's coming back! To be already and not yet at the same time, that's who Jesus is. He's already, and He's not yet. He's already Savior, but He will be King.

He's already Lord, but He will be Lord of Lords.

He's already died, but He will live.

He's already saved, but He will celebrate.

He's already, and not yet. He's been here, but He's coming. He's Bethlehem, but He's also New Jerusalem. He's the old earth and the new earth. Now behold I show you a new heaven and a new earth. For the old earth passed away, and behold a new earth, He's already coming back.

Emmanuel—God with us, for us, as us, never left us, coming back to get us!

NOTE

1. "In the Garden," by C. Austin Miles (1868–1946), Ph.D.

Christmas Honors the Common Person

ROBERT H. SCHULLER

BASED ON LUKE 2

The Glory of Christmas Pageant, held each year in our Crystal Cathedral, is a beautiful ministry that introduces many to the church and to Jesus Christ. The pageant wows people of all ages as angels fly high over the audience and children carry baby lambs to the cave of the Nativity. There are the intimate scenes that move us with deep emotion to respond to the true message of Christmas. And there are the unplanned scenes that happen, giving great entertainment and laughter to the audiences.

Throughout church history, great cathedrals and small village churches have kept the glorious Christmas story alive through pageants large and small. One such Christmas pageant was presented by the children of a little country church in Iowa.

The star of that pageant was a little fellow named Howard, who was big for his age and rather awkward. He was given the role of the innkeeper. Howard was so excited that he rehearsed his one line until he could say it perfectly. His line was, "There's no room in my inn." When Mary and Joseph came to him onstage, he was to face them gruffly and say, "There is no room in my inn."

When the pageant finally took place, on opening night Joseph came with Mary, who was almost stumbling, tired in distress. They came up to little innkeeper, Howard, and Joseph said, "I'm looking for a room for my wife." And Howard, who had memorized his line, suddenly saw Mary, and felt terrible. A tear welled up in his eye, rolled down his cheek, and he said, "Oh, come on in. You can have my room!"

THE HONORABLE INNKEEPER

That leads me to the person I want to honor today—the innkeeper. Through the centuries, he has been put down too often by ministers, Sunday school teachers, and pageant writers alike, as if he was to blame because he had no room for Mary and Joseph. Now the truth is, it really wasn't his fault.

Why do we lay such a guilt trip on the innkeeper? The Bible does not accuse him; why should we? I suggest we take a positive-thinking attitude toward the innkeeper. It is amazing how often Bible verses, Bible characters, and Bible stories have been distorted by interpreters who project their negative analysis into the Bible.

THE INNKEEPER GAVE HIS BEST

As far as we know, Joseph did not complain that there was no room for them in the inn. And according to the Scriptures, Mary did not complain either. Do you know why? It is because they knew that the innkeeper gave them the best that he had. "And what was that?" you ask. A stable?

What was the stable? The stable was actually a cave in the hillside where the cattle lived. I have visited the shepherds' fields and the caves where the sheep and cattle are kept. It was an awesome experience to enter one such cave where perhaps our Lord was born.

I submit that the innkeeper needs a pat on the back, to be complimented, because when you stop to think about it, the stable had a lot of advantages over the inn, especially for a pregnant woman about to deliver a child.

To begin with, the inn was not the best place, as you already knew. After all, it wasn't a Marriott hotel, or an International Hilton. The Inn of Bethlehem. What was it? It was a place where the masses collected. That included the ruffians, the thieves, the heavy drinkers, and the rowdy men. The inn was not really such a choice spot.

The truth is, if there had been room for Mary at the Bethlehem Inn, there would not have been a soft bed for her. She would have had to lie down on the hard floor, very probably dirt. There was not a cushion. When you stop and think of it, only God could have planned it so beautifully.

The inn would have been jammed and packed. Had there been room left, there would have been the embarrassment of the sounds—Mary's groaning and the natural screams of a teenage mother bearing her first child—which would have traveled through the entire inn. And there was no privacy!

So the stable was better than the inn. It had privacy. No one would overhear her in her labor out there. No one would be able to probe with leering eyes upon a woman in the moment of birth. It had privacy; and privacy is probably the most important human value, especially during the sensitive time when a mother is birthing a child.

The stable was also safe and secure. No thieves and ruffians there! In any one of the inns, what would you do with your possessions, your coins, and your silver? What would you do with your prize pieces? You couldn't put them under your pillow, for there was none. What would have happened to the gold, frankincense, and myrrh in the crowded inn? In the safety of the stable there wasn't the fear of anybody cutting your throat with a knife in the middle of the night.

The stable was private. The stable was safe. And the stable was warm. At that time of year, the nights are cold in Bethlehem. There were no furnaces or fireplaces in the inns to warm the air for a woman giving birth to a child. But the stable was warm.

Why was the stable warm? I know. I was born on an Iowa farm, and the temperatures there often dropped to twenty degrees below zero. We would freeze walking through the cold blizzards, but when we stepped into the barn, even though the walls were made of wood only one inch thick, and even though snow would drift through the cracks, the barns were always warm. Why? Because the cattle with their wide nostrils would exhale their warm breath, breathe in the cold air, warm it in their lungs, and blow it out again. Even the coldest barn can be warmed by just a few cattle.

Isn't it amazing? God planned it so beautifully. The inn was crowded, so consequently Mary and Joseph were led to the perfect place for Jesus to be born—private, safe, quiet, warm, and soft. For here the straw could be the mattress. No straw was ever carried into an inn.

GOD HONORS THE COMMON PERSON

Mr. Innkeeper, we salute you! The common profession—an innkeeper. The common profession—Joseph, a carpenter. The common occupation—a shepherd. Christmas honors the common person. The innkeeper was God's answer to prayer in one of the most important moments in human history. Yet he had no idea he was taking care of the Savior when he gave the best that he had.

I have four questions to ask you:

Does God still come unexpectedly to you and me in our crowded living?

How does God come?

Why does God bother about coming when we are too busy for Him?

Is there room in your life for God?

Let's look at the first question. Does God still come knocking unexpectedly at your home or your heart asking for a room? The answer is "Yes, He does!" And how does He do it? He does it usually in the form of a positive idea. If you will grab hold of God's dream for your life, make room for it, and give Him the best that you have, something beautiful will happen—far more than what you ever expected.

Is there an idea or a dream that is lingering in the back of your mind this Christmas season? You have said to yourself often, "If only I could . . . ," or, "I wish it were possible . . . ," or, "Once I dared to dream, but I wonder if I could do it again."

Is there some long-lost hope that you just cannot forget? God often comes through these thoughts. It is God at work in you.

Usually when He sends you an idea, you are not prepared for it. Your reaction is, "I've got my hands full. I don't have time to do what I'm doing now. I'm too busy already. How can I possibly venture into a new territory?"

GOD COMES UNEXPECTEDLY

And when God comes it always seems impossible. That is because God can work effectively only with people who have a positive faith. That means people who are willing to make a commitment even when it still seems impossible.

Does God still come? Oh, yes, He does . . . through ideas and dreams and through uninvited and unexpected challenges for which you seem so ill prepared. He also comes through problems, through difficulties, and even through suffering.

Jesus Christ is born this year! He is coming through words and through songs that will touch your heart. He wants to be born again today in your heart and soul. Will there be room in your inn? He wants to fill your simple little hut or home with a glory that will be the glory of Christmas.

Like the innkeeper, give Him the best you have. Give Him your heart, now, wherever you are. Christmas is a time to fall on your knees to hear the angels sing and to receive the Holy Child.

PRAYER

Thank You, Jesus . . .
   for coming to the lonely person who needs love
   for coming to the guilty person who needs forgiveness
   for coming to the doubting soul who needs faith
   for coming to the alienated one who seeks a meaning-
      ful relationship
   for entering the searching mind and heart
   for filling the empty life
   God, You are coming now for me. You are being born within me. You are saving me. It is a Merry Christmas! Amen.

Pregnant with Possibility

ROBERT SMITH JR.

BASED ON LUKE 1:26–38

Christmas is not about demystifying the mystery or unscrewing the inscrutable; rather, it is about God doing something that defies description. It is about the most incredible, unimaginable, and incomparable act in human history, the incarnation, in which God became who God was not—human—and yet remained who God was—divine. It is an event that does not make sense.

Christmas is the miraculous, the greatest miracle in history in terms of the transition from the cradle to the cross. The wood that comprised the cradle is the same wood that makes up the cross. And since they are made of the same wood, the cradle cannot be mentioned apart from talking about the cross.

PLANT CIGARS AND GROW CIGAR TREES

In his autobiography, *Notes from a Wayfarer,* Dr. Helmut Thielicke, a twentieth-century German theologian, tells about an experience in 1955 in post–World War II war-torn Germany. Times were so hard that Thielicke's four little children took their mother's cookbook and began licking the pages. He knew what it meant to have his home bombed. He knew the devastation of being uprooted and separated from his family.

Thielicke, a great cigar smoker, had a son named Rainer, who was born in 1949. Someone had given Thielicke a box of fine cigars that mysteriously vanished. The family searched for the expensive cigars, but they were nowhere to be found.

One day Mrs. Liesel Thielicke was raking the rose garden and found some half-decayed cigars buried in the soil. Upon being suspected, Rainer revealed to Dr. Thielicke, "You were actually only supposed to learn about this later, when the cigar tree had grown." Rainer had watched his mother planting flower bulbs in the garden and reasoned that a cigar tree would produce enough cigars to help pay off the mortgage for the house while at the same time fulfill his father's frequent need to smoke.

Thielicke exclaimed, "Naturally we could only praise him for his good intentions." How can you scold innocent faith like that? Now, we know that cigars do not produce cigar plants and cigar trees; that's ridiculous. It's a botanical and biological impossibility. But that's what Christmas is all about. Christmas says, "If you plant cigars, God will grow a cigar tree from them." Christmas is confirmation that God can do that which makes no sense.

How in the world could God defy anatomical laws by taking a virgin and implanting the seed of the Son in her womb; then, after letting Him develop for nine long months, she remains a virgin even after He is born. Mary was a virgin before Jesus' birth, a virgin during His birth, and a virgin after His birth. The *New England Journal of Medicine* can't make sense out of it.

But in the Christmas event, God says that if we take cigars and put them in a garden, God will grow cigar trees. And that means, taking our own ridiculous circumstances and planting our cigars and watching God grow cigar trees from them. Even when people are saying, "It won't work out. There's no hope for our situation," we must keep planting our cigars. God can cause a miracle to grow from them.

That's what Christmas is really all about. It's an inexplicable miracle that transcends and goes above the laws of nature.

John Robert McFarland wrote a book titled *Now that I Have Cancer . . . I Am Whole*. In it, he writes that the doctor had given him one year to live. Upon hearing the news, he was angry and frustrated. He began experiencing the stages of grief identified by Elisabeth Kübler-Ross—denial, anger, bargaining, depression. But then God stripped him of his illusion that he was in control of his life. And when God stripped him of that, McFarland recognized that God was in control, and he began to find freedom and fulfillment in a God who was able to control not only his life, but also his destiny and circumstances. He then was able to live the rest of his time liberated from taking total responsibility for his life.

At Christmas, you and I should recognize and celebrate that we are not in charge of our lives. Yes, it's shattering to the ego to admit that. But if one blood vessel breaks in the wrong place in our bodies, if one pink slip is issued, if one relational rift is experienced, if one midnight phone call is made, if just one accident occurs, the bottom may just drop out of our lives.

When we realize God is in charge of our lives, then we start prefacing our declarations with words like, "If the Lord will . . ." That sounds old-fashioned, but we must come to the time in our lives when we recognize that all we have is now.

If you were lying on your deathbed, what would matter most? If God said, "I'm going to let you lie on your deathbed and give you time to think about what's most important in life," how important would jewelry be? How important would furs be? How important would cars be? How important would titles be? What would mean most to you then is the only thing that you and I have—relationship—relationship with God and relationships with people whom we love. Now, if that's true while you are lying on a deathbed, why can't it be true when you are vibrant and healthy? A relationship with God and our relationships with our loved ones are the most important things in life. If God has given you a family, treasure them. If God has given you friends, treasure them. Friends and family will add more to your life than a dollar bill could ever do.

Christmas reminds us that God is in charge and in control. Luke 1:26 tells us that Joseph and Mary were betrothed. In other words, the parents had already arranged the marriage, but the wedding had not taken place yet. I once had a student who, upon his return to his homeland in Asia, would meet his wife. He had never seen her before because his parents had arranged the proceedings. They were betrothed; they were committed to each other, but the marriage had not been consummated. This was also the arrangement between Joseph and Mary.

The angel Gabriel told Joseph, "Look, I have news for you. You and your wife are going to have a child, but it won't be your baby." That news was about as devastating as God saying to Hosea, "As a good pastor, I know that you need a good sister from the church to be your wife. You need someone who's upright, someone with integrity, and someone who people respect. I have the right wife for you. She doesn't sing in the choir and she's not in the nurses' guild. She lives in the red light district and she's going to be the first lady of your church." That's devastating!

GOD WILL MESS UP YOUR LIFE

On the opening page of his book *Jesus Mean and Wild: The Unexpected Love of an Untamable God,* Mark Galli says, "God loves you and has a difficult plan for your life." Scott McKnight commends this work, for in his opinion this book provides a much needed portrait of Jesus: "Finally a Jesus who has potential enough to cause commotion and even chaos." We talk a lot about how when you serve God, He makes everything all right. But God is not primarily in the process of bringing order into our lives, as we understand order. God is in the process of bringing disorder so that He can re-arrange our lives in such a way that we prioritize our lives according to His divine alignment. So when you sing, "Come to Jesus; He'll make everything all right," understand that it's not as simple as all that. Jesus may take it and make it all wrong first; then He'll make it all right. God will mess up your life in order to give meaning to it; break up your life in order to make it whole; empty your life in order to fill it; reduce your life to weakness so God's strength can be perfected in your weakness.

The angel delivered a message to Joseph that God wanted him to marry Mary, even though she was pregnant with someone else's child. Now, Joseph had already decided to put Mary away privately. He didn't want to have her stoned, which would have been within his right to do.

According to natural perception, Mary had committed adul-tery. It just does not make for a convincing story for a fiancée to say, "Honey, I'm pregnant. The Holy Ghost did it." That's just not very convincing.

Upon receiving the divine message, Joseph had two choices. First, he could trust the divine revelation God had given him through Gabriel that Mary had not been unfaithful.

His other choice was to yield to his concern for human reputa-tion, because people can count. Marrying a woman who was al-ready pregnant would give people an opportunity to calculate the time between the marriage certificate and the baby's birth certifi-cate. Doing so would severely damage his reputation in the tiny town of Nazareth. People would say that he had violated Mary's virginity before the wedding.

So what do you do if you're Joseph? Do you protect your reputation or do you yield to the divine revelation of God? Be fore-warned, when you decide that you're going to follow God, it may mean there will be suspicion. Allegations will be made. There will be questions. You'll be second-guessed and criticized.

If you're going to follow the Lord, you're going to risk your reputation when it comes to the full revelation of God. Some of your best friends may walk away from you because they think you've gone loony. They'll say that you've lost your mind.

Christmas is about putting aside your human reputation and accepting His divine revelation, even when it doesn't make sense.

GOD WANTS TO IMPREGNATE US

Upon hearing that she was going to have a child, Mary's question, understandably, was "How is this going to be? I'm a virgin." God wants to impregnate each of us at our virginal points.

There are some points and places in each of our lives that God has never touched—never caressed, never embraced, never kissed, never held, never trod across. Those are virginal points, and we dis-allow divine encounters there because we feel that's our private do-main. We don't even want the hand of God to be placed there. But God says, "No, I want to touch you in the virginal points. This has been your own pet peeve for a while, but you're undeveloped. You can never have possibilities as long as you don't let me touch you there. You'll never be fully grown if you don't let Me encounter you there. You'll never overcome that weakness if you don't let Me transform you there. You will never know what it's like to have a family that is really together until you let Me come into those vir-ginal areas where no one has ever touched before." The nineteenth-century Scottish preacher Alexander Whyte should verbalize our prayer sentiment: "Lord, I give myself to you, and what I cannot give, I invite you to take."

If you really want to experience Christmas, God is saying, "Take down the fences. Tear down the barriers and let Me come to your virginity. Lose your virginity with Me."

There are people who need to lose their virginity to God. As long as we are virginal, we'll never reproduce, and God wants us to be productive. God wants to encounter us in places where we've never been touched before. He wants us to be pregnant with possibility.

The angel Gabriel told Mary that she was highly favored of the Lord, even though she was pregnant and unmarried. "Highly favored" is a grace term. Mary was chosen by grace. She was pregnant with possibility.

I don't understand grace; I don't even understand its definitions. There is truly something amazing about grace. I have never been able to grasp the fullness of grace; it's too wonderful for me to understand. But my wife helped me to approach an understanding of grace through an experience we had with a pet.

We had a cat named Tim who was over twenty-two years old when he died. Tim was a member of the family. My wife loved Tim dearly, and it broke her heart when he died. She mourned him like a member of the family. Then her best friend Alice told her about a stray cat that was hanging around at her former church and, in light of her recent loss of Tim, encouraged her to go over and get the cat. She was a black cat just like Tim.

My wife went over there the next day, and sure enough, the cat was there. When she reached for the cat, the cat didn't resist. She put the cat in her car and the cat has been living in our home ever since. She (my wife named her Sheba) no longer has to worry about finding food to eat or being attacked by dogs. Now she's living in a controlled-temperature environment, gets medical attention, and receives constant love and attention.

But the cat was not a pedigree. She was just an alley cat that my wife pulled off the street. She possessed nothing that made her worthy of all that attention and care. But my wife overlooked all of that and said, "I'm going to make you my cat, but not because there's something special about you or because you're so significant. It's not because you're so wonderful and beautiful, but just because I love you. You haven't earned it. I just saw you for the first time and decided to bring you home with me and let you enjoy my home and its comfort just because I love you. You're my cat, Sheba."

That's wonderful, isn't it? But if we think that's wonderful, let's just think about what God has done for us. We must never get a big head thinking that the Lord must be blessing us because we're doing something good. He blessed us when we weren't doing the right things. He blessed us, protected us, and preserved our life.

You know what God says? "I love you just because I do. And no matter how bad you are, I can't love you any less. No matter how good you are, I can't love you any more. I just love you."

God says, "I'm going to choose you and bring you out of the world. I'm going to fill you with my Holy Ghost. I'm going to dump grace on you. I'm going to extend your life. I'm going to supply your every need—not because you did anything special, but just because I love you." Now that's grace. We are blessed because we're grace-selected.

Mary was grace-selected to be the mother of Jesus. Gabriel told her, "Mary, fear not." We are told there are 365 "fear nots" in the Bible. If that's true, then there's a "fear not" for every day of the year. God wants us to live without fear.

Gabriel said, "Fear not," because Mary was troubled. She'd never had this kind of greeting before. Gabriel informed Mary that she was grace-selected; highly favored. Then he explained that she was going to have a child, a son, and His name would be Jesus, because He shall save His people from their sin.

Not only that, He would be great, and He would be called the Son of the Most High God. He's not just the son of a high god, but the Son of the Most High God—the God who is above all. My mother used to put it this way, "He not only rules, but He super rules."

When Mary said, "How can this be? I'm a virgin," she was trying to wed the inexplicable with the explicable; and it doesn't work. Some people try to figure God out. One cannot conceive the inconceivable. One has to accept that God works in mysterious ways His wonders to perform.

Notice, Mary did not say, "This cannot be." She asks, "How?" Don't forfeit the greatest miracle in your family, in your ministry, in your life, by telling God "This can't be." The creature should not say that to the Creator.

The finite cannot tell the infinite what cannot be.

The limited cannot declare to the limitless what cannot be.

The mortal cannot tell the immortal that something cannot be.

But Gabriel didn't respond to the *how*. Gabriel tells her about the *who*. "The power of the Lord shall come upon you and the Holy Ghost shall hover over you so that this holy thing that's going to be born shall be called the Son of God." We may never know the answer to the how. As long as we know the who.

We must not worry about the how. We must not waste time staying awake all night long trying to figure out the why or the how. Because while we are trying to figure it out, He already has it worked out. Worry is interest paid on trouble before it falls due; often it never falls due. Trust Him. We must not worry about the how. If we have the who, the why and the how must remain in a posture of submission.

Gabriel told Mary, If you need a witness, don't take my word for it. Your relative Elizabeth was in an impossible predicament, too. She was barren and past reproductive possibilities. She and old Zec have been waiting for a long time. But she's already six months pregnant. What would her gynecological team say? How would Medicare process the forms? What would the senior citizens' ministry say? Everybody's going to laugh because they can't explain how it happened. Zechariah and Elizabeth had been waiting a long time, even past the point of reproductive possibilities.

How long have you been waiting for an answer to prayer? An answer to deliverance? An answer to bringing together a disordered and fractured family? How long can you afford to wait for the prodigal son or the prodigal daughter to come back home? How long can you afford to wait for that scholarship? Even when it looks as if possibility has expired, can you look hopelessness in the face and say, "I still have hope"?

In the first two chapters of Job, he had no idea he was in the book. In fact, he was minding his own business while God was talking behind Job's back. Job had no idea. Then, when Job lost everything, for thirty-five chapters, God didn't say anything. How long can you afford to wait for God to speak? Finally, God talks in chapters 38–41. Can you wait thirty-five chapters to hear from God?

Right now you may be in chapter 15 of your journey. Then you have twenty-two more chapters to wait. Can you wait twenty-two more chapters before God will speak?

Some of you are in chapter 36; you only have one more chapter to go. But you're ready to give up and throw in the towel. You're ready to give up on your relationship. You're ready to do something illogical. You're ready to do something unthinkable.

You're getting ready to panic. But if you can just hold out till tomorrow and if you can just keep faith through the night, everything will be all right. You only have one more chapter; if you could just wait one more chapter.

Zechariah and Elizabeth kept on dreaming, and one day their

son John was born. And Simeon, after he held the Baby Jesus, said, "Let your servant depart in peace, because now, after all these years, I've seen your salvation" (Luke 2:29, 30).

God is not going to let certain things evade us until it happens, if we walk by faith. Some things will never be fulfilled in this life, but some blessings will come our way if we just trust God for the next chapter. Without God, nothing is possible. But with God, nothing is impossible. All things are possible with God for God makes the impossible possible!

Mary responded to Gabriel's announcement: "I am your servant. So may it be unto me." She moved from "How shall it be?" to "May it be." That's quite a move. And God is waiting on us to move from "How shall it be?" to "Lord, may it be."

Mary didn't ask, "Lord, why me?" She didn't say, "Lord, not now." God is not going to force us to yield to pregnancy with divine possibilities. He wants to influence us so that we will say, "Lord, have Your way."

Jesus prayed three times, "Father, if it's possible, let this cup pass from me." But the third time he said, "Not my will, but Thine be done." Don't think for one moment that if we don't yield to the Lord that God is going to allow His program to self-destruct. Don't think for a moment that if we choose not to yield to the will of God that somehow God's plan will be thwarted. If you choose not to yield to Him, God will go on to someone else who's willing.

Mary could have said, "Lord, not me." And guess what? Jesus would have been born of some other virgin. God is not depending on one person to do His will. Mordecai reminded Esther, "If you remain silent at this time, relief and deliverance will arise from another place" (Esther 4:14). God is seeking people who will say, "Not my will, but Thine be done."

Look at Mary. She said, "Let your will be done in my life." Well, it was a real Christmas for the virgin Mary because she said, "May it be unto me. . . ." She did not miss Christmas.

When Mary found out that she was pregnant, she moved from "How can this be?" to "Lord, may it be." She was pregnant with possibility.

Pregnancy implies that something inside has the potential to grow. God wants to move us from "How can this be?" to "Lord, may it be." God wants to make us pregnant with possibility.

Prepare the Way of the Lord

WALLACE CHARLES SMITH

BASED ON MATTHEW 3:1–10
John's preaching on repentance in the wilderness had attracted a motley and oddly configured crowd on this day, recorded in the third chapter of Matthew's gospel. Among them was the usual assortment of humanity's poor, afflicted, and broken. Those who were the dirty and unwashed, the unscrubbed and poorly, had arrived that day at the Jordan.

But these beaten-down, broken pilgrims had come with penitent minds. They fully understood the need for turning away from the evils of the world toward a Lord of hope and Sovereign of possibilities.

Those poor persons appreciated the necessity for a fresh start and an altered life course. The famed songwriter-poet Bob Dylan wrote, "When you ain't got nothing, you got nothing to lose." Those despised, disenfranchised, denigrated members of Jewish society who bought John's message at the Jordan fully understood that they had to lay their all on the altar. They had nowhere else to turn.

But there was another crowd present on the banks of the Jordan. They seemed to be attempting to sneak into "the frat" of the disinherited. But they represented another mind-set. Among the crowd this day were scribes and Pharisees. The text says, "When John saw many of the Pharisees and Sadducees come to his baptism, he said unto them, O generation of vipers, who hath warned you to flee the wrath to come?" (KJV).

This was surely discourteous behavior on John's part. He must not have known who and what these scribes and Pharisees were. These separated, saintly, and select ones functioned as the crème de la crème of the religious world. They were the religious pillars in a crumbling world. They were the faith rock in societal shifting sand. They held together the unraveling fabric of a world threadbare from oppression.

For four hundred years there had been no prophets. For four hundred years the demanding, troubling, trying commands of Isaiah, Jeremiah, and Ezekiel had been quieter than moonlight on a snowfall.

For forty decades the people had endured without a word from the Lord, and in that absence, the scribes and Pharisees had been the spiritual and religious wood that kept the fires of righteous fervor burning.

Yet, it was to this already religious, faithful-to-date, spiritual crowd that John cried out: "Repent, for the kingdom is at hand." John was not ignoring the need for Roman soldiers, tax gatherers, and prostitutes to alter their courses, but he was targeting the saved, satisfied, and sanctified who believed that claiming Abraham as their father would ensure that their souls were safe.

One problem self-righteous people have is confusion about the fact that they too are in the wilderness. This prophet, wearing tailored camel hair, was delivering a message to every man, woman, boy, and girl.

Regardless of how long we have been in church, we've got some wilderness to deal with. In spite of our upbringing, training, or competence, no matter what committees we have worked on, boards we have served, or contributions we have offered, the season of Christmas is when we should take stock of our souls, selves, and spirits and work as adequately, vigilantly, and valiantly on our relationship with God as we do in wiring toy trains, decorating trees, and baking and freezing sweet potato pies. Repent, for the kingdom of heaven is at hand.

Our church conducted a survey a few years ago and discovered that some people do not attend church school because they feel they do not need to. All of us, like sheep, have gone astray. None of us is immune to having some time in the wilderness, for which we need to repent.

What is repentance? In the Greek it is *metanoia,* meaning a changing of mind. Repentance mandates an altering of priorities. Repentance demands a reversal from sin and a redirection toward God.

I remember watching a football contest waged on the gridiron of one of the nation's most prestigious schools. The quarterback ran toward right end. The flanker came back, took the ball, and along with the blockers, ran toward left end. In football this play is called a reverse. In theology one calls it repentance.

What is repentance?

Deuteronomy 30:1 (KJV) states: "And it shall come to pass, when all these things are come upon thee, the blessings and the curse, which I have set before thee . . . and thou shalt return unto the Lord thy God and shalt obey God's voice according to all that I command thee this day . . . then the Lord God will turn thy captivity." That's repentance.

Isaiah declared: "Seek ye the Lord while He may be found, call upon Him while He is near. Let the wicked forsake their way and the unrighteous their thoughts, and let them return unto the Lord, and God will have mercy and abundantly pardon" (55:6–7, KJV). That's repentance.

The Chronicler declared: "If my people, which are called by my name, will humble themselves and pray and seek my face and turn from their wicked ways, then will I hear from heaven, forgive their sins and heal their land" (2 Chronicles 7:14, KJV). That's repentance.

Repentance is the soul's maintenance plan. At prescribed intervals, even the most efficient and effective automobiles must be brought to an authorized establishment for maintenance—the timing analyzed, the oil supply replaced with fresh lubricant, the fluids and charges examined, monitored, and reinvigorated. That's routine maintenance. Likewise, periodically, the heart must return to its designer, the soul placed on a lift and scrutinized, the grime of disobedience and inauthenticity replaced by fresh mercy and grace fluids. That's repentance.

Some of us get nowhere because we have been driving unmaintained souls, poorly serviced spirits, improperly diagnosed hearts.

Not just occasionally, but constantly, we must repent. We must ask God to forgive us for our sins of omission, that which happened and which we did not intend; and of commission, that which we meant to do.

Repentance is asking mercy for each soul we wound. Repentance is seeking forgiveness for all the hearts we break. Repentance begs for grace when we, through our insensitivities, destroy lives, destroy homes, and wound the innocent.

We do not have to take a wrecking ball and knock down someone's house. Whenever an uncharitable thought delivers destruction, repentance is required. Each unkind word, which carries venom, calls for repentance. All unsympathetic behavior, which dips the arrows of darkness into the poison of destruction, mandates repentance. We all, like sheep, have gone astray.

John said to us all—rich, poor, young, old—"I am the voice of one crying in the wilderness."

In the long night of dislocation,
In the creeping process of aging,

In the bitter realities of loneliness,
Against the ravaging, raging fires of uncertainty and doubt,
It is not Santa who saves you.

"Repent, for the kingdom of heaven is at hand." Repent, John preached, for the kingdom of God looms as an imminent reality.

DENYING PAST LIMITATIONS

What is repentance? It is, first of all, denying the limitations of the past, and second, defining ourselves along kingdom values.

Some persons cannot achieve, accomplish, or succeed because they are carrying too much "I can't" around with them. Many persons have mathematics phobias. Someone told us in eighth or ninth grade that we could not do math and we have been afraid to try it since.

Repentance is turning away from the old ways and turning toward God. Regardless of the limitations life has placed on us, repentance instructs us to deny the past's power to define. "Build your hopes on things eternal, hold to God's unchanging hand."[1]

If the power of the past laughed at you because you were short; made fun because you were tall; didn't select you for the team because you were overweight; beat you up because you were skinny; denied you work because you were black; asked you to take notes because you were a woman; told you your worship was ignorant and nonliturgical because you were Baptist; said your intelligence is suspect because you believe there is a God, turn from the past's power and allow yourself to be defined by the Spirit of God.

Repentance will set you free. Some of those same negative definitions from the past caused us to develop destructive lifestyles. Somebody beat us up, so we bought a gun. If we were told we were unattractive, we became promiscuous. If we were never loved, we wounded and hurt others. There is no definition placed on us by the world that we cannot overcome if we are willing to redefine ourselves by the Spirit of God.

John called the scribes and Pharisees vipers because they wanted to sneak into the kingdom. They wanted solutions without repentance.

We must turn our backs on those ancient devils that we have allowed to define us and accept new names, new identities, and new lifestyles.

A cube of ice on a hot day will survive only for a short period of time.

Whatever we have permitted to be our definition cannot last if it is contrary to the will of God. Murdering people with our words cannot exist in a kingdom of truth.

Treating our bodies and others uncharitably and irresponsibly will not stand in a new world marked by accountability.

Repentance is breaking free from the definitions of the past and turning toward our God.

THE INTERSECTION OF JUDGMENT AND HOPE

Repentance is also when we understand that salvation comes at the intersection of judgment and hope. Matthew said that the ax is laid to the root of the tree, not just the branches (3:10). Jesus spoke of the patient owner who waited while the keeper of the garden took another year to work on an unproductive fruit tree, pruning, fertilizing, and watering (Luke 13:6–9). But after clippers come the ax. God is going to set this world on fire. A day of judgment shall come. We must be reminded that we cannot dilly-dally, play, and believe that we have limitless time. Repentance comes when we realize we must turn from our destructive pathways.

The ax will be laid to the root of the tree. Now is the day of salvation. When we have lied and fabricated to cover up and then we go one prevarication over the line, people begin comparing notes of what we said to whom. The out-of-control spark that we tried to hide looses itself and runs unchecked like a raging fire until our reputations are ruined, our families destroyed, and our futures clouded.

The ax will be laid to the root of the tree. Aching loneliness drives one to multiple partners, illicit contacts, and immoral intersections. Nights are filled with strangers' embraces, as we attempt to drive off the pain of empty existence; but then the diagnosis returns HIV positive. The ax will be laid to the root of the tree.

All of life is a rehearsal for eternity. Some will make the crew; some will not. Seek God while God can be found.

On the Niagara River for years there was a sign just at the falls, which said, "Past Redemption Point."

How long will we deny the nobility in our souls and wallow with the swine, fraternize with worms and maggots, accept vipers and vermin as our roommates? The ax is laid to the root of the tree. Now is the day of salvation. Prepare ye the way of the Lord.

While vacationing in Maui a few years ago, we took a motor tour on a road that was marked "Hazardous Ahead, Proceed at Your Own Risk." We didn't take it but others did. We were told that although the road appears perfect upon debarkation—wide, well paved, brightly lit—after a time it begins to narrow. The surface is not well kept, the blacktop turns to concrete, broken and crooked. After a while, the road becomes gravel, finally dirt. On muddy days, only those with four-wheel drive have any hope of safe passage.

But know this: when it pertains to matters of the heart, there has never been a four-wheel-drive vehicle that safely negotiates the roadway to destruction. This hell-bound highway is broad and beautiful when we begin. Copious fellow travelers provide plenteous accompaniment on the path. But soon the road narrows. The street cracks. The going crosses into treachery. The amount of little white powder it once took to get high is no longer sufficient. More and more drugs produce dwindling results. We spend more money we don't have. Credit cards are run up, gambling bills are incurred, bank accounts looted. The ax is laid to the root of the tree.

John the Baptist said that the road ahead is filled with destruction; death awaits, along with unspeakable agony, tragedy, and heartbreak. But there is a road sign warning us, and that is the hope: Take this exit or drive untold miles out of the way.

The warning sign is the hope: Prepare ye the way of the Lord. Make straight in the desert a highway for our God. Repent, for the kingdom of heaven is at hand.

While traveling in Europe I lost my passport. One was issued me from the British consulate; I have retained it. For a week I was a citizen of the British Isles.

What John offers is not a temporary traveling document, but a passport issued by the angels, signed by creation, stamped with the blood.

One is coming who is the Son of Salvation:
Light of joy.
Hope of the penitent.
Jesus, we love to call his name.
Jesus, our hope and our salvation, our all.
"There's not a friend like the lowly Jesus."
"Jesus the name that calms our fears."

Saviour, more than life to me. I am clinging, clinging close to Thee.
Let Thy precious blood applied, keep me ever, ever near Thy side.
Through this changing world below, Lead me gently as I go.
Trusting Thee I cannot stray, I can never, never lose my way.

Every day, every hour, let me feel Thy cleansing power.
May Thy tender love to me, Bind me closer, closer, Lord, to Thee.[2]

NOTES

1. "Hold to God's Unchanging Hand," F. L. Eiland, Ph.D.

2. "Savior, More Than Life to Me," Fanny Crosby, Ph.D.

Joseph: The Portrait of Obedience

Dave Stone

BASED ON MATTHEW 1:18–25; 2:13, 19–22

Why Joseph? Think about it, really. Joseph is one of the most forgotten members of the first Christmas pageant. After all, the little bit of information that we do know about him wouldn't look too impressive on a résumé.

Joseph didn't have much money and he earned his living as a carpenter. Now there's nothing wrong with being a carpenter, but wouldn't it have been more fitting for the Messiah's earthly father to be a powerful governor, a wealthy merchant, a teacher of the Law, or some other respected Jewish leader? Why Joseph?

Next to Mary, Joseph doesn't get much attention.

The fact is, it's usually hard for a man to exist in the shadow of his wife. The male ego can be incredibly sensitive. Think about the female movie stars or other high-profile women who married obscure, unknown men. Those marriages often struggled or dissolved because of the wife's notoriety.

Remember when Kansas senator Bob Dole ran for president? Many felt that his sharp and politically savvy wife, Elizabeth, who served as secretary of labor at the time, would have made a better candidate than he. Once a photographer took a picture of Bob Dole helping his wife make the bed. The photographer said, "It's nice of you to do that. Is it just for the picture?"

Bob Dole answered, "Are you kidding? I make the beds all the time. She's doing it for the picture!"

Joseph was a behind-the-scenes guy who played his seemingly minor role with amazing integrity. In fact, in all the Bible, Joseph is never quoted—not even once. He seems as common as his name.

Why Joseph? I want to paint a portrait of Joseph that will help answer why our heavenly Father entrusted him with the responsibility of being His Son Jesus' earthly father.

Joseph's portrait can be summed up in one word—obedience. That is the quality that made this common man so uncommon. And although not much is known about him, when you begin to dig into his life, and the lives highlighted in the Bible, you'll see that all roads lead to obedience. There are at least three lessons that can be learned from the obedience of Joseph.

OBEY, EVEN WHEN IT'S EMBARRASSING

If you are familiar with the Christmas story, you know that this was uncharted water. No engaged woman would admit to being pregnant, while in the same breath contend that she had remained pure. Furthermore, no engaged man would believe such a story.

Now put yourself in Joseph's shoes. You are betrothed to a respectable young woman who has been the picture of innocence and purity and a model of integrity. Then one day, you find out that she's pregnant and you are definitely not the father.

That is exactly what Matthew says happened: Mary was pledged to be married to Joseph, but before they came together, she was found to be with child through the Holy Spirit. Because Joseph, her husband, was a righteous man and did not want to expose her to public disgrace, he had in mind to divorce her quietly.

Joseph basically had three options according to the Law. He

could have her stoned to death for her unfaithfulness—but since few men were that coldhearted, that right was seldom exercised.

Second, he could have brought her out into the marketplace and publicly exposed her infidelity and her pregnancy. Although DNA testing wasn't available back then, I firmly believe that any engaged man who had been pure could give a convincing argument for why he wasn't the father.

Women had no credibility in that culture. Making a scene and a public spectacle of Mary would have provided an outlet for Joseph's vengeance and pain, while at the same time served to protect his good name in the community—not a bad choice if you don't know the rest of the story.

The fact that Joseph opted for the third choice gives us some powerful insights to answer the question "Why Joseph?" The Bible says that Joseph was a righteous man who did not want to expose Mary to public disgrace. He had decided to divorce her quietly rather than humiliate her.

In those days, when women were considered property or producers of children, this was an incredibly self-effacing act on Joseph's part. By choosing this quiet route that allowed Mary to retain some dignity, he opened himself up for even more accusations. Even more impressive than Joseph's noble choice is the fact that he chose this course of action even before he received a revelation from God. Joseph's decision reveals his obedience to a way of life that says, "I will honor others above myself."

Joseph extended grace and chose to allow his fiancée to save face. Matthew 1:20–24 says that after he had considered this course of action, an angel of the Lord appeared to him in a dream and said, "Joseph son of David, do not be afraid to take Mary home as your wife, because what is conceived in her is from the Holy Spirit. She will give birth to a son, and you are to give him the name Jesus, because he will save his people from their sins" (NIV). "All this took place to fulfill what the Lord had said through the prophet: 'The virgin will be with child and will give birth to a son, and they will call him Immanuel'—which means, 'God with us' " (NIV).

When Joseph awakened from the dream, he did what the angel of the Lord had commanded him and took Mary home as his wife. Joseph was so intent on being obedient that he immediately went through with the wedding.

The Bible says that he took Mary home as his wife. Did you catch the order? He married her and only then did she move in with him. These days, many people live together before marriage. When they do so, several things happen: they break God's command to save sexual intimacy for the marriage bed; they statistically increase the odds of divorcing if they do marry; and they increase their odds of being in an abusive marriage. But Joseph, ever obedient, followed God's order.

Obedience to Christ can be embarrassing at times. You might be embarrassed in a public restaurant to bow your head and pray for your meal, but you do it to express thanks. Your parents or your children might not understand why you give 10 percent of your income to the church, but you want to obey God's Word. Coworkers might shake their heads when they learn that you turned down a promotion because of the time it would take away from your children, but you choose what is best for your family.

It's easier to gloss over the truth, or to see if you can get by without disclosing all the details of a situation. But obedience demands that we follow through and be honest. That's not always easy, and at times it can be downright embarrassing, like the night I was trying to deliver an anniversary gift to my wife. I borrowed my next-door neighbor's truck, and after we got the furniture into our home, my wife, Beth asked, "Are you sure you can back John's big truck into his garage?"

I told her, "Oh, that's no problem at all. I'm good at this!" So I backed it in, giving special attention and detail to the mirrors on either side. And I did get in without hitting the mirrors. The only problem was that I backed the truck into their other car! It just came out of nowhere!

Well, the Bible says to go immediately to the person you have offended (Matthew 5:21–26), but they weren't home at the time. When they didn't answer their cell phone, my son said, "I think they were invited to dinner up at a neighbor's house." So I called up there, and when the daughter answered, as she passed the phone to my next-door neighbor, I had her quote to him, "Love your neighbor as yourself."

I thought that would kind of be a good way to pave the way in case things did turn violent. And that verse was passed along and he kind of laughed and said, "Did you wreck my truck?" "Well, kind of," I said. "I ran your truck into your Lexus." Then I asked, "What year was that Lexus anyway? Was it like a '91 or an '88?" He corrected me. It was a 2005!

My neighbor was very understanding and gracious about the whole incident. But the difficult part for me was the days afterward, listening to voice mails from all the other neighbors who were at the party. They all took delight in my mishap, leaving messages like: "This is Billy's Driving School, and we have an opening. Please call us back at 1-888-Learn-to-Drive."

As embarrassing as it was to wreck two of my neighbor's vehicles, my embarrassment cannot compare to what Joseph endured. Joseph was obedient to God's plan even though it was embarrassing to his reputation. His decision to be obedient also had long-term consequences that would prove embarrassing as well. Even years later, when Jesus returned to Nazareth to teach, some comments were made to cast doubt on his heritage and legitimacy. With no regard for himself or for the embarrassing consequences, Joseph was obedient to the Lord.

DAVE STONE

OBEY, EVEN WHEN IT'S INCONVENIENT

This situation for Joseph wasn't inconvenient just for the moment; it inconvenienced his entire adult life. For one, having a child this early in a marriage can be an inconvenience that brings additional stress. Another thing: traveling by donkey for eighty-five miles from Nazareth to Bethlehem with a new wife who was due to give birth at any moment was very inconvenient. But there were other inconveniences as well, like the numerous schedule changes that had to have hampered Joseph's advance planning.

On several occasions, Mary and Joseph had to stop what they were doing and move, like, to a whole different country.

Matthew 2:13 says, "When [the Wise Men] had gone, an angel of the Lord appeared to Joseph in a dream. 'Get up,' he said, 'take the child and his mother and escape to Egypt. Stay there until I tell you, for Herod is going to search for the child to kill him'" (NIV).

Sometime later, Matthew records for us: "After Herod died, an angel of the Lord appeared in a dream to Joseph in Egypt and said, 'Get up, take the child and his mother and go to the land of Israel, for those who were trying to take the child's life are dead.' So he got up, took the child and his mother, and went to the land of Israel" (2:19–21, NIV).

Verse 22 shares another change in plans: "But when [Joseph] heard that Archelaus was reigning in Judea in place of his father Herod, he was afraid to go there. Having been warned in a dream, he withdrew to the district of Galilee."

Through all of this Joseph had to be thinking, "Why all the midnight wake-up calls and impromptu trips, Lord? I've got orders to fill and chairs to build. I can't just skip out on my customers. They depend on me. No offense, God, but do you really have a plan that you are unfolding, or are you just making this up as you go?"

Obeying the Lord was inconvenient at times, but Joseph led

his family as the Lord directed and he made certain that they followed God's plan for the Jewish people, through their animal sacrifices and annual trips to the temple.

Obedience to God is easy when it neatly fits into our plans, but obedience is difficult when it's inconvenient.[1]

We all have our own will, our own agenda, and Joseph had to surrender his plan to God's plan. Frank Sinatra sang "I did it my way," but Joseph didn't; he did it God's way. The rumors were inconvenient, the constant moving was a pain, and the pressures of raising God Incarnate would prove to be quite unsettling. But Joseph waited on God's timing, and through the years that must have been an incredible act of obedience and patience.

Obedience to Christ can mean speaking up to a person at the ball game whose speech is totally inappropriate. Obedience may mean driving a separate car on an out-of-town trip to avoid giving the wrong impression or appearance when traveling with someone of the opposite sex.

It's inconvenient for parents to search high and low with their teens for modest yet stylish clothing, but obedience to Christ compels that to happen. Obedience may take the form, as it did with Joseph, of simply loving your spouse and your family and being open to the Lord's leading on when and where to serve.

One of my favorite stories is of Robert McQuilkin, former president of Columbia Bible College and Seminary in South Carolina. Several years ago, he retired from his position in order to care for Muriel, his wife of forty years. Giving up his career was an inconvenience, but he chose to be obedient to his vows as a husband.

OBEY, EVEN WHEN IT DOESN'T MAKE SENSE

If you have committed to sexual purity, it grates at you to have that purity impugned. And then, to wait even longer would seem senseless. But according to Matthew 1:24, 25 (NIV) "he did what the angel of the Lord had commanded him and took Mary home as his wife. But he had no union with her until she gave birth to a son."

The world would say to Joseph that it was senseless to wait until after Jesus was born for the privilege of having relations with his wife. But Joseph waited patiently for several more months.

Maybe he felt like it was the right thing; maybe he felt the timing would be more appropriate after the baby had been born; maybe the angel had cautioned him to wait. Or just maybe, Joseph remembered Isaiah's prophecy concerning the Messiah: "Therefore the Lord himself will give you a sign: The virgin will be with child and will give birth to a son, and will call him Immanuel" (7:14, NIV).

Sometimes God's plan doesn't seem to add up, but He knows what he's doing. Perhaps God wants to show you that He's trustworthy, and at the same time test your obedience to Him.

Naaman was a respected, skilled military commander who was diagnosed with leprosy, a terrible skin condition. In 2 Kings 5, Elisha, the prophet of God, told him to go and dip in the Jordan River seven times and he would be healed.

Naaman told his servant, "That's senseless! Why doesn't he just wave his hand over me? Or what's wrong with the water in Damascus? Why the Jordan?"

The servant responded, "If he had asked you to do something major you would have done it; so why not try this?" At that, Naaman humbled himself and obeyed.

He must have looked at his skin after each dip, not seeing even the slightest sign of healing. But he kept going back in. After the sixth dip, he looked no different than he did after his first immersion. And Satan was probably tormenting him with messages like, "You call this obedience, Naaman? This is embarrassing, inconvenient, and senseless. Walk out of the water now, because you are going to feel mighty foolish when you dip one more time and you're still the same leprous loser you were before. I guarantee you that the God in heaven will laugh and thank you for the entertainment!"

But Naaman obeyed God and went down one more time; and 2 Kings 5:14 (NIV) records: "So he went down and dipped himself in the Jordan seven times, as the man of God had told him, and his flesh was restored and became clean like that of a young boy."

And God wants our obedience even when it doesn't seem rational.

As the years went by Joseph must have prayed, "When will everyone know that this boy is Your Son? When will my obedience be vindicated?" At times he had to think, "This doesn't make sense, God." But the Lord was unfolding His will and using Joseph's obedience to do so.

And so you still come to worship even when you don't feel like it. Or you put the brakes on the engagement because she's not into living as if the Lord is the most important part of her life.

Choosing to be obedient may not make sense in your head or in your heart, but you remain true to the One who spoke the universe into existence! It is one thing to know God's plan for your life, but it is something completely different to submit to His plan. Obedience flies in the face of self-will and intellect.

We like to think that we have it all figured out. Maybe you feel that you've waited long enough for God to unfold His will; but God is saying, "Hang in there; be obedient. You just have to dip one more time."

When my daughter Sadie was twelve, she was very excited about going to a Christmas party with a group here at church. It was the first Friday in December and she had been counting down the days. But early on that Friday morning when she went in to the bathroom to shower for school, I had placed a letter on her mirror. In the note I told her that she wasn't going to school that day, and that she should pack warm clothes for three nights.

Although she didn't let it show, I knew she was disappointed that she wouldn't be at the party for the gift exchange. She had overheard Beth and me talking in the kitchen the day before about a speaking engagement I had in rural Kentucky. By then I knew that she was thinking: "I'm going to be out in the boonies for the weekend, stuck with my dad."

Beth said, "Trust your dad; you'll have fun."

Before the trip I had arranged for different people to leave voice mail messages on my phone for Sadie. So as I drove, she listened to messages from different people, each of them saying, "Don't worry about missing your party. You just trust your father." All along the way, she heard the message "Trust your father." Then her small group leader from church called and said, "We'll miss you, but I wish we could be where you're going. Just trust your father."

And while I had Sadie looking for something in the backseat, I pulled into the airport. I had her total attention as we went to the ticketing area. I looked at her and said, "I'm preaching in New York City this weekend, and three months ago I bought you a ticket in case you would like to go."

She'd seen the lighting of the tree at Rockefeller Center on television a few nights before and was just intrigued with Times Square and the excitement of Christmas there. She had a great time visiting those places she'd seen only on television.

She had an opportunity to stand in front of the great Christmas tree at Rockefeller Center and she visited Times Square just before she went to see *Fiddler on the Roof.* Sadie rode subways, bargained with street vendors for Christmas gifts, and went ice-skating at Rockefeller Plaza. She even got to take a picture with Nick Lachey. To top it all off, she got to hear me preach three times! What more could a twelve-year-old want?

Sadie telephoned her girlfriends at home while the party was going on, but she was glad that things had unfolded the way they did.

She didn't throw a fit when she saw that letter on the mirror.

She didn't say, "I don't want to go anywhere with you! This is my big party!" Instead, she just quietly packed her bag and tried to be upbeat because she knew that wherever we were going was important to her father.

In her mind, I bet she thought her obedience would be embarrassing because she'd told all of her girlfriends that she would be at the party.

Her obedience was inconvenient. She had to make up two days of homework from missing school.

And while she was packing her bag, she had to think, "This doesn't make sense. I don't even know where my father is going to take me."

But today she would say that weekend is her favorite memory.

As her dad I said no to her party but yes to an incredible adventure that she'll remember for the rest of her life.

Where would your heavenly Father like to take you if you just trusted Him? It might not be where you're expecting. Instead of someplace humdrum and routine, perhaps He wants to take you on an incredible adventure of faith, service, and fun; but it begins with your obedience.

And maybe, someday, your heavenly Father will look at you and say what I said to Sadie in the middle of Central Park: "Thanks for trusting your father."

And so I say to those of you who have been waiting for a godly spouse, don't lower your standards—trust your Father.

And to those of you who have been stuck in a job with no other Christians—hang in there and trust your Father.

And to those of you who are considering Christianity, I encourage you to trust your Father.

And your heavenly Father invites you to confess that you're a sinner, repent, believe that Jesus is God's Son, and be obedient in Christian baptism. The Bible reveals His good plan if we will only be obedient to it.

NOTE

1. Bob Coy tells of talking with one of his members who had an ethical dilemma at work. The boss was asking all of the waiters to report how much tip money they received each day. But all the servers had gotten together and decided to report less than their actual tip earnings, believing that if they played their cards right, everyone might get a significant increase in their hourly wage.

Bob told the young man that he had to be obedient to the Lord's calling on his life and tell the truth. The young man did as his pastor advised and gave an honest report. His was significantly higher than all of the others. Each week he kept turning in the true numbers and he became the brunt of hatred and opposition from his coworkers. His fellow servers would look for opportunities to try and trip him or cause him to drop plates of food or spill drinks. The cooks began preparing his orders last. Of course, the result was that the amount of his tips began to go down.

Determined to hold to his Christian convictions, the waiter hung tough for weeks. Bob Coy said that the young man came back to his office sometime later and said, "Yesterday, the head of the restaurant chain was in and he wanted to see me. He asked if my tip numbers that I had been turning in had been accurate, and I told him they were."

The man said, "We're looking for managers for this organization who are honest and able to maintain their integrity—even when it isn't popular." On the spot he was named the new manager of that very restaurant. And those coworkers who had made his life miserable for weeks had to answer to him.

Now God doesn't always unfold His will that way—but isn't it cool when He does? Divine vindication doesn't usually happen overnight; as in the waiter's case, it takes time. And while we wait we must remain steadfast in our obedience.

That's not easy.

Christmas! So What!

Gardner C. Taylor

BASED ON LUKE 2:9–11, 13–17

Christmas! So what! I hope that your lips will never curl in that kind of sneer about the blessed day that marks the birth of our Savior. Still, there are people for whom Christmas will not have the same meaning that it has for some of us.

A columnist in the *Atlanta Journal* once wrote an article about "counter-Christmas." He meant to show that there are people for whom Christmas means exactly the opposite to what it is fitted to mean, and what many of us take it to mean. There will be people on that day who are "counter-Christmas," or "anti-Christmas."

If you look at Christmas purely as a human holiday, a happy season, a celebration, then some anti-Christmas things will result from the day. House fires increase at Christmas because of defective electrical wiring. Armed robbery, as we well know, increases at Christmas because some people want to get good things by bad means.

There are anti-Christmas sentiments and anti-Christmas events around us. Injuries and deaths by automobile accidents will go up because some of us associate too much liquor with Christmas.

"If Christmas is better than other times for some of us, it is worse than other times for others of us," the columnist stated. "Christmas intensifies loneliness and grief for many. Some will remember more sharply and sorrowfully at Christmas that last year at this time the home circle was unbroken, but now there are vacant chairs and empty hearts. Some, out of loneliness enlarged by the day it is, will celebrate, if that is the word, Christmas in barrooms and bus-terminals, in jails and, yes, in luxury apartments and lovely, split-level suburban homes where lonely people console themselves with drink and television and tranquilizers, waiting for the telephone that does not ring or a letter that does not come."

I met a prominent man in a service station a few days before Christmas one year. "How is your family?" I asked.

"We divorced a year ago, and living alone in that two-story house is hell," he said.

I looked into his eyes in the chill evening light and could not force out the words "Merry Christmas."

Maybe the things I have mentioned do not specifically touch you, but we are all candidates for a sad Christmas in one way or another. How can we escape it? What cure have we for the cynical words that any one of us might be brought to utter?

"Christmas! So what!"

I think we must get back to the original pattern to see whether our sense of Christmas is cut along the right lines. Let us pry away the crusts that have grown around Christmas and see what is really there. We sing Irving Berlin's fetching ballad "I'm Dreaming of a White Christmas."

It may not snow and we need to find Christmas in that other song of the season, "O come, all ye faithful, joyful and triumphant. . . . O come let us adore Him, O come let us adore Him, Christ the Lord."

THE FIRST CHRISTMAS

Let us get back to the first Christmas as a pattern and see what made it a great day of joy and gladness. Some simple shepherds half asleep heard the hills ring with a music never before heard among the sons of men.

Does that not say that the loftiest things of God are open and available to the humblest and simplest of us? These shepherds heard the heavenly announcement, "Unto you is born this day in the City of David a Savior, which is Christ the Lord." How many centuries had poised, so to speak, on tiptoe to hear that word? How many sceptered kings and jeweled potentates have there been who would have given a king's ransom to be original hearers of the song of the angels, "Fear not, for behold, I bring you good tidings of great joy, which shall be to all people"?

How kind of God to let simple, common laborers be the first to hear the angels' anthem. How long in the choir practice rooms of heaven must the angels have rehearsed that song, revered imaginations wonder, and now some humble workmen doing the night shift hear that song. Does it not say supremely what God is forever saying, that "the highest truth is born in the humblest places and the richest blessings of God are clad in the simplest garb"?

Those of us who cannot pretend to possess sparkling wit and humor or blinding brilliance might well say, "Thank you, God, that the dearest things You have are not shut off from the likes of us."

The shepherds heard the song of the angels amidst the silent hills and dull surroundings of their daily work. Why will we not see this? Why will we not understand that there are no dull days, no ordinary life in a world where God lives and works? The Christmas story bears witness to the reality, the actuality, the living presence, if you will, of that unseen order which envelopes like a soft and delicate atmosphere our ruder, coarser world of sight and touch and thickness.

There is another world around this world of flesh and things. He is deaf and spiritually blind who does not know that above us and around us there is a finer, higher world of sweet mysteries, and peculiar joys, and excitements we cannot explain, and a gladness so real and so total we can only cry when it fills us.

There is another world. Handel said of that oratorio we love so well, *Messiah*, that it was, in a way, given to him. He said, "I thought I did see the heavens open and the Lord God on His throne."

"How did you think up those angels you described this morning?" said a parishoner in old Plymouth Church to Henry Ward Beecher when he came out of his pulpit one Sunday in my dear old borough, Brooklyn.

"Think them up? Man, I saw them," replied the preacher.

There is another world, and pity the man or woman who has not seen that world and heard the song of the angels. I am touched inexpressibly when I ponder the delicate and haunting visions of our slave forefathers in the midst of circumstances too harsh even for those of us who are their children to contemplate.

In bitter and inhumane circumstance, listen to them speak of another world, where the angels sing, enveloping their cruel, cold existence: "Looked all around me! Looked so fine! I asked the Lord if all were mine."[1]

HEAR THE ANGELS SING

Have you heard the song of the angels, the tidings of a world of beauty and wonder around this common life? Did you ever sit among your family and, strangely, feel a thankfulness that made you somewhat shamefacedly brush a tear away? You heard the angels sing!

Did you ever do something you knew you ought to do and then felt strangely cleansed and pure? You heard the angels sing!

Did you ever long for something good and worthwhile and despaired that it would even happen? And then it did and you felt so happy, so thankful. You heard the angels sing!

Or there was the death of someone for whom you cared, and even while you wept, a peculiar peace came over you as if someone was singing, "It is well with my soul." You felt sad, but with a hope and a peace you could not explain. You heard the angels sing!

Go, hear! The shepherds made a response to the tidings of the angels. They did not dismiss it all as fantasy. They said among themselves, "Let us now go even unto Bethlehem, and see this thing which is come to pass, which the Lord has made known to us."

Let us go and see. There are so many riches in Jesus Christ, the tidings of which have already come to us—and that we might have in fullness and joy if only we would "go and see."

Trace your blessings. Track what we call our good fortune and we shall see God clearly in our lives. Go back into the hills of your blessings, look for the mountain springs far up and away that are the source of the river of goodness flowing in your life, and you will cry, "I will lift up mine eyes unto the hills whence cometh these healing waters."

Think of today, or yesterday, or tomorrow; consider how many good things are in your life; and then look for that hand which has in its opening palm ten thousand blessings, and then thank Him, saying, "This is the Lord's doing; it is marvelous in our eyes. This is the day which the Lord has made, we will rejoice and be glad in it."

Praise God from whom all blessings flow,
Praise him, all ye creatures here below,
Praise him above, ye heavenly host,
Praise Father, Son and Holy Ghost.[2]

These shepherds did another thing. When they had heard and when they had gone to see, they went then to tell. Listen to the old story: "And when they had seen the Christ Child they made the news known abroad. And all they that heard wondered at those things which were told them by the shepherds." How we need to report to our friends the blessings we know and the joy of Christ.

Let me ask you to do one thing on Christmas morning, only one. Take down that precious little book which tells the story of Jesus. Read it again as if you had never seen it before. See again the world of spirit which envelopes our hard and cynical old world as subtly, but as surely, as the air fills the eternal spaces.

Hear again the song of the angels, God's own announcement of His care and His coming. Hear the angels say: "Fear not" the unseen places, the world of the Spirit; the doings of God are things of beauty, not of horror.

The unseen world—even unto death, before which men have crouched in terror—is a land of light and love, eloquent with glad tidings, aglow with the shining face of God Himself. Hear the music of the angels midst the ugly noises of corruption and cynicism and hatred and prejudice and war and anger and muggings and robbery.

Hear the song the angels sing: "Behold, I bring you good tidings. Good news! Jesus has come! Good news! Christ is born! Good news! Glory to God in the highest and on earth, peace to men of goodwill." It shall be! It shall be!

NOTES

1. "Every Time I Feel the Spirit," Negro spiritual.

2. "Praise God from Whom All Blessings Flow," Thomas Ken, Ph.D.

A Creative Christmas

FRANK A. THOMAS

BASED ON LUKE 2:7

It would be a good thing to remember during this Christmas season that popular culture would have you experience the mood of Christmas without doing the work of Christmas.

The mood of Christmas is shopping, reindeer, turkey, and egg nog, sleigh bells, Nat King Cole's "chestnuts roasting on the open fire," Santa Claus, mistletoe, and presents. But the work of Christmas is different from any of that.

But what is the work of Christmas? That question can best be answered with another question: what is the most important gift for you this Christmas?

In answering that question, some people may think of that television commercial where the husband puts a bow around a new car and presents it as a gift to his wife on Christmas day. Others may think about a diamond ring, a new iPod, Xbox, or laptop computer.

But the most important gift of Christmas is the gift of relationship—friendship, support, love, and caring. There is no more valuable gift at Christmas.

We tend to take relationships for granted—the fact that there are people in our lives who will care for us, who will give us time and attention. A good and loving relationship is a gift. But how can you give that gift for Christmas?

You may be thinking about the gift of relationship as some cheerful connection that stirs good and positive feelings. That's the mood of Christmas, but that's not the work of Christmas.

The work of Christmas—which yields the spirit of Christmas—is not only loving those who love and care for us. Christmas is also loving those who do not love you and caring for those who do not care for you. Christmas is giving the gift of relationship to somebody who may not reciprocate.

It's not easy loving and caring when those expressions are not returned. The easy thing to do at Christmas is to ignore unpleasantries and focus on trivia and frivolity, but Christmas is about peace on earth, goodwill, and joy to the world. What better time than Christmas to demonstrate love and peace in your home, your neighborhood, your job, your church, and your world?

I remember growing up and my parents bought us gifts, wrapped them, and placed them under the tree. We anxiously opened our gifts, only to find underwear, long johns, and pajamas. I remember saying to my parents, "This is not Christmas! You all have to buy this stuff anyway." Our parents gave us what they could afford. But didn't you just hate those kinds of Christmas presents when you were a kid?

Christmas is not about doing the things that you are supposed to do anyway, like buying pajamas and underwear and making it a Christmas gift. You are *supposed* to spend time with the people that you love and that you feel good about. That is the mood of Christmas, but not the work of Christmas.

The work of Christmas means being creative rather than trying to find Christmas at the shopping mall. Why is it that we think there is only one way to express love at Christmas—buying somebody a present? How unimaginative!

Mary and Joseph got creative about Christmas. There was no room for them at the inn, but that did not stop Christmas. They were poor and came to Bethlehem with no place to lay their heads, but that did not stop Christmas.

The first Christmas was about the gift of relationship: Joseph and Mary went out back to the stable, wrapped the baby in cloths, and lay him in a feeding trough as the shepherds and the Wise Men worshiped Him. They refused to be hindered by what they did not have at the first Christmas and focused instead on God's expression of love in the miraculous Gift that God had given humanity.

Why do we think that Christmas has to be our way or no way? I find in Luke 2:7 a creative Christmas. The first Christmas was about relationship—God came to humanity to bridge the chasm left by sin.

I remember one year when we wanted my son to come to Memphis for a family Christmas but we found out at the last minute that he could not come because of work responsibilities.

Deeply disappointed, I sat down and decided that maybe we needed to get creative at Christmas. If he could not come to us, we would go to him. So his mother, his sister, and I got in the car and drove ten hours to have Christmas with him. We gave him the gift of relationship.

There was no shopping involved and no credit card purchases the year that we went to visit my son. There was only the determination to find a way to be together and celebrate love and relationship.

You may think the holiday season is already stressful enough and wonder: "Why should I extend myself and go the extra mile?" You should do it because this is the true meaning of Christmas.

The babe in Bethlehem came because God got creative. God realized that we would not come to God, so God came to see about us, just as I went to see about my son.

God got creative and came to us to create right relationship. God had already created the world, but when that baby came into the world it was the creation of right relationship. It was a creative Christmas.

So, if God can extend God's self for you, why can't you extend yourself for God? This is the work of Christmas—to extend to others the love of God that you have already received by virtue of that babe in the manger.

A Good Place to Stop

KENNETH C. ULMER

BASED ON LUKE 2:1–14

When I was little, our family would take a vacation every year. We would go north one summer and south the next, as we had relatives in both parts of the country. Before the trip, my dad would always plot our route. After a while, of course, he knew the routes and we would take the same highway each year. But it always dawned on me that Daddy had already preplanned our stops; he had set our destination. It was clear that Daddy had planned to travel so far and then stop. He had timed and calculated everything; he knew how far he could go before we would run out of gas and need to re-fill. Over the years we would find ourselves stopping at the same places each trip, whether going north or south. Often Daddy would say, "We're coming on a good place to stop."

In studying the birth of Christ and the early portion of His life, you will notice that there were several preplanned stops. And through studying this Word, I promise that God will show you a couple of good places to stop along your journey into your destiny.

Luke 2 unfolds the story of how Jesus was born—how Caesar Augustus ordered a census for all of the nations governed by Rome; how Joseph went out from the city of Nazareth into Bethlehem because he was of the house and lineage of David. So, having taken Mary as his wife, Joseph left Nazareth to go into the region of Judea, into Bethlehem, located about six miles from Jerusalem.

The Bible says that Mary was "great with child." And so while they were there in Bethlehem, Mary brought forth her firstborn son and wrapped him in swaddling clothing, strips of linen, and laid him in a manger. There's some debate as to whether it was a manger or a feeding trough. Others say the manger was the edifice itself, that it was more like a cave, not so much like a barn, as we see sometimes in pictures. In those days, the manger was really more like an area carved out of stone.

But Mary laid him in a manger because there was no room for them in the inn. While Joseph and Mary were busy with the birth of Jesus, somewhere near Bethlehem was a group of shepherds keeping watch over their flock by night.[1]

Suddenly, the angel of the Lord came to the shepherds, and the glory of the Lord shone round about them. They were very afraid, but the angel said unto them, "Fear not, for I bring you good tidings of great joy which shall be to all people. For unto you is born this day in the city of David a savior which is Christ the Lord. And this shall be a sign unto you. You shall find the babe wrapped in swaddling clothes and lying in a manger." And suddenly there was with the angel a multitude of the heavenly host, praising God and saying, "Glory to God in the highest, and on earth, peace, good will toward men" (Luke 2:10–14, KJV).

What the shepherds witnessed was so magnificent that they decided to go and see what the heavenly commotion was all about. They left everything and quickly went to Bethlehem, where they found Mary and Joseph with the babe lying in a manger. After they had seen it, they made known everything that was told them concerning this child. When Mary heard what the shepherds said, she kept quiet and reflected on what they told to her. Meanwhile, the shepherds returned to their fields, along the way glorifying and praising God for all the things they had heard and seen.

A GOOD PLACE OF BIRTHING

Because everything took place in Bethlehem, that's a good place to stop. The name Bethlehem means "House of Bread." Sometimes you'll pass by a Jewish synagogue or temple and you'll see Beth-something, like Beth Israel. *Beth* simply means "house." *Lehem* means "bread," so Bethlehem means "House of Bread."

It was at Bethlehem that the babe was born. Now pay attention to this: your Bethlehem is the place where God has ordained what He has placed in you to come forth. John writes of Jesus: "In the beginning was the Word, and the Word was with God, and the Word was God . . . and the Word was made flesh" (John 1:1, 14, KJV). This "Word" *(logos)* has a two-sided meaning: it means "reason, idea"; and then it means "speech," or "declaration." Jesus was God speaking, but He was also God's idea. So Mary was carrying the idea of God in her womb.

God plants in you a God idea. A God idea will always surpass a good idea. The God idea is that which God places in you—something that grows in the womb of your spirit and is ordained to come forth at your Bethlehem. It is the place where your destiny unfolds. It's the place where God takes you—where the ideas, the call, the purpose He's planted in you comes forth.

A GOOD PLACE OF FRUITFULNESS

In the Old Testament, Micah 5 refers to this Bethlehem as Bethlehem-Ephrathah, meaning "Bethlehem in the district of Ephrathah." We might say it like, "Inglewood, in the county of Los Angeles." Ephrathah means "fruitfulness" or to be fruitful. So Mary and Joseph went to Bethlehem because it was not only the place where the divine idea of God would come forth, but also where the idea would become fruitful.

In the Bible, Bethlehem is not only called Bethlehem-Ephrathah, but it is also called Bethlehem of Judea, as opposed to a city called Bethlehem Zebulon, which is another region. Bethlehem of Judea means that Joseph and Mary left Nazareth and went through Judea on their way to Bethlehem.

Bethlehem is the place where God takes you that moves you into your destiny. It is the place that validates His purpose for your life, that speaks of the fruitfulness of your life under His hand. Bethlehem is the place of delivering and bringing forth what God has placed in you. It is the place where your labor will bring forth fruit to honor God. Bethlehem is the place of success, of productivity.

A GOOD PLACE TO PRAISE

But Bethlehem is also a place that is in Judea. Everything that happened in Bethlehem happened also in Judea. Judea, we might say, was a large state, and really kind of like California. So it would be like Inglewood, in the county of Los Angeles, in the state of California.

Bethlehem, located in the region of Ephrathah, in the state of Judea. The word "Judea" means "praise," and is related to the word "Judah."

So God brought them into a place of deliverance and a place of fruitfulness, and also caused them also to be in the context of praising Him. So it is praise where His journey begins. And His journey begins in Bethlehem, the place of bread, the place of fruitfulness, and the place of praise.

So Bethlehem is a place where you are not only productive, but are fed. It is a place where you are fed the Word. It is the place of the Word. In 1 Corinthians 10:16–17, Paul wrote that the church is a place of bread. So church ought to be a place where you come to be fed, a place that inspires you to be all that God has called you to be.

A GOOD PLACE TO GROW

After leaving Bethlehem, Luke 2:39 says, they returned to Galilee to their own city of Nazareth, and the child grew strong in spirit, filled with wisdom, and the grace of God was upon Him. It is just before that verse that Matthew inserts the journey to Egypt. Luke does not record that they were sent to Egypt to protect Jesus. Jesus was born in Bethlehem, but it was in Nazareth that He grew.

Each of the verbs in verse 40 is in the imperfect tense, which means it would be more accurately translated: "And the child was growing and the child was waxing [or getting strong] in spirit and the child was being filled with wisdom, and the grace of God was being on him."

Nazareth was also a good place to stop. Birth takes place in Bethlehem, but birth is not the end of the journey. He went to Nazareth to grow. The text implies that He grew physically, intellectually, and spiritually. The text implies that Jesus was growing up.

Some of us are growing older, but not necessarily growing up. The imperfect tense of the verbs in verse 40 speaks of a process. In other words, it is not something that happened overnight. You don't grow overnight. Children do not become grown overnight.

The text implies a process, and in that process Jesus was growing. He was growing in Nazareth—interesting play on words. The word "Nazareth" comes from the root word *nazare,* which meant "root." The prophet Isaiah said that the Messiah shall come as a root out of Jesse, who was the father of David (Isaiah 11:10).

The word for root means "stump" or "root that is beneath the soil," or "root that is remaining." It speaks of what happens when a tree is cut down and all that remains is the root. Isaiah not only speaks of the birth of Christ; he goes all the way to Calvary, and talks about the Suffering Servant who gives His life as a ransom for sin.

At Calvary He was cut down, but the remainder of that which was cut down was a root or a stump. The Christ was to grow out of the stump that was left. So when the Bible says He grew in Nazareth, it's an interesting play on words that He grew in the place of a stump.

Somebody knows what it's like to be cut down—plans, dreams, ideas, visions, and goals, for whatever reason, short-circuited, waylaid, changed, altered, cut down. Now, here's the catch. Where the devil messed up was, he may have cut down the tree, but he should have uprooted the stump. Because if you've got a stump left, if you've got enough faith to make a root, if you've got enough vestige of hope left, you've got enough for a whole new crop to come up on.

God may have sent you to a place called Nazareth, a place where you don't have anything left but a stump. It's the place where it seems dark and discouraging. It's when your plans and dreams seem to have come to nothing. Yet before it's over, God does something underneath the soil. God does something to the root.

I don't care who's cut you down, God says you've got enough stump left to go on and grow and bring Him glory and be productive. God takes you to a place where sometimes all you have left is a stump so He can raise you up the way He intends.

When Jesus went to Nazareth, He got stronger in spirit; that's underneath the skin. God was doing something in Him that folks outside couldn't see. That means, as Paul says, God was strengthening Jesus in the inner man. God was making Him do push-ups and pump iron on the inside.

Not only was Jesus growing stronger in spirit, He was being

filled with wisdom, which is the ability to activate knowledge to a positive end. Wisdom is not just taking more notes; wisdom is not just getting more information. Wisdom is what you do with it—how you activate it, how you dissect it, and how you use it.

Wisdom is the God-given ability to handle life. It is taking information and processing it to a positive end. Luke also says, "The grace of God was upon him." The word "grace" means "favor." I don't know of any other theological concept I struggle with more than favor. I struggle with favor; it is such a fascinating dimension of the nature of God. It is when God moves on your behalf.

Favor is not just the idea of grace in the sense of God granting you what you don't deserve; it's also God moving on your behalf. It is favor with God, but it's also God granting you favor with people. It's when God prepares people for you, because with the power of God in your life, everybody can't handle you. That has to be something that God does in their spirit, to get them ready for what He's already done in your life. It's the favor of God.

NAZARETH IS A GOOD PLACE to stop. How's it growing? How are you growing in your spirit? Are you seeing the favor of God and the wisdom of God, giving you the ability to handle stuff that you could never handle by yourself? It is the favor and wisdom of God that gives you the ability to see yourself handling stuff that, if you saw someone else in that situation, you would wonder how could they handle it. How's he going to make it through that? How's she going to bounce back?

Nathaniel, one of Jesus' disciples, asked the question, "Can any good thing come out of Nazareth?" (John 1:46, KJV). Some conclude that Nathaniel was asking, "Can anything good come out of a place like Nazareth?"

Nazareth had a reputation as a wicked city, a godless city. But there's no evidence in history, sacred or secular, that validates Nazareth as an evil city. In other words, it was just a rumor that Nazareth was bad, with never a shred of historical or archaeological evidence to validate that claim. So to come through Nazareth also symbolizes coming through the rumors and suspicions that folk place on you without really knowing who you are.

Another implication is in the sense of the prophetic position of Nazareth. Nazareth is never mentioned in the Old Testament. Bethlehem is mentioned, as are Jerusalem and Judea. So when Nathaniel asked the question, it meant, "Can any good thing come out of this town with no theological, prophetic, or historical significance?" Saying that nothing good has ever come out of a place doesn't mean it's a bad place; it just never produced anything good.

So the question is, can any good thing come out of a place that's never produced a good thing? I love how Philip answers Nathaniel: "Come and see." In other words, Philip was saying, "I'll show you somebody," pointing to Jesus.

God wants to take you to Nazareth and show the world that if it looks at you, it'll see somebody who came out. It'll see someone who came through. It'll see someone who came from a place where no good has ever come.

God says when you go to Nazareth because of His favor, He is able to bring something good out of the place that has never produced good. He is able to allow you to go through stuff that, under any normal circumstances, should have wiped you out. But because of His favor on you and His giving you wisdom, He puts you on display: "Look over there! I'll show you somebody. She's been through something, but she's better for it." "He's had to undergo something, but he came out the other side."

God wants to make you an example. God wants to show you to the world and say, "She made it."

Further into chapter 2, Luke tells us that Jesus' parents went to Jerusalem every year at the feast of Passover. When He was twelve years old, they went up to Jerusalem to celebrate the Passover. Jerusalem is a good place to stop. Jerusalem is the place of the Temple, the place that symbolizes the presence of God.

A GOOD PLACE TO WORSHIP

Joseph, Mary, and Jesus went up to Jerusalem to celebrate the Passover. Every year the Jews would go to Jerusalem to reflect on their journey. The Passover symbolized the celebration of God delivering their forebears out of Egypt.

Jerusalem is a place to celebrate the favor of God, demonstrated by the fact that you are able to celebrate the goodness of God. The Passover celebration recalled God's favor in allowing the angel of death to pass over the Israelites. Had he not passed over their forebears, they would not have been able to celebrate. So they went to Jerusalem to celebrate God's favor, mercy, and God's grace upon their ancestors and upon them. Jerusalem is the place of worship.

The journey began in Bethlehem, a good place to stop, and progressed to Jerusalem, a place of worship and another good place to stop.

DURING THE CHRISTMAS SEASON, admittedly, there have been times when I've celebrated the holidays without giving much attention to the biblical account of Christmas. In other words, I often have celebrated Christmas, but not meditated on God's revelation of what Christmas is all about and the blessing that God released into the world when He sent His Son.

Don't miss Him! Celebrate, yes—parties, family, food, friends, fun, yes, yes, yes. But don't miss the opportunity to lift Him up.

I met a Muslim man who kept telling me, "Bishop, you've blessed me. God has blessed me through you, and I've seen your faith." The man was about to open a bank, and you have to have big bank to open a bank. The man told me about how he had seen our ministry struggle and the opposition we'd faced. But then he said, "What I've seen in you has inspired me in my business. I saw you come through opposition and ridicule. I've been through some hard times in my business, and every time I thought about what you went through. What I've seen in you has blessed me."

Don't miss Jesus! A Muslim and a Christian were talking about Jesus and salvation and Christ and the blood of the Lamb—all because he saw something in me.

That's what God wants to do with you! There are some people on your job who cannot figure you out. They don't know what makes you tick. They see you take a licking and keep on ticking. They cannot figure out what's up with that. It's God giving you an open door.

You have an opening; don't miss it. Give a testimony for Jesus. Don't tell them how smart you are; say a word for Jesus. Don't tell them how many degrees you have; say a word for Jesus! Don't tell them how strong you've been; say a word for Jesus! Don't miss Him!

Bethlehem is a great place to stop. Nazareth, a place to grow, is a great place to stop. Jerusalem, a great place to stop, is a place to worship Him, because He has passed over because of God's favor.

You are alive today because of His favor. You've come through another year, not because you were so ingenious, creative, cool, and smart, but because of favor. There are people who faced what you've gone through and didn't make it.

In this season of celebrating the birth of Christ, I will not miss the Christ of Christmas. My life is a testimony of His love, His mercy, His grace, and His favor.

I am a walking miracle. I should have been taken out a long time ago; had no business getting this far in the first place. I'm a walking miracle!

When Jesus left Jerusalem at age twelve, he went back to Nazareth. Why? Because there was still some growing to do. That means God is not finished with you yet. After you worship Him, you go back and grow some more.

You can't grow unless you eat, and so you take bread with you. He is the Bread of Heaven—out of Bethlehem, the House of Bread.

When the Magi came to Bethlehem, they gave Him gifts. Won't you bring Him a gift? The greatest gift that you can give Him is the gift of yourself.

NOTE

1. The Bible says the shepherds were watching their flock by night. The fact that they were watching their flock by night implies that it was probably not in December, because it is unlikely that the shepherds would graze sheep in the field in winter weather. So more than likely, Christ was born in late summer, maybe early fall. Some have speculated that Christ was born as early as May or as late as September. But unless it was an unusually warm winter, the birth of Jesus likely did not occur in December.

God's Timing and Our Timing

William D. Watley

BASED ON LUKE 2:6

In detailing events relating to the birth of Christ, Luke explains, "While they were there, the time came for her to deliver her child."

While Joseph and Mary were where? While Joseph and Mary were in Bethlehem, far away from their home, far away from their family and friends, the time came for her to deliver her child.

While Joseph and Mary were in a city that was so crowded with people they could not find suitable lodging, the time came for her to deliver her child.

While Joseph and Mary were on a trip that was anything but pleasurable, the time came for her to deliver her child. The delivery of the child might have been more timely if Joseph and Mary had been on a business trip that they expected to make money from, or if they were on vacation in a very relaxed atmosphere. However, the trip they were on was one that would cost them money, and was anything but pleasurable because it was one over which they had no control.

A decree had gone out from the Roman emperor that the world, as he knew it, that portion of the world over which he had authority and control, should be taxed. Everyone was to go to the place of his or her birth to register for taxation. Joseph and Mary were in Bethlehem because they had no choice. While they were in a city where they had no friends and family, and that was so over-crowded they did not have suitable lodging; while they were on a trip that would cost them money, and one they would not have made if they had a choice in the matter, the time came for her to deliver her child.

As beautiful as the Christmas story is, the fact of the matter is that the Savior was born at a really inconvenient time. Had any one of us been in charge, we probably would have scheduled Jesus' birth at a more convenient time. We probably would have chosen a time when Joseph would not have been under the stress of trying to find lodging for his pregnant wife, when Mary would have had more comfortable surroundings and the Lord Jesus would have had a more suitable environment to lay his head.

When one considers the mean conditions in which Jesus was born, it seems to me that God could have picked another time and place to bring his only begotten Son into the world, particularly when one considers how long the coming of Jesus had been proph-esied and anticipated. Centuries before the birth of Christ, the prophet Isaiah had declared, "A child has been born for us, a son given to us; authority rests upon his shoulders; and he is named Wonderful Counselor, Mighty God, Everlasting Father, Prince of Peace" (9:6, NKJV).

Centuries before he was born, Joshua had seen the captain of the Lord's hosts (Joshua 5:14–15, KJV). Centuries before he was born Jeremiah had talked about a mighty battle-ax who would be the weapon that we could wield in times of battle (51:20).

Centuries before He was born Ezekiel had seen a wheel in the middle of a wheel that was the center of everything that moved (10:10).

Centuries before he was born Daniel had seen a stone hewn out of the mountains without human hands, which would bring down every other mountain and would become a mountain itself that would fill the whole earth (Daniel 2). With all of the prophetic expectation announcing and heralding His coming, one would think that the advent of God's long-anticipated Deliverer would come in a more glorious and powerful way. When one looks at the conditions in which Jesus was born, one wonders why God chose to bring forth Jesus at that time and in that place.

The timing of God is often a mystery to those who believe and follow God. More than one believer has looked at certain occurrences in his or her life and asked not only, "Why Lord?" but also, "Why now?"

More than one believer has asked, "Why is this happening to me at this point in my life, my career, or my marriage? Lord, you know everything that I am going through. Why are you adding this load to the burdens that I am already carrying? Why is this happening to our family at this time?"

Or, "Lord, why isn't this happening at this time? Lord, you know how much I need to be delivered from this situation. Why are you taking so long to move or to answer my prayer?"

"Lord, you know how badly I need a job. When are you going to open up a door?"

"Lord I am up to my neck and I'm about to drown. When are you coming to see about me?"

"Lord, I have prayed and fasted. I have studied Your Word, and I have claimed the promise. What more do I need to do to see some movement regarding this situation?"

"Lord, the situation is going from bad to worse while my enemies continue to gloat about my defeat and my downfall. How much longer and how much more will I have to endure before you move?"

"Lord, I have been struggling with this problem and trying to climb this mountain a long time. When will I see a breakthrough?"

A minister was pacing up and down in his study in a very agitated state. When his wife happened to walk in and observe him, she asked what was wrong. He looked at her and said, "I am in a hurry and God is not. I need God to move right away and God seems to be taking God's own sweet time."

One of the greatest challenges of a believer's faith walk is trying to come to grips with God's timing. Sometimes it seems that God is out of sync with what needs to happen, according to our timetable. That seems to be the case in the text. According to the Word of God, "In those days a decree went out from Emperor Augustus that all the world should be registered. This was the first registration and was taken while Quirinius was Governor of Syria. All went to their towns to be registered. Joseph also went from the town of Nazareth in Galilee to Judea, to the City of David called Bethlehem, because he was descended from the house and family of David. He went to be registered with Mary, to whom he was engaged and who was expecting a child. While they were there, the time came for her to deliver her child" (Luke 2:1–5, RSV).

In those days, when the emperor Augustus and the empire that he ruled were at the height of their power . . . Jesus was born.

In those days, when the world as they knew it was focused on the edicts and whims of Rome . . . Jesus was born.

In those days, when there seemed to be no end to Roman tyranny and power . . . Jesus was born.

In those days, when the religious leadership had lost their prophetic zeal so that they could safeguard their own personal kingdoms and fortunes and maintain good relationships with the government so that they could continue to get their "faith-based" grants . . . Jesus was born.

In those days, when traditional religion had lost much of its fire and its focus and had become so much form and ritual . . . Jesus was born.

In those days, when many of the faithful were being lulled to sleep with the pabulum of a prosperity gospel and noisy praise that had no real power . . . Jesus was born.

In those days, when the rich were getting richer as the poor were getting poorer as they labored under excess and heavy taxation and exploitation . . . Jesus was born.

In those days, when there had been no prophetic voice in the land for over four hundred years, God brought forth Jesus to establish the fact that God's power was so great that even when evil is at the height of its game, God is still God. God is so awesome that God can shake evil with its military might using a baby who was born to a mother on a dirt floor in an animal shelter.

Since God is still God, anytime that God moves is the right time. God's miracles happen at any time and at any season because God's power works independently of us.

A discouraged and embattled minister who was undergoing a vicious attack in the media called one of my spiritual mentors for counsel and comfort. The minister wondered if his reputation would ever be restored because he did not see how he could possibly experience a comeback without his reputation. After listening to the minister, the mentor advised, "Sometimes God has to show us that He can bring us back without using what we think we need to come back. Sometimes you don't need what you think you need for God to do what God wants to do in your life."

When the enemy has us under attack, our restoration, our recovery, our resurrection is not in our hands but in God's hands. God is still able to do whatever God wants to do when God wants to do it, no matter what we have or do not have. Your restoration is not in your hands; it is in God's hands.

People who tell us that we are down too far to get back up, and that we are so damaged that we will never be what we once were, don't know about the power of our God.

People who tell us that our life is over and that we might as well get accustomed to living in the shadow of what we used to be don't know about the power of our God.

The hellhounds that attack us may be beyond our power, but they are not beyond the power of God.

The sickness that afflicts our bodies and our minds may be beyond our power, but it is not beyond the power of God.

There is no such thing as an irreversible or incurable illness in God's sight. The addiction, the depression, the guilt, the shame, the habits that have held us in captivity for all these years may be beyond our power to control and contain, but they are not beyond the power of God.

In the name of Jesus every person can be free! We can be healed and we can be delivered. The devil is a liar! God still rules and Jesus Christ is still Lord over all of life and over death itself forever and ever.

We think we need a certain amount of money. We think we need to have certain people on our side. We think we need to be a certain age or at a certain station. We think we need to have a mate or a particular mate to get to where God wants to take us or to have what God wants us to have. Whether we have what we think we need or not, God is able to restore us, bless us, make us, keep us, fix us, save us, deliver us, make ways for us, work miracles for us, no matter what the outward circumstances of our lives.

The circumstances of our lives are problematic for us but not for God. God is God, no matter the circumstances. God is not moved by conditions; God is moved by faith and by obedience.

As Joseph and Mary journeyed in faith and in obedience, God brought forth Jesus despite the conditions in which they found themselves. Without the comforts of home, family, and friends, without proper medical attention, on the floor of an animal shelter, far away from whomever and whatever Mary and Joseph thought they would need to bring forth Jesus, God brought forth His only begotten Son.

When Joseph and Mary arrived in Bethlehem, the time came for her to deliver her baby. Centuries before they arrived, though, Micah had prophesied that the Messiah would come from Bethlehem, even though it was one of the least significant of the cities of the land (5:2). God's timing is always lined up with God's Word, and with God's long-range plan for our lives, which fits in with God's long-range plan for the world.

God told Jeremiah, "I know the plans I have for you . . . plans for your welfare and not for your harm, to give you a future with hope" (29:11, NRSV). We may not know God's plans, but God does, and we can trust God's plans. We may not be able to trust the plans of others, but we can trust God's plans.

The ancient Greeks had two ways of measuring time: *chronos* and *kairos*. *Chronos* was regular time, measured by weeks, months, and years. But *kairos* was a critical moment, a special time for transformation and action. Our birth date was *chronos,* but the time when we were born again was *kairos.* The date that we met someone special was *chronos,* but the day we fell in love was *kairos.* We keep time by *chronos,* but God moves by *kairos.* God moves when the time is right to demonstrate His sovereignty in all situations. When we are waiting on God to move we are waiting in *chronos;* but God acts in *kairos,* when there is no doubt that God is moving.

Only God could bring forth a baby king, born on a dirt floor when Caesar Augustus was at the height of his reign, who will one day reign in the same place where Caesar Augustus thought that he was invincible.

"In those days a decree went out from Caesar Augustus that all the world should be taxed." That's *chronos.* "This was the first registration and was taken while Quirinius was governor of Syria. All went to their own town to be registered." That's *chronos.* "Joseph also went from the town of Nazareth in Galilee to Judea, to the City of David. He went to be registered with Mary to whom he was engaged and who was expecting a child." That's *chronos.* "While they were there, the time came for her to deliver her first child." That's *kairos*. "And she gave birth to her firstborn son and wrapped him in bands of cloth, and laid him in a manger, because there was no place for them in the inn." That's *kairos*.

As Luke 2 continues to unfold the Christmas story: "In that region there were shepherds living in the fields, keeping watch over their flock by night. Then an angel of the Lord stood before them, and the glory of the Lord shone around them, and they were terrified. But the angel said to them, Do not be afraid, for see—I am bringing you good news of great joy for all the people: to you is born this day in the City of David a Savior, who is the Messiah, the Lord. This will be a sign for you: you will find a child lying in a manger. And suddenly there was with the angel a multitude of the heavenly host, praising God and saying, 'Glory to God in the highest heaven, and on earth peace among those whom he favors.'" That's *kairos*.

"When the angels had left them and gone into heaven, the shepherds said to one another, 'Let us go now to Bethlehem and see this thing that has taken place, which the Lord has made known to us.'" That's *kairos*.

"So they went with haste and found Mary and Joseph, and the child lying in the manger. When they saw this, they made known what had been told to them about the child." That's *kairos*.

"But Mary treasured all these words and pondered them in her heart. The shepherds returned, glorifying God for all they had heard and seen, as it had been told them." That's *kairos*.

Accept the Gift

STEVE WENDE

BASED ON MATTHEW 1:18–25

Christmas is, for me, a time to celebrate with others the fact that God comes seeking after us. God comes searching after us to give us a gift that we can find in no other way. It is the most important gift we can ever receive.

To talk about a God seeking after us sounds a little odd, a little upside down. Usually, when people in our culture talk about God, they talk about their searching after God. People talk about the fact that they are seeking God, that they have questions and they want to find answers. When people talk this way, there are always other folks who, of course, want to provide those answers.

People will say, "Well, I want to tell you about God," and they write philosophies and publish books and go on television and write articles for the paper, and all that is fine. I do not want to be critical of anybody, I just want to point out that we are so small and God is so big, that if we go searching after God to try and figure Him out, it's going to take a long time. And so when somebody wants to tells us who God is, his or her opinion, we almost have to ask, "Why should we listen to you?"

When you get right down to it, if we're going to try to figure out God and figure out how we connect with God, your opinion or mine really doesn't do the trick. What we really need is for God to tell us who God is. What we really need is for God to reach out to us—to come seeking us—to tell us how we connect with God. Anything else is going to be inadequate.

That's what the first Christmas was all about.

Two thousand years ago, God reached down to this earth to reveal Himself to us. In the midst of a planet of people arguing about who God is, God changed the conversation, brought light into the darkness, and let us all see for ourselves by becoming flesh in Jesus.

Years ago, when I was a Boy Scout, we went to Philmont Scout Ranch in New Mexico. One of the things we did was go down into an old, out-of-use gold mine. Our guides took us deep into the mine; it was very dark. After a point, they said, "We're going to turn out the lights. Don't worry about it, just put your hand on the shoulder of the boy in front of you."

After they turned out the lights, they said, "Just walk straight forward. You can't be hurt; the ground is level. We're going to take you into a different place."

And so we walked through the dark—pitch dark—into a different part of the cave. We could feel the cool wind blowing on our faces. Then they said, "Now just kind of feel around and see if you can figure out where you are."

And so we very carefully felt around and discovered an ore cart, an old pickax, an old shovel, and what we thought was a hurricane lantern. Because our pupils had dilated after being in the dark all this time, they said, "Shield your eyes. We're going to turn on the lights and let you see where you are."

When the lights came on, we opened our eyes to the most beautiful, magnificent cavern I had ever imagined in my life—sta-lactites, stalagmites, and colors of all sorts. What I remember most about that experience is what we had discovered while we were feeling around in the dark. We actually had figured out some things accurately. Yet, if you take all the things we had accurately discovered in the dark about that space, it was only maybe 2 percent of the total. We had missed the other 98 percent, which suddenly became visible in the light.

At Christmas, God acted through Jesus to turn on the light so that as the world looked at Jesus, it could see the other 98 percent of the core truths about God that, until then, we could argue about, disagree about, but never resolve. Because no one had seen God face-to-face. When we talk about Christmas, we're talking about God reaching out through Jesus, so that in the midst of this world unresolved about God, arguing about God, not able to reach God, God could reach out to us. He could show us Himself, reveal Himself to us, and so begin to clarify who He was. But then in addition, God is so good, as He reached out to us in that way, He not only told us something, showed us something, He also gave us something.

Can you remember as a child thinking that when you got older you wouldn't be afraid? Can you remember when you were a child thinking that when you got older you would never feel lost or alone? Can you remember thinking when you were a child that when you got older you would never tremble at the darkness? Now you're older; yet everyone who reads this message knows what it's like to feel lost and alone in the face of a cruel creation.

When God reached out to this world at Christmas, He came to do more than show us something and tell us something. In His goodness, God also came to give us something; namely, in the midst of a broken and isolated creation, filled with people pushing away the love for which they yearn, He came to give us Himself.

God gave us Himself so that, as we would accept Him into our lives, taking His hand and letting Him walk with us, leader and Lord, friend and lover of our souls—as we would allow that to happen, He could fill an emptiness inside of us that could be filled in no other way. And we, who are so often lost and alone, could be found—found in our Father's arms and found in our Father's heart.

Throughout the Christmas season we buy presents for other people and they buy gifts for us. But Christmas is about another present, a gift that God personally came to give. It is the only present that matters. It is the present of God wanting to give His heart to you, that His heart might dwell inside you, that you are willing to receive His hand of leadership and love in yours.

And if you will not take that present, there's not a single other present that anybody's going to give you that matters. But if you accept that present, if you will keep His hand in yours all the days of your life, you will have all that you'll ever need.

It can be scary at first, when you begin to realize what Christmas is really all about—that God really is reaching down from highest heaven into your heart to offer you the gift of Himself and asking you to take Him by the hand. It can be incredibly scary to reach out and receive that hand and put your hand in His. In this topsy-turvy world it can be very difficult to keep your hand in His and not let it go. But it is crucially important—for your future, and for your life—that you do so.

One of my favorite authors is Dr. Leo Buscaglia, who has gone on to be with the Lord. One of my favorites, of all the stories he told, took place when he went in the hospital for surgery. Dr. Buscaglia was not what the doctors would call a good patient. He was offended at being sick and definitely did not want to go in for surgery. He decided that the best way to deal with this was to pretend it wasn't going to happen. He told everybody who knew him, all his friends and family, to stay away; he did not want visitors after surgery. He emphatically told the medical staff that he did not want visitors after surgery.

Dr. Buscaglia recalled that he woke up after surgery feeling like he'd been hit by a truck! The first thing he wanted was visitors. He wanted visitors desperately. The medical staff had told him that physically he was going to be okay; but he felt so alone, so isolated. He felt the despair welling up inside him. But he had told everybody, "No visitors." They even had a big yellow "No Visitors" sign on his glass cubicle in the intensive care ward.

But he wanted so badly to talk to somebody. He wanted to reach out, but he had tubes going down his mouth so he couldn't speak a word. He was lying in his hospital bed feeling the despair rising up as if it would drown him when, all of a sudden, he saw a head moving over the glass pane. He recognized the head as belonging to one of his oldest and dearest friends. This man stood over six feet tall, but he was leaning over as if he could become inconspicuous. The friend had snuck into the intensive care ward, avoiding detection by the nurses. He had ripped the "No Visitors" sign off the door and threw it on the ground and walked over to see Leo.

Dr. Buscaglia, remembering that moment, said, "When that friend took me by the hand, it was as if life itself was flowing into my veins. I tried to say, 'Thank you for coming even though I had insisted that you not come.' But I couldn't talk because I had tubes going down my mouth. All I could do was burble. Finally my friend reached over, slapped me on the lips gently, and said, 'Oh, hush up, Leo. I know you told me not to come, but I didn't believe you. I decided I was going to come anyway.'"

Christmas is about God looking down on a planet filled with sinful people, papered with No Visitors signs, and saying, "I'm going to come anyway."

Christmas is about God being born in Bethlehem to a nation impoverished, subject to another nation, a terrible situation filled with pain, and saying, "I'm going to come anyway."

Christmas is about that boy growing up into a man, reaching out to the leaders of the nation and being rejected, and having them plot His death, but saying, "I'm going to come anyway."

Christmas is about the cross. Christmas is about that man being nailed to the cross and then laid in a tomb with a stone rolled over it to seal it shut, and then kicking that tomb aside like a child kicking a No Visitors sign on the floor and saying, "I'm going to come anyway."

Christmas is about God reaching out to this world through that man—that He might offer you the gift of Himself, so that as you take His hand in yours you may receive His heart into yours—so your future might be surrounded by His love forever.

Christmas is nothing less than the invasion of this planet by grace and God saying to you that He wants to bring that grace into your heart. Please, with all that is within me, I plead with you to accept the gift. Put your hand in His. Never let it go, and He will put heaven in your heart. For you, Christmas will come.

PRAYER

O God, we have looked forward to this Christmas season all year long. O Lord, the darkness that overcomes our self-generated imitations of Your light is shattered by the bright and shining star of Bethlehem.

Help us to hunger for Your presence again—in the ways Your people sought Your presence, eagerly awaiting Your interruption of hope and peace, of joy and love—into our daily existence. We pray that the light of Bethlehem's manger will be received by all upon whom Your favor has shone. For the downtrodden, grant energy for another time to trust; for the hungry, bring the bread of life; for the thirsty, pour out your righteousness as the prophet Amos foretold.

Lead us to look for Your divine message in all things. Like the shepherds, grant us the desire to search for that great joy and good news. Like Joseph, speak to us in our dreams when the only thing we can really claim is the love we share with one another, that we might know Your divine will. Like Mary, help us to live as a people who believe that all things are possible with You, and that without You, nothing is possible.

May Your Holy Spirit plant within us an insatiable desire for Your righteousness to reign on earth. Not through somebody else, not through another idea, but through each one of us. We do not yield the language of our faith, O God, to anyone; for this is Your night.

You are the God of Abraham and Sarah, and so we say, "Merry Christmas." You are the God of Ruth and Naomi, so we shall greet one another in the name of Christ. You are the God of our mothers and our fathers, and we boldly stand on the shoulders of history and proclaim every fiber of our being that makes this a holiday.

Draw us ever nearer to Bethlehem's manger. For this we humbly pray in the name of Emmanuel, God who has chosen to be with us. Amen.

The Value of Creating Family Traditions

PAULA WHITE

BASED ON DEUTERONOMY 4:9–10; 11:18–19
Christmas is a time of establishing and celebrating many traditions. There is great value in taking the time to establish traditions for your family. Now, as never before, the family is under attack by the enemy. We need to strengthen our families, and one of the greatest ways research teaches us is through building and creating traditions. There's such value in that.

Family gives us a sense of belonging. It gives us a sense of security, of identity, of connecting with one another. Whatever the makeup of your family, whether it's a single mother, an elderly couple, or whether it is young children with two parents, I want to help you be the strong family that God intends.

The Bible declares this in Deuteronomy 11:18–19 (NKJV): "Therefore you shall lay up these words of mine in your heart and in your soul, and bind them as a sign on your hand, and they shall be as frontlets between your eyes. You shall teach them to your children."

Deuteronomy 4:9–10 (NKJV) says, "Only take heed to yourself, and diligently keep yourself, unless you forget the things that your eyes have seen and lest they depart from your heart all the days of your life. And teach them to thy sons and thy sons' sons."

In other words, what God was telling us is, "Traditions: create them for your family." He was speaking specifically through the Word of God.

Here is what a tradition is: a practice or belief that creates positive feelings, handed down from generation to generation.

The reason I say it creates positive feelings is that people always return to the place of pleasure. When you create a family tradition—and this is the value of it—tradition brings a sense of connectedness; it brings a sense of oneness.

You see, families begin to say stuff like, "We always put sauerkraut on our mashed potatoes. That's one of our family traditions."

Why? My husband, Randy, did it as a young boy. His grandmother did it; his great-grandmother did it. And so it's our family tradition, not only to have mashed potatoes, but to have sauerkraut with mashed potatoes.

Then, of course, many people know about one of our greatest family traditions that we so look forward to. Our children are grown, my youngest is twenty; we have three grandchildren. But even now on Christmas we still run into the family room, where the Christmas tree is. Before the first gift is opened, before any celebrating takes place, before we have a meal, or before we even light up the tree, the first thing we do is gather together and Randy prays over us. Then we all begin to thank God for the many blessings He has given us.

We give thanksgiving through prayer to God and we pray together as a family. Then, Randy opens up the Bible and reads the Christmas story from the first two chapters of the gospel of Matthew. It is our family tradition.

Now, I can't tell you every gift I've gotten every Christmas. I can remember some things—a few outfits here, a piece of jewelry there. But the one thing I can always remember—always—is our family reading the Christmas story together.

It's our tradition. I remember us praying together. It's the tradition. And I remember that there can't be a meal without potatoes and sauerkraut. It's the tradition.

In other words, family traditions help to create and establish values. Values cultivate connection and promote a sense of identity, a feeling of belonging. Values also promote a feeling of safety and security by providing a place of familiarity. In other words, it's a landing pad.

I think there's not a better time than the holidays to begin creating traditions. The number one holiday when we create traditions to help us stay connected is Christmas, but you can do it at any time, all year long.

A family tradition might be eating a meal together every day. Do you know that by eating together you lower the chances of your child becoming addicted to any kind of disorder, whether that is alcoholism, drug addiction, or an eating disorder?

You may ask, "Just by having a family meal together" Yes. Sharing a meal together as a family also provides a place to communicate, to talk and say, "How was your day?" It becomes a routine and something of value that keeps your family connected.

In a society that's tearing us apart, one in which everyone's going their own way and doing this and doing that, I urge you at Christmastime to create a tradition.

Like what, Paula? Oh, bake cookies together. Every single year maybe you build a gingerbread house together and you eat it on Christmas Day. Or maybe you go down to the shelter and feed somebody and minister to them, as we do on Thanksgiving; that is our family tradition. It's a family tradition: before we eat our family meal, we take the first several hours of our day and feed people who are less fortunate than we. It's our way of saying, "Thank You, God, for all the blessings."

Now, what are some practical ways to do this? Here are some practical suggestions:

1. Aim for a moderate number of traditions. In other words, don't try to take on everything. Say, "We're going to do one thing." Negotiate with the family; do a survey. Say, "Johnny, what would you like to do? Susie, what you would like to do?" Remember, it's creating a place of pleasure that produces positive feelings. People always return to the point of pleasure. It creates that memory. You can walk in a house and smell a smell and it will take you back to a tradition: *Sniff.* "I remember this; it's just like Grandma's." We've learned that people who have traditions survive tough times a whole lot better than people who don't. It becomes the fabric that—even during difficult times like the death of a loved one, or even through a divorce or something that is so difficult and devastating—helps keep us connected.

2. Some more practical ideas are to establish new traditions. If certain ones aren't working, then go back and ask, "What would I like to do differently?"

3. Make sure that you have spiritual traditions. That's what God taught us: teach your children, because traditions show a sense of your value of faith. People establish traditions like setting out cookies for Santa Claus, and all that's fun and all that's great. But don't forget to always remember that somewhere in the process of establishing your traditions, your children are emulating not what you say, but what they see you do. How do they see your faith in action? Create a tradition that shows not just what you say about God, but what you really believe about God. If I'm connected to someone, I can believe that I'm safe and secure; and out of that security, I can do just about anything I set my mind to. And we know the greatest place of security.

It's not in the hands of another human being, but in the arms of Jesus Christ. That's why He says, "Through me you can do all things."

God has such great things for you and your family. I believe there's a miracle wrapped in a package waiting for you to unwrap it.

You ask, "Paula, what unwraps my miracle?" The answer is, your faith. And if you will take your faith and just open up the gifts that God has for you, you are going to be astonished at how transformed everything in your life is going to be.

So from Pastor Randy, my children, our grandchildren, the whole White family, we say to you, Merry Christmas and Happy holidays. God bless you.

An Amazing Contrast

Marcos Witt

BASED ON ISAIAH 9:6

Isaiah poses an amazing contrast in his prophecy: "For unto us a child is born . . . and the government shall be upon his shoulder." That's an amazing contrast when you think about it—a child and a government.

When many of us think about Christmas and we celebrate the season, we reflect on images of the Christ Child lying in the manger, wrapped in swaddling cloths. We talk about the Christ Child and we see images of the babe, not really considering that the child grew up to be a powerful man who changed the course of history, and He continues to change the course of human existence to this day.

That child born in the stable became a conquering king, and the Bible says the government shall be upon His shoulder. He's the King of Kings and the Lord of Lords; the government is on His shoulder and He's no longer a child lying in a manger. He is now a King seated at the right hand of God on an eternal throne of righteousness. All power and authority has been given to Him. He's been given a name that is above every name.

If you ever worry about how things might be going in your life, you just need to remember that the government is on His shoulders. See, a government is an entity that governs, and because He's seated on the throne, you can rest assured that He's governing. His righteousness is correct and just.

If you've ever been worried about your family or the direction of one of your family members, turn it over to the King of Kings—because the government is on His shoulders.

If you've ever been concerned about your finances or your future, turn them over to the King—the government is on His shoulders. I can guarantee you that your next year is going to be even better than this year—because the government is on His shoulders. Greater things and greater days are in store for you because the government is on His shoulders.

If only we could just see the baby in the manger, seated now on the throne, and understand that He is the one who governs in all righteousness and authority, you and I would live much more peaceful lives.

WONDERFUL COUNSELOR

Isaiah continued his prophecy: "And he shall be called Wonderful, Counselor." Have you ever been in need of counsel? Have you ever needed advice that you could trust and depend on? The advice I can give you this morning is to get as close as you possibly can to the Wonderful Counselor because His counsel is good. He will give you good advice. He will point you in the right direction.

The Bible says He will put your feet on a rock, and you will not be moved. He will give you the counsel you need to guide your family in the direction they need to go, because He is the Wonderful Counselor.

MIGHTY GOD

Isaiah then refers to the Coming One as the "Mighty God." I love that sound: Mighty God. See, there are kingdoms that rise up and try to dethrone Him, but there is only One who can sit on an eternal throne, and that is the Mighty God. He's mighty to save; He's mighty to deliver. He's mighty to heal; He's the Mighty God.

I love the Scripture that says He's the captain, that He's the Lord of the hosts of heaven. The word "hosts" means "many." Get a picture in your mind that the hosts of the Lord are surrounding you. The armies of the Lord are in full regalia, ready to fight for you. They are ready to take on your battles and to take on the enemy in Jesus' name.

The babe in the manger is the Mighty God who will deliver you from any and every calamity. He's the one who will fight for you, and I guarantee you that He will fight for you better than you can fight for yourself. So let Him fight your battles.

Call on His name! Speak it with boldness! See, there's something about calling out the name of Jesus that makes the demons tremble. They remember Calvary's cross, where He took authority over them. Christ took the keys of death, hell, and the grave, and He reigns today as a Mighty God.

EVERLASTING FATHER

Isaiah prophesies that the Christ is the Everlasting Father; that's the Father who never runs out. That's the eternal Father. It doesn't matter what kind of experience you had on this earth with your terrestrial father; in Christ you have an Everlasting Father. His arms are stretched open wide, ready to hug you and take you in and comfort you and console you.

The Bible explains that He has sent His Holy Spirit, and the Bible calls the Holy Spirit the Comforter. The Comforter is here

today to embrace you and to dry up each and every one of your tears. He is your Everlasting Father looking out for each and every one of your needs. You can rest assured today that your daddy, the Everlasting Father, is in control.

PRINCE OF PEACE

Finally, Isaiah describes the Coming One as the Prince of Peace. I like the sound of that. A lot of single ladies are waiting for their prince to come along. Well, the Prince of Peace is here right now.

During the holidays, the cities are not peaceful, and Houston is no exception. The roads and highways are not peaceful; some of the malls and stores aren't very peaceful either. But this we can know for sure: no matter where we are, no matter where we drive, the Prince of Peace is on board with us. Because of that, we can have the peace that passes all understanding. You need the Prince of Peace on board with you.

You know, Christmas can be interesting when families get together, because we all have that one family member who keeps things stirred up. You know what I'm talking about. We all have that one relative who keeps things tense—the king or queen of keeping it on edge.

Instead of being aggravated or irritated, the family gathering at Christmas is a great opportunity for you and me, who are champions in this world, to show that we can have peace in the midst of the storm because the Prince of Peace walks alongside us and the Wonderful Comforter dwells inside us. My desire is that the Prince of Peace will dwell in your household and among your family during this Christmas season.

NEVER AN END

Isaiah closes this verse with this very powerful declaration: "The increase of his government and his peace will never see an end."

Many people believe that life is just going to get worse and worse, and they want us to believe that, too. But as long as you and I have the Prince of Peace, the Mighty God, the Wonderful Counselor, the Everlasting Father, living with us, things are just going to get better and better and better.

There will never be an end to His kingdom; it's just going to get better. The news reports may seem to get worse; but in Christ, everything will get better and better.

PRAYER

Father, I thank You for Christmas, when we come together to celebrate the birth of Your Son, Jesus Christ. Thank You for that wonderful gift of eternal salvation that You've given us through Him who came to us as a helpless child, lying in a manger.

God's Gift to Us

JEREMIAH A. WRIGHT JR.

BASED ON LUKE 2:11

By grace are you saved. Salvation is God's gift to you (Ephesians 2:8–9, NKJV). An old hymn of the church that is rarely sung—in this age of upbeat, bass-line pumping, New Jack gospel music—speaks to that same truth:

> *Thank you, Lord, for saving my soul.*
> *Thank you, Lord, for making me whole.*
> *Thank you, Lord, for giving to me thy rich salvation so full.*[1]

GOD'S UNEXPECTED GIFT

Salvation is God's gift to us. The babe in the Bethlehem manger is God's gift to us. The angels announced, "To you is born this day, to you is given this day a savior." The mere fact of the announcement implies that God's gift to us was unexpected.

These shepherds were not expecting any tremendous breakthroughs. They were not expecting a word from the Lord; no messages from on high.

I go to church expecting to hear a word from the Lord. It may come in the morning message, or it may come in the morning hymn.

A lot of churches don't sing hymns anymore. A lot of new Christians don't even know hymns; they don't know white hymns and they don't know black hymns. I had an opportunity to conduct a series of lectures in South Africa; one of the lectures was on black sacred music. Providentially, later on that day, after the music lecture, we saw a group of black South Africans from one of the townships—teens, young adults, middle-aged folks, and folks my age—marching on the capital, singing a song and stepping the *toyi-toyi* to protest the vote that Parliament was about to take. About one hundred folks were heading to the capital, singing.

Earlier that morning, in the lecture, I had said that many black hymns are slipping away because the young people are not being taught those hymns any longer. They know contemporary worship songs, but they don't know traditional hymns. These South Africans were stepping to and singing:

Trials dark on every hand and we cannot understand
All the ways that God would lead us to that happy Promised Land
But we're trusting in His love and we'll follow 'til we die
For we'll understand it better by and by.

(That song was written by Charles A. Tindley, a black preacher from Philadelphia.)

Sometimes God speaks, but not just through the words of the hymn; sometimes it's through the melody. There are times when God speaks through the memories surrounding the hymn. For instance, when I hear, "Jesus, Jesus, O what a wonderful child," the melody brings back to me memories of Christmases in Virginia, where the saints couldn't say the word "child." What I used to hear at my grandpa's church was, "O what a wonderful chile."

Through the memories God speaks to me and says, "As I was

with you down in Virginia when you went with your momma and daddy to your granddaddy's church, I am with you today up in Chicago, when you go to your own church and both your momma and your daddy have come home to be with me." Sometimes the Lord will send a message while you are on your job. The shepherds were doing what they did for a living. The Lord sent them a word that was unexpected. The word that He sent was about His gift to us that was unexpected. The shepherds were not expecting the gift that God gave. But God specializes in the unexpected.

GOD'S GIFT IS UNBELIEVABLE

God's gift to us was unexpected, but this text also teaches that God's gift to us is unbelievable. In Luke 2:15, the shepherds said to one another, "I got to see this. I got to see this for myself because seeing is believing. And what we just heard and saw is unbelievable. We want to see if what the angels said and sang is true. This is unbelievable."

Why was it so unbelievable? Remember that Rome was in charge of everything in those days. When Jesus was in the manger, Rome ruled. Luke 2:1 says that Caesar was on the throne. Caesar Augustus was in charge of the military. Quirinius, says Luke 2:2, was the military governor sent by Caesar to put down the insurgency in Palestine.

There was a group of Palestinians who wanted the foreign troops out of their country and the superpower of the day was not trying to hear that. Nobody tells a superpower what they can or cannot do. Nobody tells the president of a superpower what he can or cannot do. He is the superpresident; he is above the law. He makes the laws as he goes along.

So the superpresident of the superpower issued a decree concerning homeland security. Everybody had to go where they were born to get a passbook. He was clearly in charge. If he wanted everybody to be registered for reasons of homeland security, it was done. If he sent out a decree, it was done. If he dispatched Quirinius and stationed his troops in somebody else's country, it was done. If he decided he wanted to spy on his own people, do wiretaps or e-mail monitoring, or arrest you and hold you prisoner without ever charging you for any crime, or without telling you or your family why you were arrested, nobody could do a thing about it because he was the emperor of the entire world empire and the head honcho of the first superpower on earth.

Caesar didn't need a coalition of the willing. He didn't need congressional approval. He didn't need favorable press coverage, and he certainly didn't need a majority vote. Rome was in charge of the military and the money. Caesar's picture was on the money. Show me somebody who's in charge of the military and the money and I'll show you where the real power is.

From the cradle to the grave, Rome was in charge. Rome was at the cradle in Luke 2:1, and Rome was at the cross and the grave in Matthew 27 and Luke 22.

A Savior who can deliver you from that kind of power must be coming with an army—an army that's out-of-sight. But the message from God is that the Savior—and this is unbelievable—is a baby. A helpless, small, tiny, poor, vulnerable baby! That is hard to believe.

Not only was the Savior a baby, He was not born in a presidential palace or a governor's mansion. A Savior! That's hard to believe.

Plus, the Savior's army that showed up in verse 13 didn't show up to fight; they showed up to sing and praise. That is truly unbelievable.

God specializes in the unexpected and God majors in the incredible. God's gift to us is unbelievable, but that's just like God. God's gift to us of Jesus the Christ is unexpected, and it is unbelievable.

GOD'S GIFT IS UNRESTRICTED

In a world that is fragmented, compartmentalized, balkanized, tribalized, exclusionary, and clubbish, this third aspect of God's gift is the most difficult to internalize. There are people who believe, "If you're not in our club, there's something wrong with you and we will demonize you to prove it."

We draw the lines for our clannish, cliquish club so strictly that we don't want anyone in our club who doesn't think as we think or look the way we look. But worse yet, we don't know how to disagree with one another anymore and stay in the same club. We will leave if we disagree with something and leave in a New York heartbeat. Our propensity for exclusion goes directly against the most difficult lesson for most of us to hear and learn. God's gift is not only unexpected, God's gift is not only unbelievable, but God's gift is ultimately unrestricted. In verse 10, the angel uses the word "all."

The message from God about the gift of God is that God's gift is for all people—not our kind of people, but all people. Not white people or black people, but all people. It is unrestricted—not some people or most people, but all people.

The angel said, "I bring you good news of great joy for all the people, a Savior is given." The Lord has come for all people. There are no restrictions on God's gift to us. God's gift to God's world is unrestricted.

A story is told by preachers in the black church tradition: All of the angels were waiting by the gate of glory because Jesus, the Prince of Peace, was coming back home after that Friday that he went to Calvary. After two angels had gone down to sit on the stone and tell the women who came to anoint Him that He was not in the grave, that He was risen as He said He would, they were all there, all the angels, waiting for Jesus to return to heaven.

Suddenly, one of them cried out, "Here He comes, but He's got somebody with Him! He's bringing somebody with Him! It must be Abraham, the father of the faithful. No, it doesn't look like Abraham. It must be Isaac, the miracle child born to Sarah. No, he doesn't walk like Isaac. It must be Jacob; he wrestled with the Lord all night long and prevailed. Nope, he's not limping so we know it ain't Jacob. Maybe it's Moses, the friend of God. He's the man who talked face-to-face with Him. No, he's too young to be Moses. Well, it must be somebody special, somebody like Enoch, who walked with God, or Elijah, who rode in a chariot of fire. Maybe it's Samuel, the last judge of Israel."

As Jesus drew near, they shouted, "Hosanna! Who is it? Who has earned the right to return to glory with the Prince of Peace?"

Jesus came up to them smiling and said, "He's a thief, a sinner saved by grace. He didn't have to earn a thing. I freely gave him passage to glory with no restrictions, no 'if' clauses, and no conditions attached."

Jesus gave the gift of eternal life to a dying, unbaptized thief who never spoke in tongues and was excluded from everybody's list of acceptable folk. The Savior is God's gift to you and me. This gift from God is unrestricted. Whatever you have done that makes you feel unworthy, you need to hear the message of Christmas with a new ear. God's gift is for you. God's gift is to you. Unexpected, unbelievable, and unrestricted, God's love is for you.

NOTES

1. "Thank You, Lord (for Saving My Soul)," by Mr. and Mrs. Seth Sykes.

Shopping for a Savior

ED YOUNG

BASED ON MATTHEW 2:11; EPHESIANS 2:8

During the holiday season, I think that most of us have one thing on our minds—shopping. In the weeks leading up to Christmas, many of us go on a shopping safari. We shop everywhere—from malls to online. We shop using magazines. You name it, and we've gone after it.

Most of us are trying to find that ultimate gift, the gift that does a couple of things. First, it reflects the personality of the person giving the gift. Second, it meets the need of the person receiving the gift. Let's face it. At Christmas, a lot of us are stressed out, wigged out, and freaked out. We've shopped till we dropped. I think we all have this desire to shop.

A man reading this message might be thinking, "Wait a minute, Ed, I don't like to shop. I'm allergic to malls. I have an aversion to going out in search of the ultimate gift." But I believe that line of thinking is false, because guys do like to shop, we just do it in different ways.

THE ULTIMATE SHOPPER—THE ULTIMATE GIFT

This shopping desire that we have, I think, comes from God Himself. Did you read that right? I think this shopping desire that we have, this mentality to be on a shopping safari, comes from God Himself, because God is the ultimate shopper. God has selected the ultimate Gift—a Gift that reflects His personality and meets the needs of the recipient. God sent us the ultimate Gift. That's what Christmas is all about. God sent us Jesus Christ.

Jesus is God and Jesus meets our needs; He died on the cross for our sins. God, being God, could have sent us joy. He could have sent us love. He could have sent us a bunch of money. But He sent us the ultimate gift—Jesus. That Gift reflects who He is and it met our deepest longings.

God also purchased this Gift. Jesus was born in a manger, which is an ordinary piece of farm furniture. Jesus was a carpenter who lived a sinless life and spilled His blood on the cross for all of our iniquities. He purchased our freedom. God offers us this indescribable Gift.

God says, "Here's this Gift. It's the ultimate Gift. If you receive it, you have the ultimate life."

Now, what do you think most human beings have done with God's Gift? Do you think most of us have bowed our knees to Him? Do you think most of us have said, "Okay, God, I get it. You've given me this ultimate Gift and I receive it." Do you think we've done that?

Well, most of us have white-knuckle gripped the shopping cart of life and we've spun our heels and gone our own way. We've said, "God, that's cool that you have given us this indescribable unfathomable Gift. But you know what, God? I am going to do what I want to do. I will find the ultimate life on my own. I will pack my cart with my stuff because, after all, it's my cart and I have the freedom of choice. I know what's best for me."

Most of us go down several different aisles.

THE AISLE OF POSITION

The first aisle we go down is called the aisle of position. We think, "If I reach that position . . . if I can gain the corner office . . . if I can have letters before and after my name, then that will do it." We try to position our carts in front of other people's carts.

THE AISLE OF POSSESSION

In the possession aisle we try to stack up a bunch of stuff—cars, clothes, homes. We are always comparing our carts to other people's carts. We say, "Oh, I've got more in my cart than my neighbors do. That's good! I've finally got more than my neighbors!"

But then, suddenly, the neighbors refinance because of lowered interest rates, and then they get more. It's a wicked game. I love what Denzel Washington said about money: "You know, money does not buy happiness, but it sure is a good down payment." He's exactly right. Money has a great numbing power. If you show me someone who has discretionary income, then I'll show you someone who has a lot of options.

So, when you are feeling sad, or kind of depressed, when you're feeling angry, you go out and buy something. You acquire something and, for a while, it has a numbing effect. Money is kind of like Botox for the soul. It works for a while, but then it wears off.

THE AISLE OF ADVENTURE

Aisle three is the aisle of adventure. We go for all the thrills and chills and the buzzes and highs. We move from trip to trip, from game to game, and from contest to contest. We can never sit still.

THE AISLE OF RELATIONSHIPS

We've piled our cart full of position, possession, and adventure but our cart is still empty. So we go down aisle four. We say, "Okay, aisle four—relationships. That'll do it! I'll just meet someone special."

So, we meet someone special and there this person is. We push our cart right next to the person. We date the person. We marry the person. We mate with the person. We crank out a couple of kids. Then we have a little house with a white picket fence, a dog and cat. Dad's involved in Little League and Mom's volunteering at the school. Everything is hunky-dory! But the cart is still empty.

But let's look past all the shopping and delve into the real issue of Christmas, the true meaning of the season. Why do people celebrate Christmas anyway? Do all these people shopping and celebrating Christmas know how to get to heaven? After all, getting to heaven is the ultimate thing because it's all about a gift.

The Bible says that we should just receive the Gift that has already been given for us. That's what Christmas is. It's simply making a manger out of our hearts and lives and allowing the Baby Jesus to be born there. And once we step over the line, once we turn our carts around and do a 180, once we unclench our white-knuckle grip on the rail and drop to our knees, then, the Bible says, we have the ultimate position. It says we are children of God.

We're adopted into the family of God (Ephesians 1:5). If you study the term "adoption" in the Bible, you will learn that parents could not disown an adopted child. When we are adopted into the family of God, we have the ultimate position.

We also have the ultimate possessions, because when those

rough winds hit, we can tap into God's strength. When we have a bout with doubt, we can tap into His bank.

We also have adventure. Think about the adventurous aspect of the Christian life.

Do you wonder why you are so lonely? Do you wonder why you feel like your life is not clicking? Do you wonder why you have all the stuff you dreamed about but you are still missing it? I'll tell you why. It's because you're not living your life on the track it was designed for. In other words, you are not allowing Jesus to push your cart and your life. You've not unclenched your white-knuckle grasp on the handles. You've not shopped till you've dropped to your knees. And until you do that, your life is never going to be the ultimate.

God designed us for this life. He gave us unique abilities to be pushed down His track. Yet most of us in our autonomy say, "Well, I'll push my own cart."

During the Christmas holiday season, a lot of us move our carts dangerously close to Jesus and some of us even pick up the Christ Child and put Him in the cart. We say that there is always room for a baby in the cart. We can strap Him into our cart, and we can strap Jesus into all the other stuff in our lives.

You see, He fits perfectly into our lives when we limit Him. We say things like, "Okay, Jesus, You stay there. Shhhh. You stay there. Here's a pacifier. I've got all my positions and my possessions and my adventure and my relationships, and I will make a little room for You in my cart, Jesus. Because after all, you know, I'm Catholic . . . , I'm Lutheran . . . , I'm Baptist . . . , I'm a good guy. I'm compartmentalizing my faith. I've got a little religion. I've got my recreational life, my personal life. Jesus, don't look back at the other parts of my life now."

But once we give our carts to Christ, we have the ultimate position, ultimate possessions, ultimate adventure, and ultimate relationships. We're related to the Lord Himself. We're his children.

We've been adopted into His family. And because of that, we are right vertically. Then we are right horizontally, with other people.

SHOP UNTIL YOU DROP

I think most of us need to do what the Wise Men did years ago. The Wise Men were shoppers. They were shoppers, women. Over two thousand years ago, they were searching and they were seeking—they were shopping. They were brilliant men, heavy hitters, and prosperous guys. They were connected to the natural sciences. The Bible says they did this in Matthew 2:11: "They saw the child with his mother Mary, and they bowed down and worshipped him." They shopped until they dropped.

TODAY IS TOMORROW

Years ago my son, in anticipation of Christmas, kept asking me the same question fifteen times on Christmas Eve: "Dad, is today Christmas?" I said, "No. It's tomorrow."

"Dad, is today Christmas?"

"No, it's not. Tomorrow is."

Finally, he got wise and changed his question. He asked, "Dad, is today tomorrow?"

And when I thought about that, I thought about human beings. At this point, God is ambushing a lot of people with His love, His grace, and His conviction because their carts are empty.

You know when your cart is empty. A lot of you say, "Well, maybe tomorrow I can do it. Maybe tomorrow I can do this deal. Or maybe . . ."

"Hey," God is saying. "Today is tomorrow."

What's wrong with right now? What's wrong with doing the deal right now? If you are counting on being a good guy, or a nice girl, or just having good intentions to get you to where you need to

SHOPPING FOR A SAVIOR

go, it's not going to happen for you. You're facing a Christ-less eternity.

Aren't you exhausted? Is the rubber on the wheels of your cart worn out from all the shopping and seeking and searching? Why don't you shop until you drop? Why don't you drop to your knees and say, "Jesus, have your way with me. Have your way with me," A lot of you have been doing a lot of shopping at Christmas and in your lives. It's time for you to do some dropping.

Acknowledgments

This book was the God-given brainchild of a gifted editor, Malaika Adero, who one Sunday while listening to a sermon in church envisioned how powerful the preacher's message could be in book form.

An incredible collection of Christians made her vision a reality. Adrienne Lotson compiled the first list of preachers to invite to the project. Hargis Thomas, Carl Jeffrey Wright, Bruce Barber, Johanna Castillo, and Olivia M. Cloud, who brilliantly edited this book, expanded the list exponentially. Without them, the Revelations 7:9 range that is Christianity in America today—and that this book has sought to capture—would not have been a possible quest.

One word—faithful—describes those who transcribed tapes and word processed hundreds of documents. Sherry Bailey of Complete Word Processing Services and Carolyn M. Davis of Word for Word Publishing, both true handmaidens of God, brought their decades of book publishing experience and their love of God's Word to this project. They were more than conquerors in every challenge. Jina Bostick, Elgalyn D. Wells, Earlene Greene, Mallori Mackbee, and Diva Rios provided them invaluable assistance.

The Simon & Schuster team members are pros. Thank you, Krishan Trotman, Michelle Lomuscio, Nancy Inglis, Christine

Saunders, Joyce Andes, and Jeanne Lee for applying the excellence of trade publishing to Christian subject matter with great sensitivity.

Hundreds of church secretaries and pastor's assistants showed what Christian conduct truly is, as they responded to calls, faxes, and e-mails regarding the making of this book. The public does not see what you do, but God knows your fine work. So do we, and we appreciate you! Thank you.

And most of all, to the preachers, you deserve double honor. This book is a tiny show of force in the battle to reclaim righteous observance of the birth of Jesus Christ. Your reflections take Christmas out from under the lenses of shopping, wrapping, and doing and put it at the center of a magnifying lens for the only true and living God. Thank you each for your preaching and for sharing your inspiring words in this book. May you continue to be powered up by God's spirit and blessed beyond imagination!

Biographical Sketches of Contributing Preachers

DANIEL AKIN, PH.D., has written or contributed to nearly a dozen Christian and scholarly books and Bibles. He is the president of Southeastern Baptist Theological Seminary in Wake Forest, North Carolina, where he also serves as professor of preaching and theology. He was the New Testament editor for Thos. Nelson's popular *Believers Study Bible*, author of *1, 2, 3 John* in the New American Commentary Series and *God on Sex*, and a coauthor of *A Theology for the Church*. During the past twenty years, missions have taken him to Australia, Thailand, Paraguay, and Sells, Arizona, where he worked among the Papago Indians.

MELVIN BANKS SR. is the founder and chairman of Urban Ministries, Inc. (UMI), one of the leading publishers of Bible studies and books, magazines, videos, and other Christian education resources for churches in the African American community. Based in the Chicago metropolitan area, UMI reaches nearly 100,00 teachers with Sunday school and vacation Bible school materials that facilitate communication of Christ-centered lifestyles, biblical principles, and Christian moral values to adults, children, and teens. He founded UMI in 1970 to produce Christian resources specifically geared to the needs and life concerns of urban people, particularly African Americans. These resources have earned recognition by the Evangelical Press Association. Four of UMI's eight videos have earned Chicago Emmy and Angel Awards.

He is also founder of the Urban Outreach Foundation, which conducts leadership training institutes.

He is author and editor of a number of books and Bible studies, including *Winning and Keeping Teens in Church*.

NATHAN D. BAXTER is a third-generation Pennsylvania clergyman, and is presently bishop of the Episcopal Diocese of Central Pennsylvania. He was formerly rector of historic Saint James Episcopal Church, founded in 1744, renowned as a leading institution in the founding of our nation, whose ministry today is grounded in a diverse worship life of fifteen weekly services, ranging from traditional Anglican liturgies to services for young children to Saturday jazz masses. Prior to Saint James Church, he was dean of the National Cathedral in Washington, D.C., where he led many national worship events, including President George W. Bush's first presidential inaugural service; the White House Millennium Prayer, at the request of President William J. Clinton; and the internationally televised National Day of Prayer and Remembrance Service at the cathedral following the terrorist attacks of September 11, 2001. His publications include the award-winning *Challenge and Comfort: A Pastor's Thoughts for a Troubled Nation*.

A. R. BERNARD is the founder and pastor of Christian Cultural Center in Brooklyn, New York, a thriving ministry and not-for-profit organization with a membership of over 20,000. The 6.5-acre sanctuary and conference center also includes a café, flower shop, newsstand, and restaurant. A new paradigm in houses of worship, Christian Cultural Center includes among its many ministries The Bookstore, which began as a single-table operation and is now a $500,000-per-year business, providing Bibles, books, recordings, videos, and gifts to church members and ministries locally and internationally.

In 1990, while the ministry he had founded in 1978 continued to grow, he was asked to serve on the board of directors for the Christian Men's Network (CMN) to help restructure the organization. During his six years on the board, CMN grew to comprise 74 international offices with a presence in approximately 150 nations. In addition to serving as treasurer for the board, Rev. Bernard was one of their most requested speakers. With the passing of Dr. Edwin Louis Cole in 2002, Bernard became the president of CMN.

He addressed an unprecedented one million Christian men on racial reconciliation on the mall in Washington, D.C., and is a requested speaker at Fortune 500 companies as well as universities and colleges.

GEORGE G. BLOOMER remains focused on his mandate from the Lord to preach the Word of God without compromise. He is founder of the deliverance ministry, Bethel Family Worship Center of Durham, North Carolina, known as "the church on Dowd Street." He is author of eight books, including *Witchcraft in the Pews.*

CHARLES E. BOOTH has served as pastor of Mt. Olivet Baptist Church in Columbus, Ohio, for the last twenty-eight years. A Proctor Fellow, he earned his doctor of ministry from United Theological Seminary (UTS) in Dayton, Ohio, and currently serves as professor of preaching at Trinity Lutheran Seminary in Columbus and a doctoral mentor at UTS.

He led peace marches through the neighborhoods surrounding Mt. Olivet and a bold campaign to close down crack houses and combat violence in these communities. Under his leadership the church completed a multimillion-dollar building program, is preparing to begin work on a Family Life Center, and founded a fully accredited Christian academy stressing excellence in academics, African and African American history, and Christian education.

He has traveled the world preaching and teaching the gospel, served on the advisory board of *The African American Pulpit,* and is author of *Bridging the Breach: Evangelical Thought and Liberation in the African-American Preaching Tradition.*

MARK G. BOYER has been a Catholic priest for thirty years in the Diocese of Springfield–Cape Girardeau, Missouri, and is the founding pastor of Saint Francis of Assisi Parish. He has taught at Missouri State University for more than eighteen years. He is author of twenty-eight books on biblical and liturgical spirituality and of numerous articles.

CECELIA WILLIAMS BRYANT is an episcopal supervisor in the Fifth Episcopal District of the African Methodist Episcopal Church, headquartered in Los Angeles. She cofounded the first A.M.E. church in a Francophone country, Bethel A.M.E. Church in Abijan, Ivory Coast. Missions have taken her throughout the Caribbean and South America, as well as to Sierre Leone and other parts of West Africa. She chaired the first convocation in the A.M.E. Church on the status of women. She was a founder of Gethsemane Outreach and Women's Center in Baltimore, Elnita McClain Women's Center in Houston, and the Davidson Houston Academy in Dallas. She is author of five books.

JOHN R. BRYANT has pastored three churches (Bethel A.M.E. Church, Fall River, Massachusetts; St. Paul A.M.E. Church, Cambridge, Massachusetts; and Bethel A.M.E. Church, Baltimore, Maryland). He holds a D.Min. from Colgate Rochester Divinity School and has preached and taught on more than twenty-five college campuses and on five continents. As a Peace Corps volunteer in West Africa from 1965 to 1967, he eventually oversaw 101 churches and 25 schools there. He currently presides as bishop over the A.M.E. Churches in fourteen states west of the Mississippi.

KEITH A. BUTLER is the founder and senior pastor of Word of Faith International Christian Center.

Word of Faith International Christian Center was founded on January 14, 1979, and has a congregation of more than 21,000 members and more than 300 employees. The main church is located on a beautiful 110-acre campus in Southfield, Michigan, where multiple services are held in the 5,000-seat auditorium.

Bishop Butler pastors not only the Word of Faith Christian Center in Southfield but also satellite churches in San Francisco, California, and Toronto, Canada. He also oversees the international operations in England, Bulgaria, Africa, and Brazil.

With the support of his lovely wife, Pastor Deborah L. Butler, and their children, Pastor Keith A. Butler II and his wife, Minister Tiffany Butler, the proud parents of Alexis Nichole and Angela, Pastor MiChelle A. Butler, and Minister Kristina M. Butler, Bishop Butler continues to plant churches worldwide. He ministers extensively in churches, conferences, and seminars throughout the United States and abroad, with an emphasis on instruction, line-upon-line teaching, and a no-nonsense, practical application of God's Word.

Bishop Butler is also the author of more than a dozen books.

ANTHONY CAMPOLO has served American Baptist Churches in New Jersey and Pennsylvania, and is presently associate pastor of the Mount Carmel Baptist Church in West Philadelphia.

He is a media commentator on religious, social, and political matters, having guest-hosted many television programs, including *Nightline, Crossfire, Politically Incorrect, The Charlie Rose Show, Larry*

King Live, and *CNN News.* He cohosted his own television series, *Hashing It Out,* on the Odyssey Network, and presently hosts *From Across the Pond,* a weekly program on the Premier Radio Network in England.

He served for ten years on the faculty of the University of Pennsylvania and is professor emeritus of sociology at Eastern University in St. Davids, Pennsylvania.

Founder and president of the Evangelical Association for the Promotion of Education (EAPE), Dr. Campolo works to create, nurture, and support programs for at-risk children in cities across North America and has helped establish schools and universities in several developing countries.

He is author of thirty-two books.

JOSEPH CHAMPLIN served as pastor in three parishes in the diocese of Syracuse and has been a Roman Catholic priest for over fifty years. Currently semiretired, he is the sacramental priest at Our Lady of Good Counsel Church in Warners, New York.

After studying at Yale and Notre Dame and attending seminary in Rochester, New York, he served as associate director in the Liturgy Secretariat for the National Conference of Catholic Bishops, traveling more than two million miles and lecturing on liturgical and pastoral matters. He also conducted retreats for priests and missions for parishes.

He has written fifty books, including *What It Means to Be Catholic* (St. Anthony Messenger Press). More than twenty million copies of his publications are in print. His most popular volume is *Together for Life* in both English and Spanish, now with over nine million copies in circulation (Ave Maria Press/Liguori Publications). He has appeared in a dozen videos and made numerous television appearances. *Take Five* (Ave Maria Press) and *A Catholic Perspective on the Purpose-Driven Life* (Catholic Book Publishing) were published in Fall 2006. *Juntos Para Toda La Vida (Together for*

Life) has consistently been at the top of the best-selling Catholic Spanish books list.

DAN CHUN is pastor of First Presbyterian Church of Honolulu and cofounder and chairman of the board of Hawaiian Islands Ministries, a group that does leadership development for all of the churches in Hawaii. He cochairs Hawaii Together, the governor's task force for the community in response to the war.

As part of Promise Keepers, he has spoken to more than 250,000 men in stadiums and sports arenas around the country about how to be a better father, husband, employee, and friend.

Dan Chun is fourth-generation Hawaiian born, and his grandfather was houseboy to Queen Liliiuokalani at Iolani Palace and was there on the day of the military takeover. He is an award-winning film producer and former TV News reporter for KGMB-TV (a CBS affiliate). He earned his doctor of ministry from Fuller Theological Seminary.

EMANUEL CLEAVER is currently serving his first term in the U.S. House of Representatives. First elected to public office in 1979 as a city councilman, he later served as mayor pro tem of Kansas City and then made history as the first African American elected mayor of the city. During his two-term stint as mayor, he was president of the National Conference of Black Mayors. Cleaver, who holds a master's in divinity, is an ordained Methodist minister and still serves as senior pastor at Saint James United Methodist Church in Kansas City.

SUZAN JOHNSON COOK was the first African American woman to be elected to an American Baptist church in its two-hundred-year history and was the first woman elected president of the Hampton University Ministers' Conference, which represents all the historically African American denominations. She is the New York City Police Department's only female chaplain. She has served on the Domestic Policy Council in the White House and with the HUD secretary for faith initiatives. Her eight books include *Too Blessed to Be Stressed* and *Live Like You're Blessed.*

KEVIN W. COSBY is senior pastor of Saint Stephen Baptist Church in Louisville, Kentucky, which has been recognized as one of the one hundred largest churches in America and one of the six super-churches of the South. Saint Stephen recently built a thousand-seat satellite church in Jeffersonville, Indiana. Cosby is also president of Simmons College of Kentucky. He lectures at universities and institutions around the world and is the author of three books.

MICHAEL ERIC DYSON is professor in the humanities and of religious studies at the University of Pennsylvania, and taught at DePaul University, Chicago Theological Seminary, the University of North Carolina at Chapel Hill, Columbia University, and Brown University. A teen father who once lived on welfare, he earned a Ph.D. from Princeton.

An ordained Baptist minister, often described as the hip-hop intellectual, he is a social analyst and best-selling author of books on Malcolm X, Martin Luther King, singer Marvin Gaye, and Bill Cosby. In his latest, *Come Hell or High Water,* Dyson offers a searing assessment of the meaning of Hurricane Katrina. He is one of the world's leading scholars on the hip-hop music genre and the culture that surrounds it, as well as its roots in African and African American cultures and influence on American popular culture.

Dyson is host of a daily syndicated talk radio program, *The Michael Eric Dyson Show,* which is heard every weekday on the Syndication One Radio Network (Radio One). He is also a regular commentator on National Public Radio and the HBO-TV program *Real Time with Bill Maher.*

WILLIAM S. EPPS is the eighth pastor to serve at the historic Second Baptist Church in Los Angeles, California. He is president of a nonprofit church-based community organization that seeks to improve the quality of life in the South Central community and serves as adjunct professor of preaching at Fuller Theological Seminary, Pasadena, California. He is editor in chief of the *National Baptist Voice,* the official publication of the National Baptist Convention, and author of *What Did Jesus Say? A Daily Devotional Journal* (Judson Press).

KEN FONG is senior pastor of Evergreen Baptist Church in Los Angeles. Born and raised in Sacramento, he is a third-generation American of Chinese ancestry. He made a decision to follow Christ while in junior high school. Two powerful forces overshadowed any fleeting thoughts he had about someday becoming a pastor: his desire for material security and his belief that he was too "Americanized" and too cool to be a Chinese pastor. He earned a degree in biological science, and although it was assumed he would one day become a doctor, he started working with youth in a Chinese American church. He later chose to enroll in Fuller Theological Seminary in Pasadena, California, and after he completed his M.Div., he was appointed associate pastor at Evergreen as this English-speaking Japanese American ministry was beginning to answer God's call to include Chinese Americans. His passion burns for ministry approaches that are culturally attuned to reaching Americanized Asian Americans, especially the unchurched. His vision is to develop a fresh model of church, one that will be both multi-Asian and multiethnic, one that loves God and loves people.

BILLY GRAHAM. The Reverend Billy Graham has preached the gospel to more people face-to-face than anyone else in history—more than 210 million people in 185 countries and territories. The Billy Graham Evangelistic Association, which he founded in 1950, has reached hundreds of millions more through television and radio, film and the Internet. Reverend Graham lives with his wife, Ruth Bell Graham, in the mountains of North Carolina.

JOEL C. GREGORY is professor of preaching at George W. Truett Theological Seminary of Baylor University in Waco, Texas, and Distinguished Fellow of Georgetown College. His speaking takes him annually to hundreds of venues and dozens of locales. He has spoken in forty-six states and in Latin America, England, Europe, the Far East, and the Middle East. He has been guest preacher at Westminster Chapel, London, the Barcelona Olympics, Interlaken, all six Southern Baptist seminaries, and scores of university campuses. He addressed the Baptist World Alliance in Seoul, Korea, and has served as a trustee of the International Mission Board of the Southern Baptist Convention.

He was formerly pastor of the historic First Baptist Church of Dallas, the largest church in the Southern Baptist Convention, where he preached to President George H. W. Bush. He also pastored Travis Avenue Baptist Church, the largest Baptist congregation in Fort Worth.

He was a weekly speaker on the "International Baptist Hour," a weekly radio program networked on more than five hundred stations and one of the two longest-running national religious radio programs. He also served as preacher on the nationally televised "Baptist Hour" broadcast.

He is author of five books, editor of two, and coauthor of three.

FORREST E. HARRIS SR. is president of American Baptist College in Nashville, Tennessee, and assistant dean for African American church studies at Vanderbilt University Divinity School.

He pastored the Oak Valley Baptist Church, Oak Ridge, Tennessee, where he brought together community organizations and founded a development corporation, and Pleasant Green Baptist Church in Nashville, where he established the first church-based community development corporation in Nashville and an interreligious and interracial organization of Nashville congregations.

As director of the Kelly Miller Smith Institute on the Black Church at Vanderbilt, he coordinated a national ecumenical dialogue of more than 12,000 participants on "What Does It Mean to Be Black and Christian?" This national discussion resulted in the publication of two books.

A member of the Ecumenical Association of Third World Theologians, Dr. Harris has traveled to South Africa, China, and Canada to deliver papers on topics related to human rights and global and ethnic conflict.

MARILYN HICKEY founded Denver's Orchard Road Christian Center with her husband, Wallace Hickey, in 1960. (The couple celebrated fifty years of marriage in 2004.) The church started with twenty-five people and is a Charismatic center ministering to thousands and hosting well-known speakers and worship leaders from around the world. With daughter Sarah Bowling, Marilyn initiated city prayer, a monthly citywide prayer meeting that now includes 120 local churches representing diverse denominational and ethnic groups. Marilyn's ministry includes a daily TV program, *Today with Marilyn & Sarah* (cohosted by Sarah and reaching potentially 1.5 billion households), international crusades and ministry training schools, Bible teaching seminars, and humanitarian aid. Often the invited guest of world leaders, Marilyn has ministered in more than one hundred nations, including Australia, China, Ethiopia, Germany, India, Israel, Italy, Jordan, Kazakhstan, Morocco, Pakistan, Russia, Spain, Sudan, Thailand, the United Kingdom, Uzbekistan, and Vietnam. She and Sarah publish a quarterly newsletter, *connect*, and have written scores of books and released over 1,500 CDs, DVDs, and tapes.

DONALD HILLIARD JR. serves as senior pastor to Cathedral International–the Historic Second Baptist Church–which under his leadership has grown from 125 members in 1983 to six thousand members today in three locations in New Jersey: Perth Amboy, Asbury Park, and Plainfield. Cited by the American Baptist Churches (USA) as a model for church growth, Cathedral International has sixty ministries, including a community development corporation, an umbrella organization providing numerous outreach services to the local community, a child-care center, a counseling center that provides therapy for both the church and the community, a Bible Institute that partners with Oral Roberts University in offering theological studies, and a family life center that hosts banquets and receptions and provides space for a creative dance center and youth activities. The church offers economic empowerment opportunities for entrepreneurs and constructs affordable housing. The church has been cited by the city and state as a major catalyst for the renewal and development of downtown Perth Amboy.

Via Streamingfaith.com and the Word Network, the gospel from Cathedral International reaches millions of homes across the globe.

Hilliard is author of six books and ministers at churches, conferences, and conventions internationally. He reaches corporate America as a Christian motivational speaker

He serves *The African American Pulpit*, the leading academic periodical on black preaching, as an executive advisory board member; and is a current board member of *Gospel Today*.

BARBARA KING is the founder/minister of the Hillside Chapel and Truth Center in Atlanta, Georgia. She began this nondenominational, ecumenical ministry in 1971 with twelve members in her living room. The Hillside complex today covers nearly twelve acres, with a growing congregation numbering more than ten thousand.

Through its numerous outreach projects, Hillside has an important role in the development of metropolitan Atlanta.

Hillside espouses international ministry, and King has traveled extensively in the United States and to Finland, Russia, England, Israel, Egypt, Kenya, Senegal, South Africa, the Caribbean, Brazil, and British Guiana. Hillside was the first African American New Thought ministry to establish a sister church in South Africa (in May 1994). King has been invited to the White House by President George W. Bush and was regularly invited by President William Jefferson Clinton and Vice President Al Gore. She participated in the 2005 Clinton Global Initiative, to focus the world's leading minds on the most challenging global dilemmas.

She is author of seven books; hosts a television program, *A New Thought, a New Life;* and appeared on Oprah Winfrey's *Remembering the Spirit.*

JACQUELINE E. McCULLOUGH, a second-generation preacher, is senior pastor and founder of The International Gathering at Beth Rapha, in Pomona, New York. Her vision for evangelistic ministry is expressed in the international reach of Daughters of Rizpah, a nonprofit religious organization, where she serves as president/ CEO.

After earning a doctor of ministry from Drew Theological Seminary in Madison, New Jersey, she engaged in postgraduate study at the Jewish Theological Seminary.

She is a prolific author of books and contributor to such publications as *Gospel Today, SpiritLed Woman,* and *The African American Pulpit.* A songwriter and worship leader, she has released two praise and worship CDs. She has been a featured speaker at Azusa Conference, *Essence* Music Festival, Hampton Minister's Conference, Gospel Music Workshop of America, and Woman Thou Art Loosed and a guest on numerous television and radio programs, including *BET Tonight with Tavis Smiley, Bobby Jones Gospel, The 700 Club*, and on Trinity Broadcasting Network.

VASHTI MURPHY MCKENZIE made history as the first female bishop of the African Methodist Episcopal Church. Her statement "The stained-glass ceiling has been broken" was quoted on the front page of *The New York Times*. Her current role as president of the church's council of bishops, the executive branch responsible for its operation worldwide, is also a first for a female. She is, at the same time, serving as the presiding prelate of the 13th Episcopal District, which encompasses Tennessee and Kentucky.

She served as bishop in southeastern Africa. She began her ministry in Maryland where she developed numerous ministries and faith-based community programs.

A former journalist, she is the author of several books, including *Journey to the Well*.

BERTRAM MELBOURNE is interim dean and an associate professor of Biblical language and literature at the Howard University School of Divinity. Born on the island of Jamaica, Dr. Melbourne served in the West Jamaica Conference of the Seventh Day Adventists as pastor/evangelist and youth and education director. He is author of two books and has written articles for other books and publications. He is an accomplished poet, and a number of his poems have been published by the National Library of Poetry. He has taught, lectured, and preached nationally and internationally in Africa, Australia, Bahamas, Canada, the Caribbean, Fiji, Great Britain, Korea, New Guinea, and the Solomon Islands.

ELLA PEARSON MITCHELL was the first female dean of Sisters Chapel at Spelman College in Atlanta. She has also taught at the American Baptist Seminary of the West and Proctor School of Theology in Richmond, Virginia. She earned a master's degree at

Union Theological Seminary and Columbia University and a doctor of ministry from Claremont School of Theology, while instructing there.

She edited several groundbreaking books on women in the preaching ministry: *Women: To Preach or Not to Preach* and four volumes of *Those Preaching Women* (all Judson Press).

She is well known for innovative team-teaching and team-preaching with her husband, Henry Mitchell. *Together for Good: Lessons from Fifty-five Years of Marriage* is their joint autobiography. Their sermons are in *Fire in the Well* (Judson Press). In 2006, she and her husband, whom she met in seminary sixty-five years ago, celebrated their sixty-second wedding anniversary. The Mitchells currently reside in Atlanta, Georgia.

HENRY H. MITCHELL was founding director of the Ecumenical Center for Black Church Studies, in Los Angeles. He earned advanced degrees from Union Theological Seminary in New York City and Claremont School of Theology, California (Th.D.), and his academic career included appointments at Proctor School of Theology, Virginia Union University (Dean), and Colgate Rochester Crozer Divinity School. He and his wife, Ella (see above entry), team-taught homiletics at the Interdenominational Theological Center in Atlanta for a dozen years.

He is author of six books, one of which, *Celebration and Experience in Preaching*, was named as one of the top ten clergy books of the year by the American Academy of Parish Clergy. His *Black Church Beginnings* (1650–1900) is a radical rewrite and correction of early black church history. He is coauthor of four other books, including a joint memoir with his wife of their first fifty-five years of marriage and *Fire in the Well.*

In "retirement" in their late eighties, the Mitchell team still preach and write (author or edit) whenever or wherever they are requested.

OTIS B. MOSS III currently serves as pastor of Trinity United Church of Christ under the leadership of senior pastor Rev. Dr. Jeremiah A. Wright Jr.

Prior to joining the pastoral staff at Trinity United Church of Christ, Reverend Moss served as pastor of the historic Tabernacle Baptist Church in Augusta, Georgia, which during his tenure grew from 125 members to more than 2,100.

Still under forty, he started Issachar Movement, a consulting group designed to bridge the generation gap within churches and train a new generation of prophetic church leadership. He received his undergraduate training in religion and philosophy from Morehouse College, where he was a Ford Foundation Scholar, was named by the NCAA as an all-American track and field athlete, and graduated with honors. Completing graduate work at Yale, he was awarded the Mays Scholarship in Religion and the Magee Fellowship.

Newsweek magazine cited him as one of God's foot soldiers committed to transforming the lives of youth. Belief.net called him one of the future religious leaders who will impact the African American church. *The African American Pulpit* recently named him one of the "twenty to watch" ministers who will shape the future of the African American church. He is the youngest lecturer ever to speak at the Hampton University Ministers and Musicians Conference, the largest African American ecumenical conference in the nation.

He is a frequent guest commentator on Naomi Judd's show on the Hallmark Network, *Naomi's New Morning*.

His essays, articles, and poetry have appeared in several periodicals. *Redemption in a Red Light District* is his first book.

MYLES MUNROE is a multigifted international motivational speaker, author, lecturer, educator, government consultant, adviser, and businessman, who addresses critical issues affecting every aspect of human, social, and spiritual development. He is the founder and president of Bahamas Faith Ministries International, an all-encompassing network of ministries, headquartered in Nassau, Bahamas.

Dr. Munroe holds bachelor of arts degrees in education, fine arts, and theology from Oral Roberts University and a master of arts degree in administration from the University of Tulsa.

In 1998, Dr. Munroe became the youngest honoree to receive the Officer of the British Empire (OBE) Award, which was bestowed by the Queen of England for his contribution to the growth and strength of the Bahamas. He was also the recipient of one of the highest awards of the Government of the Bahamas Silver Jubilee (SJA) for his outstanding contribution to the growth and strength of the Bahamas.

Dr. Munroe and his lovely wife, Ruth, are the proud parents of two college students, Charissa and Chairo (Myles Jr.). Dr. Munroe is the sixth child born into a family of eleven children raised in a Christian home in Nassau, Bahamas, where his father is a Baptist minister and his late mother was a missionary.

Better known as Mr. Purpose, Dr. Munroe had every opportunity to become a loser, but chose to become a winner by daring to reach higher, go farther, see over, and grasp something greater, which has allowed him to reach millions of people around the world and help them discover their destiny, purpose, potential, and leadership ability.

WILLIAM (BILL) E. PANNELL is special assistant to the president and senior professor of preaching at Fuller Theological Seminary in Pasadena, California, where he was first appointed, more than thirty years ago, assistant professor of evangelism. He has served on Fuller's board of trustees, as dean of the chapel, and as director of the African-American Studies Program. A gifted preacher and professor of homiletics, he has nurtured several generations of

Fuller students from the classroom to the pulpit. He is author of numerous articles and books.

Victor D. Pentz is senior pastor of the Peachtree Presbyterian Church of Atlanta, Georgia, the largest congregation in the Presbyterian Church USA, with just under nine thousand members. It is widely recognized for its commitment to local community and global missions, having built Habitat for Humanity homes throughout Atlanta, as well as in Americus (Georgia), Hungary, Ireland, South Africa, Honduras, South Korea, the Philippines, and Egypt. Prior to coming to Atlanta, Dr. Pentz was senior minister of First Presbyterian Church of Houston, Texas, and under his leadership that church established the Nehemiah Center, a nationally recognized center of learning for inner-city children.

He has served as chaplain for the flight crews of three space shuttle launches, traveled extensively in Israel, Egypt, Greece, and Turkey, and preached at Roman Catholic services in Bethlehem.

His sermons have been syndicated for *Preaching Today,* a national tape resource for ministers. He contributed to *The Leadership Handbook of Pastoral Theology,* vol. III (Baker Books), and has published articles in *Christianity Today, Leadership Journal, Men of Integrity, Christian Networks Journal,* the *Wittenberg Door,* and other magazines. He serves on the board of contributing editors of *Preaching* magazine. His television ministry following the tragedy of 9/11 was featured in "Yahoo! Internet Life."

W. Franklyn Richardson is senior pastor of the historic Grace Baptist Church in Mount Vernon, New York, and Port Saint Lucie, Florida, a two-location congregation of more than four thousand members. He has served Grace since April 1975. Dr. Richardson is an alumnus of Virginia Union University, Yale University, and United Theological Seminary.

A community builder and organizer, his visionary leadership is responsible for two community development corporations that have constructed affordable housing at a cost of more than $65 million. He served on the central committee of the World Council of Churches, which represents more than 400 million Christians in 150 nations.

He has preached on several continents, and for the past thirty years his sermons have been broadcast throughout the New York, New Jersey, and Connecticut area on WVOX radio and nationally televised every Sunday morning. He is author of the acclaimed book *Power of the Pew,* and has written articles on faith-based community development.

ROBERT H. SCHULLER is founder of the internationally acclaimed Crystal Cathedral Church in Garden Grove, California. He came to Garden Grove, California, in 1955 to found a congregation of the Reformed Church in America. With his wife, Arvella, as organist and $500 in assets, he rented the Orange drive-in theater and conducted Sunday services from the roof of the snack bar.

He is the author of more than thirty books, five which have appeared on the *New York Times* best-seller list.

ROBERT SMITH JR. is professor of preaching at Beeson Divinity School of Samford University, Birmingham, Alabama. He served as pastor of the New Mission Missionary Baptist Church in Cincinnati, Ohio, for twenty years.

WALLACE CHARLES SMITH is senior minister of the historic Shiloh Baptist Church of Washington, D.C., one of the oldest African American churches in the city. With a membership of more than four thousand persons, Shiloh's congregation has a long history of community outreach and family-empowering ministries.

He is a popular guest lecturer and teacher. He is a member of the board of trustees at Eastern Baptist Seminary and a member of the general council of the Baptist World Alliance, a worldwide fellowship organization representing Baptists in more than 160 countries. He served as a member of a reconciliation team to bring black and white Baptists together in South Africa. He has traveled extensively and has preached in South Africa, Argentina, Zimbabwe, and Cuba.

Among his many community responsibilities, he assists churches in securing grants for needy persons in their communities. A longtime member of the Progressive National Baptist Convention, USA, Inc., he has taught leadership courses, led seminars, and is a trustee of the Board of Home Missions.

He is contributing editor of *The Pulpit Digest*, has written numerous articles, including guest editorials for *The Washington Post*, and is the author of a book, *The Church in the Life of the Black Family* (Judson Press).

DAVE STONE has for the past seventeen years shared the preaching responsibilities with Bob Russell at Southeast Christian Church, a nondenominational congregation in Louisville, Kentucky, where more than eighteen thousand worshipers attend services each weekend. In January 2006, the Reverend Russell graciously passed the baton of leadership for the church to Dave.

He has spoken at regional and national conventions in thirty-five states. His most recent book, *Refining Your Style*, won the *Preaching* magazine "book of the year" award.

GARDNER C. TAYLOR, in more than a half century of ministry, has contributed to the kingdom of God as a pastor, a civil rights activist and leader, and a preacher of international renown. His remarkable gift as a preacher has earned him a place among the pantheon of great American preachers.

Taylor is now pastor emeritus of Concord Baptist Church in Brooklyn, New York, and his tenure (1948–1990) was marked by tremendous growth. Ten thousand people joined Concord under his pastorate, and a number of ministries were developed to serve the Brooklyn community.

He led fund-raising in New York on behalf of Dr. Martin Luther King and the civil rights movement and advocated for better conditions for minorities in the North, as well. He fought housing discrimination against Hispanics and African Americans. He was arrested for public protest on behalf of minority trade workers.

A principal organizer of the Progressive National Baptist Convention, he served as the organization's second president in the early 1960s.

His skills at proclaiming the Word have been honored by invitations to appear an unprecedented five times before the Baptist World Alliance. He has preached to national denominational gatherings in seven nations around the world.

He has taught preaching at Harvard, Princeton, New York, Union, and Colgate Rochester seminaries. In 1979, *Time* magazine named him one of the seven greatest Protestant preachers in America, dubbing him "The Dean of the Nation's Black Preachers." A survey in *Newsweek* magazine named him one of the twelve greatest preachers in the English-speaking world.

He delivered the sermon at the Inaugural Prayer Service of President William Jefferson Clinton, and in August 2000, President Clinton bestowed upon him the nation's highest honor, the Presidential Medal of Freedom.

He continues to proclaim the gospel through writings, speeches, and a tireless preaching schedule.

FRANK A. THOMAS is senior pastor of Mississippi Boulevard Christian Church in Memphis, Tennessee. Having earned a doctor of ministry from Chicago Theological Seminary, he has taught preaching for many years at the doctoral level at several distinguished seminaries.

He is the chief executive officer of Hope for Life International, Inc., which is the nonprofit that owns *The African American Pulpit* (TAAP), a quarterly journal that serves as a repository for the very best of African American preaching and provides practical and creative resources for persons in ministry. It is the only African American–owned, nondenominational preaching and ministry journal in the country and has a subscription base of more than seven thousand.

He has authored several books, including *They Like to Never Quit Praisin' God: The Role of Celebration in Preaching* (Pilgrim Press, 1997), a book on preaching methods.

KENNETH C. ULMER is senior pastor of Faithful Central Bible Church in Inglewood, California. Under his leadership since 1982, the church has grown from 350 people to more than 13,000. The church purchased the Great Western Forum, formerly the stadium of the Los Angeles Lakers, which allowed the church to easily accommodate this incredible growth.

He envisions Faithful Central as a conduit of God's love and power as it reaches out to Los Angeles and makes an eternal impact across the globe. He has a passion for realizing and obeying God's will for his life and an inexhaustible thirst for the knowledge and wisdom of God.

WILLIAM D. WATLEY is the senior pastor of Saint James A.M.E. Church in Newark, New Jersey, a congregation of six thousand parishioners. He established a social services corporation that serves as the umbrella organization for many outreach programs, including one that provides 287,000 meals for homeless people each year. He founded Saint James Preparatory School, a state-of-the-art middle and high school for grades seven through twelve.

An innovative worship leader, he has made the Wednesday Sweet Hour of Praise service renowned for its dynamism and inspirational messages; it's attended by nearly eight hundred individuals weekly.

Holding a doctorate in philosophy-ethics from Columbia University, he has done post-doctoral research at the Ecumenical Institute in Céligny, Switzerland, and Harvard's Institute for Educational Management. He has taught extensively, serving as president and distinguished professor of religion at Paul Quinn College in Waco, Texas, and visiting professor at the Princeton Theological Seminary.

A prolific author, Dr. Watley has written a dozen books, several booklets, and many articles.

STEVE WENDE is senior pastor of First United Methodist Church of Houston, Texas, the forty-seventh pastor of this multicultural church whose history dates from 1839. Located since 1910 at the corner of Main and Clay Streets, in 1993 the church added a second campus on the west side of the city, which offers additional worship opportunities, a school, and a recreational center complete with swimming pools and softball fields. The church founded a community center, retirement home, and media ministry. Wende continues to lead the congregation in its strong tradition of spiritual formation, civic leadership, and community service.

A noted speaker who holds a master's of divinity from Yale and a doctorate in ministry from Princeton Theological Seminary, he serves as contributing editor for *Preaching* magazine. He has received many awards for his work in the areas of church growth, education, and mission outreach.

PAULA WHITE is a life coach, motivational speaker, pastor, preacher, author, humanitarian, philanthropist, teacher, TV personality, wife, and mother. Paula White Ministries' work included hundreds of large-scale outreaches to the needy and lost, an orphanage, and international relief. Her journey from a troubled past to the abundant life motivates her to touch people who find themselves without hope.

She copastors the twenty-two-thousand-member Without Walls International Church in Tampa, Florida, with her husband, Randy White, and hosts *Paula White Today*, an international television program.

She is the author of *He Loves Me, He Loves Me Not* (Charisma House) and *Deal with It!: You Cannot Conquer What You Will Not Confront* (Nelson Books). Her most recent publications are *Birthing Your Dreams* and *Simple Suggestions for a Sensational Life* (Nelson Impact).

MARCOS WITT is a musician, songwriter, singer, author, speaker, and senior pastor of the Hispanic congregation at Lakewood Church in Houston, Texas, one of the largest churches in the United States. The congregation has an active and growing membership of more than six thousand people and a TV program that airs every week in more than twenty countries and can be watched live on the Internet.

He was born in San Antonio, Texas, to a young American missionary couple who moved to Durango, Mexico, and started an outreach. After his father's tragic death, his mother, years later, remarried a man who embraced the vision God had originally given his parents, and became his father figure.

He grew up in Mexico, where he studied classical music at the University of Juárez in Durango. He eventually started his theological studies at the International Bible College in San Antonio, Texas, and is studying for his master's at Oral Roberts University in Tulsa, Oklahoma.

Twenty years ago he founded CanZion Producciones (now CanZion Group, LP) and has recorded twenty-nine cassettes, CDs, and DVDs, which have sold more than 9 million copies worldwide. Millions attend his concerts and watch his television programs every year all over the Spanish-speaking world. He has twice received the Latin Grammy in the category of Best Christian Album. His most recent recording, *Dios es Bueno* (God Is Good), was recorded in Puerto Rico and includes bachata, reggaeton, and rock.

In 1994, Marcos founded CanZion Institute, a school dedicated to the preparation of worship leaders and music ministers. More than three thousand students attend the twenty-eight campuses of the Institute in ten different countries in North and South America and Europe.

Since the year 2000, he has participated in over one hundred leadership conferences and seminars organized by LIDERE, a company dedicated to the equipping of leaders and pastors.

He is a frequent guest at the White House, representing the evangelical Hispanic community.

He has written eight books.

JEREMIAH A. WRIGHT JR. was called to serve the congregation of Trinity United Church of Christ in Chicago, Illinois, in 1972. Membership was eighty-seven adults. Membership now exceeds eight thousand. During that time the church has constructed two new worship centers and two senior-citizen housing complexes, operated a federally funded child-care program for low-income and unemployed families, run a federally guaranteed credit union (assets now exceed $3 million), and established many other ministries.

Trinity Church has for decades tithed its annual budget each year, giving a tenth of its revenues to other churches, agencies, denominational missions, and world missions in Liberia, Haiti, Ethiopia, Nigeria, Ghana, Brazil, South Africa, Ghana, and Brazil. The church opened a computer school in Saltpond, Ghana, in the summer of 2000.

Trinity makes a tremendous investment in higher education

and theological education each year, giving to the United Negro College Fund and scholarships to graduating high school members who are college bound.

Under Pastor Wright, Trinity ordained thirty-eight seminary graduates and currently assists sixty-five members in accredited seminaries throughout the country.

Trinity has also "birthed" four new congregations in the United Church of Christ—two in Atlanta, one in Gary, Indiana, and one in Milwaukee, Wisconsin.

Four of the new pastors serving those new congregations attended seminary with financial assistance from Trinity Church, and all were ordained by Pastor Wright after completing seminary.

He earned his doctorate from the United Theological Seminary, with training by the renowned Dr. Samuel DeWitt Proctor.

ED YOUNG is the founding and senior pastor of Fellowship Church, Dallas–Fort Worth, Texas, one of the ten largest churches in America. Located on a main campus of 141 acres, the church also operates four satellite campuses: in downtown Dallas; Plano; north of Fort Worth; and Miami, Florida.

Known for his candor when talking about leadership and the inner workings of a growing church, Young provides resources for church leaders through CreativePastors.com and the Creative Church Conferences. Ed Young Ministries airs a weekly televised program on networks throughout the U.S. and Europe, including USA, TBN, Daystar, and CNBC Europe. His weekday radio program is broadcast in major cities throughout the U.S.

He is author of nearly a dozen books.

Permissions Acknowledgments

SCRIPTURES COPYRIGHT